POSITIVE FRE

Past, Present, and F

EDITED BY

JOHN CHRISTMAN

Pennsylvania State University

CAMBRIDGE
UNIVERSITY PRESS

CAMBRIDGE
UNIVERSITY PRESS

Shaftesbury Road, Cambridge CB2 8EA, United Kingdom

One Liberty Plaza, 20th Floor, New York, NY 10006, USA

477 Williamstown Road, Port Melbourne, VIC 3207, Australia

314–321, 3rd Floor, Plot 3, Splendor Forum, Jasola District Centre, New Delhi – 110025, India

103 Penang Road, #05–06/07, Visioncrest Commercial, Singapore 238467

Cambridge University Press is part of Cambridge University Press & Assessment, a department of the University of Cambridge.

We share the University's mission to contribute to society through the pursuit of education, learning and research at the highest international levels of excellence.

www.cambridge.org
Information on this title: www.cambridge.org/9781108738217

DOI: 10.1017/9781108768276

First published 2022
First paperback edition 2023

A catalogue record for this publication is available from the British Library

Library of Congress Cataloging-in-Publication data
NAMES: Christman, John Philip, editor.
TITLE: Positive freedom : past, present, and future / edited by John Christman.
DESCRIPTION: Cambridge, United Kingdom ; New York, NY : Cambridge University Press, 2022. | Includes bibliographical references and index.
IDENTIFIERS: LCCN 2021020788 (print) | LCCN 2021020789 (ebook) | ISBN 9781108487900 (hardback) | ISBN 9781108738217 (paperback) | ISBN 9781108768276 (epub)
SUBJECTS: LCSH: Liberty–Philosophy. | Political ethics. | BISAC: PHILOSOPHY / Political
CLASSIFICATION: LCC JC585 .P616 2022 (print) | LCC JC585 (ebook) | DDC 320.01/1–dc23
LC record available at https://lccn.loc.gov/2021020788
LC ebook record available at https://lccn.loc.gov/2021020789

ISBN 978-1-108-48790-0 Hardback
ISBN 978-1-108-73821-7 Paperback

Contents

Contributors

JOHN CHRISTMAN is Professor of Philosophy, Political Science, and Women's Studies, Pennsylvania State University

RUTGER CLAASSEN is Professor of Political Philosophy and Economic Ethics, Utrecht University

MAEVE COOKE is Professor of Philosophy, University College Dublin

MARIA DIMOVA-COOKSON is Associate Professor in the School of Government and International Affairs, Centre for the History of Political Thought, Durham University

MICHAEL GARNETT is Senior Lecturer, Department of Philosophy, Birkbeck College, University of London

CAROL C. GOULD is Distinguished Professor and Director of the Center for Global Ethics and Politics at the Ralph Bunche Institute, City University of New York

NANCY J. HIRSCHMANN is Stanley I. Sheerr Term Professor in the Social Sciences, Department of Political Science, University of Pennsylvania

DAVID INGRAM is Professor of Philosophy, Loyola University, Chicago

MICHAEL QUANTE is Professor of Philosophy and Vice President, University of Münster

AVITAL SIMHONY is Associate Professor, School of Politics and Global Studies, Arizona State University

HORACIO SPECTOR is Professor of Law, Torcuato Di Tella University, Buenos Aires, and the University of San Diego School of Law

CHAD VAN SCHOELANDT is Assistant Professor of Philosophy, Tulane University

STEVEN WALL is Professor of Philosophy, University of Arizona

Acknowledgments

I would like to thank K. Bailey Thomas for valuable assistance in preparing this manuscript. I am also grateful, as always, to Mary Beth Oliver for endless inspiration and support.

INTRODUCTION

The Multiple Dimensions of Positive Freedom

John Christman

As several writers have noted, the word "freedom," and its conceptual twin "liberty," are ubiquitous in political discourse, despite endless controversy about its meaning.[1] Nevertheless, certain families of concepts have emerged that divide the terrain and serve as dominant centers of conceptual gravity in these debates. These include "negative" views that define liberty entirely in terms of the absence of constraints on action, republican conceptions that focus on social relations of (non-)domination, and a variety of "positive" accounts that link freedom to an effective, self-governing, well-reasoned and virtuous agency in a social context, among other factors. The purpose of this book is to explicate these positive notions and, in so doing, illustrate the importance of such ideas in the specification of the fundamental values of a just society.

Readers will likely be familiar with Isaiah Berlin's basic distinction between positive and negative conceptions of liberty, as well perhaps as Charles Taylor's parallel contrast between (negative) "opportunity" concepts and (positive) "exercise" concepts.[2] The basis for these distinctions is the contrast between understanding liberty as the absence of something – actual or potential constraints on the actions of an agent – and the presence of some other factors, such as the capability to carry out one's wishes, or the capacity to reflectively accept one's values, or the recognition by others of one's status as a social being. The number of these positive

[1] See, e.g., Axel Honneth (2014). Also, our contributors in this book all use "freedom" and "liberty" more or less interchangeably, though we do so with a sensitivity to the fact that in different political and intellectual contexts, one of these terms is more appropriate than the other. Moreover, we are looking at freedom here as a concept in social and political philosophy and hence independent in principle from the idea of free *will* or metaphysical freedom (at least at a first pass). What is crucial is that the words freedom and liberty refer to a condition of social life that is of basic value in conceptions of a just society for the modern world. For discussion of the emergence of this ideal, see Patterson (1991).

[2] Berlin (1969b) and Taylor (1979). See also Maeve Cooke's revisionary distinction between "individualist" and "communalist" conceptions in her contribution later.

factors makes for a complicated array of ideas, leading Richard Arneson to remark that Berlin's distinction is not really between two concepts (of liberty) but between one concept and a motley (Arneson 1985).

I think, however, that there is a more productive way to map this terrain, and I will try to do so very briefly in this introduction, laying out some conceptual points of convergence in various renderings of the idea of positive freedom.[3] The essays assembled here are meant to delve into one or another of these points as well as show the moral and political implications of valuing freedom in this sense. The contributors do not all use precisely the same conception or necessarily agree with each other on key issues, but together they present a closely connected array of conceptualizations that will serve as a reference point for social and political theorists who make use of ideas of freedom in their work.

I.1 The Historical Emergences of Positive Liberty

Michael Garnett, in Chapter 1, provides a sweeping and insightful gloss on the history of political thought out of which conceptions of positive freedom have emerged in different ways. He argues, as well, that a major thrust in those traditions is a search for "evaluative unification," where freedom is connected with virtue, reason, well-being, and/or oneness with God, though in various manners and degrees. Many thinkers figure particularly prominently in that history, especially for those who emphasize freedom as a social and political value. Those include figures such as Hegel, Marx, T. H. Green, and others. Green and Marx get individual treatment in the essays by Maria Dimova-Cookson and Avital Simhony (on Green), and Michael Quante (on Marx). These and other theorists prominent in this tradition are also considered by David Ingram (Chapter 5) and Maeve Cooke (Chapter 11).

But what concept, or family of concepts, emerge from this history in a way that uniquely represents a positive conception of freedom? Defenders of such a notion certainly all agree that liberty (as a social and political value) must involve more than simply the absence of interference by others, as in the traditional (negative) liberal idea. The reasons for this are multiple, and many of the essays here emphasize the contrast between positive freedom and liberal conceptions, largely on the latter's narrow

[3] This schematic overview of the concept can be seen as complementary to Michael Garnett's historical/thematic survey of the various conceptions of positive liberty, in Chapter 10.

conception of agency as well as its undertheorized understanding of the social nature of the subject and their actions.[4]

Beyond that, there is divergence in conceptions to be sure. But to some degree or another, theorists tend to focus on a few identifiable conditions as the focal point of freedom. Enabling conditions, factors internal to the agent, the social relations in which the agent is enmeshed, and the connection between freedom and moral value and/or reason are all mentioned in some way or another as relevant factors. Let us then take a brief look at these focal points and how the essays here deal with them.

I.2 Structural Conditions of Positive Freedom

I.2.1 Internal Factors

One of the central components of many positive conceptions of freedom is self-determination, or the ability of the person to be their own master. The absence of interference by others is insufficient for liberty, on these conceptions, because of the way persons can lack freedom because of their inability to determine their own actions, internally, and therefore lacking a key capacity central to free agency. Such self-determination or self-mastery can be understood as being in control of one's decisions and actions rather than being under the sway of addictions, manipulative intrusions into the decision process, or other factors that emanate from "outside" the person. Now such a view may carry with it the postulation of a "higher" and "lower" self – the self-being governed and the self-doing the governing. However, what some might see as the worrisome implications of this postulation can be avoided if the notion of self-determination is unpacked in a *procedural* manner, where conditions of authentic agency can be spelled out without the use of a bifurcated account of the agent (as in, for example, Christman 1991). The idea would be that an agent is free in this sense if the motives and values that move her to action were formed in the right way (that is, not as a result of addiction, manipulation, and so on).

Steven Wall, in Chapter 6, refers to features of internal self-mastery in terms of "mesh," "integration," and "reasons-responsiveness," and I look at this factor under the rubric of "authentic agency" in my contribution

[4] It should be noted, however, that defenders of positive freedom need not dismiss the relevance of open options and noninterference to liberty; they merely argue that it is insufficient for it.

(Chapter 7). Wall's analysis shows how seeing freedom as involving these factors should commit us to a particular connection between freedom and well-being. Similarly, Horacio Spector sees freedom as having the effective power to conceive, choose, and act in ways that realize one's idea of a meaningful life, and this means that paternalism can in certain instances be justified to a greater extent than is normally thought. However, in Chapter 9, Nancy J. Hirschmann argues that we must go further and inquire into how the social construction of desire can be relevant to a person's freedom, and she applies this insight in a special way to the condition of the disabled.

Seeing the connection between individual self-determination and freedom points up the importance of personal *abilities* of various sorts, ones which require not only internal self-control but also resources that all persons need to effectively act on their desires. Moreover, the capacity to so act requires further that one stand in certain social relations with others, both at the interpersonal and political levels. This leads to the next set of elements.

I.2.2 Capabilities

As I mentioned, many theorists view freedom in the austere, negative, sense as importantly incomplete, particularly because it omits mention of those facilitating conditions that allow actions to proceed as intended. That is to say, resources such as food, education, health care, and so on allow agents to pursue activities that they value, and lack of such "capabilities" prevent them from so acting. This is a view famously developed by Amartya Sen, who claims that freedom (as a value central to conceptions of justice) must be seen as involving capabilities to achieve valued functionings (beings and doings seen as worthwhile to the agent) (Sen 1992; see also Crocker 1980). I discuss the importance of capabilities in my chapter, as does Carol Gould (Chapter 8). Rutger Claassen does not explicitly adopt a capabilities model of freedom in his essay here,[5] but he shows that those who connect freedom with access to resources in this way, and who have egalitarian commitments, must look more skeptically at the relation between private property and political power. Specifically, he argues that defenders of positive freedom must look more critically at the

[5] Though for his discussion of the capabilities approach, see Claassen (2018a).

way private property tends strongly to affect political power in decidedly inegalitarian ways (Chapter 12). Gould (Chapter 8) and I (Chapter 7) also show how access to external resources is important for freedom, both for individuals and democratic politics.

I.2.3 Value Conditions

An additional focal point in many conceptions of positive freedom concerns whether free action must be in pursuit of rightful or virtuous aims to count as such. For example, Jean-Jacques Rousseau argued that "moral" freedom requires that one is governed only by laws one has made for oneself, but he added that freedom in society entails conforming to the general will, a volitional expression that represents one's own rational purposes as seen in the context of social cooperation with others. And famously, Kant defined freedom as inherently tied to acting from the moral law.

The relation between (positive) freedom and value is explored in several of the essays here, for example in the chapters by Wall, Quante, Dimova-Cookson, Cooke, and Simhony. This is a preoccupation for such theorists because of the need to avoid the charge made by Berlin and others that the promotion of liberty in the positive sense can lead to the unacceptable exercise of power over citizens in the enforcement of (perhaps contentious) moral principles in the name of freedom. In Chapter 3, Dimova-Cookson takes this charge and argues that indeed we must identify a sense of "moral positive freedom" in addition to "personal positive freedom" typically defended in order to capture the value-laden nature of human action as well as the connection between freedom and well-being. This latter connection is also a focal point for Wall in Chapter 6, who specifically argues that freedom (as self-mastery) can be seen to contribute to one's quality of life but only when that is seen as the pursuit of aims backed by objective reasons. Both Dimova-Cookson and Wall argue vigorously that such a position is compatible with value pluralism of the sort that Berlin so insisted upon and so avoid the worry he expressed that such ideas paradoxically allow people to be "forced to be free."

Simhony, like Dimova-Cookson, draws inspiration from T. H. Green in arguing for a notion of positive freedom as self-realization and self-development in Chapter 4. Like Spector, Simhony discusses the relation between valuing freedom and justifying paternalism, but argues (contra Berlin) that promoting positive freedom in this sense will not lead to undue paternalistic interference.

I.2.4 Social Conditions and Political Implications

Seeing freedom as a kind of self-government – captured by the requirements involving "internal factors" discussed earlier – carries with it certain implications concerning social relations relevant to the enjoyment of liberty. Many defenders of positive freedom emphasize the way that human action must be seen as constituted or shaped by social practices and political institutions, and only insofar as one has some control over those factors can one be said to be free. (As I mentioned, Hirschmann looks specifically at the social construction of the self in this light.)

For this reason, a long tradition of freedom theorists in the positive vein have sought to show a connection between liberty and *democracy*. That is, only if one can participate in a political system that structures the way one lives can one say that one governs oneself in that setting. In Chapter 8, Gould draws a direct connection between freedom and democracy, both at the political level and in the workplace. In my essay, however, I acknowledge the general importance of opportunities for democratic participation for freedom, but I resist making any conceptual ties between freedom and *citizenship* so as to better account for the experiences and aims of those struggling to attain freedom in contemporary settings without enjoying or seeking full citizenship status. Chad Van Schoelandt also draws attention to the relation between freedom and politics, in Chapter 13, by focusing on the role of public reason in establishing the legitimacy of political institutions (and its relation to the freedom of citizens). Cooke, in Chapter 11, takes a close look at the contrasting ways that Jűrgen Habermas and Axel Honneth treat the relation between self-government in the social/ethical lifeworld and modes of public autonomy in democratic practices and institutions.

Other thinkers (many of whom are strongly influenced by Hegel) go further and claim that a specific sort of interpersonal *recognition* is required for freedom, a public acknowledgment of one's identity as an agent in the world. The role of recognition in one's conception of freedom is specifically discussed by Cooke, myself, and Ingram. Indeed, in Chapter 5, Ingram points to some serious difficulties in requiring a robust requirement for recognition at the level of social identity. The ways that different social identities and roles can conflict show that a higher-order reconciliation of more localized recognitive dynamics must be postulated for a recognition-based conception of social freedom to be achieved.

As I mentioned, there is divergence among the thinkers represented here as well as some disagreements about the nature and implications of a plausible conception of freedom. In general, however, the purpose of this collection is to gather together some of the best reflections on the idea of freedom in this positive register and, in so doing, provide models of that condition that can best capture what is truly valuable about a free society and why so many have sacrificed so much to attain it.

CHAPTER 1

Unity and Disunity in the Positive Tradition

Michael Garnett

Positive freedom can be hard to pin down. While negative freedom may be characterized as an absence of coercion or physical prevention, and republican freedom as an absence of interpersonal domination, positive freedom resists such pithy treatment. Moreover, this isn't due to a lack of possible elucidations but due to an overabundance of them. The term is widely taken to refer to a variety of seemingly distinct goods, including but not limited to actually exercisable options or capabilities (Crocker 1980; Gould 1988); collective self-determination (Taylor 1979: 175; R. Dworkin 2011: 365); individual, psychological self-government (Christman 1991; Hirschmann 1996; Carter 2019); and self-realization or flourishing (Skinner 2002; Bilgrami 2018). Indeed the term's most influential purveyor himself, Isaiah Berlin (1969a), seems to characterize positive freedom in mutually inconsistent ways within the space of only a few pages.

Why is this? Part of the explanation, though not all of it, is a persistent but often unacknowledged tendency to think of the distinction between positive and negative freedom as *exhaustive*. If the distinction is exhaustive, then positive freedom is any freedom that isn't negative, and vice versa. If negative freedom is narrowly defined, as it usually is (in terms, say, of noncoercion or physical nonprevention), then positive freedom must be widely defined. "Positive freedom" thus becomes a catch-all term for any rag-tag number of heterogeneous conceptions, united only in their rejection of the negative approach. After all, one thing that capabilities, collective self-determination, psychological self-government, and self-realization all have in common is the fact that none of them is equivalent to mere

Thank you to John Christman for his valuable advice and comments, as well as for inspiring me to embark on this project. Thank you also to Susan James for very helpful conversations and comments on the chapter. Finally, thank you to Robyn Blum, Kirstin Borgerson, Danielle Bromwich, Sophia Connell, Andrew Huddleston, Hallvard Lillehammer, Douglas MacKay, and Joseph Millum for their feedback on an earlier draft.

noncoercion or physical nonprevention. If the positive/negative freedom distinction is exhaustive, this fact on its own suffices to qualify them (and many more besides) as "positive conceptions." For this reason, however, if "positive freedom" is to pick out its own distinct and internally coherent way of thinking about freedom, then the idea that the positive/negative distinction is exhaustive needs to be avoided.

Moreover, the root of this idea is a tendency to see the positive/negative distinction as a logical one concerning the underlying form of freedom claims. If the distinction is ultimately one of logical form – such as, for instance, between "freedom from" and "freedom to," or between analyses that take freedom to require the world to be a certain way and those that take freedom to require the world not to be a certain way – then it makes sense to expect it to be exhaustive. If "positive freedom" is to pick out a unified approach of its own, this way of thinking about the distinction must be avoided too. That is, even if there does turn out to be some purely formal distinction to be had here (a much-debated question: see e.g., MacCallum 1967; Christman 2005a; Nelson 2005; Elford 2013), this isn't the direction to look if we want a chance of viewing positive freedom as a coherent conception in its own right.

To do that, we need to treat "positive" and "negative" not as *descriptions* of logical forms but as *names* of intellectual traditions. Unlike logical forms, intellectual traditions are messy and historically contingent. Nevertheless, they're developed in response to intelligible philosophical problems and pressures, and manifest some degree of internal unity. Treating positive and negative freedom as intellectual traditions, therefore, allows each to be understood as its own coherent family of conceptions, and not simply as a repository of conceptions excluded by the other. The price of doing so, however, is treating the positive/negative distinction as gappy.

Recognizing the distinction's gappiness has another benefit, which is that it helps us to situate the ideas of positive and negative freedom in their proper cultural contexts. A philosophical tradition is more than just a set of positions located in conceptual space; it's a set of views developed over time by thinkers in intellectual contact with one another. This makes philosophical traditions *inherently parochial* in a way that philosophical positions, abstractly specified, aren't. I here take "positive freedom" to pick out one strand of what's generally (though inaccurately) termed as "Western" philosophy – that is, roughly, philosophical thought descended from Ancient Greece. In doing so, I take "positive freedom" and "negative freedom" to name ways of thinking that just happened to develop in particular times and places in response to local intellectual pressures, such that they're unlikely to exhaust the domain of conceptual possibilities for thinking about freedom. This opens space for thinking about other approaches too – such as the republican view, which (along with its feminist and black liberationist versions) grew in conversation with them, and views of freedom developed independently in other intellectual contexts, such as Confucian and Daoist views (Ni 2002; Jiang 2011, 2012). In addition, it points to the fact that there may yet be important areas of conceptual space still to be explored.

In this chapter, I aim to bring the positive conception into better focus by tracing the positive tradition through some of its twists and turns, and considering in what ways it might qualify as a single tradition. Drawing on the lessons of this survey, I then suggest a way of thinking about the nature of positive freedom that is both principled and historically informed.

1.1 The Positive Tradition

What, then, is the "positive" tradition? What gives it unity and coherence, and constitutes it as a single tradition? To answer these questions effectively, we'll need to do more than simply catalog different philosophers' accounts of freedom and point to their similarities and differences. To understand what really drives the positive tradition, we'll need to know not only what various philosophers took freedom to be but also, more deeply, why it mattered to them: what they took to be *at stake* in disagreements over the meaning of freedom. Only by understanding the underlying *point* of holding a positive account of freedom will we be able to fully understand what unifies it as a single tradition.

With this in mind, I suggest that we see the positive tradition as unified by unity itself: a commitment to the project of *evaluative unification*. More specifically, it's unified by a commitment to the view that freedom is necessarily coextensive with *some or all* of the values on the following list: (1) moral virtue, (2) reason and understanding, (3) well-being, and (4) oneness with God. Moreover, although "positive freedom" is now generally taken to be a political concept, its roots lie in a meta-ethical project that's concerned with the ultimate authority of moral norms. Accordingly, two principal philosophical motivations for seeking to establish this unification are to be found within the tradition – one meta-ethical, and one political – and we must distinguish carefully between them.

The central aim of the meta-ethical version of the evaluative unification project is to secure morality from skeptical challenge. It seeks to do this by showing that moral virtue is necessarily coextensive with, and therefore necessary for, the realization of (some or all of) the other values on the list. This project takes off from Plato and runs through the Stoics; Neoplatonism; much of Muslim, Jewish, and Christian philosophy in the medieval period; early modern rationalism; German idealism; and remains with us today in the form of neo-Kantian and neo-Hegelian orientations within contemporary moral philosophy.

The more familiar political version develops out of this. It's concerned with articulating a vision of the free society that might serve as a less individualistic alternative to the classical liberal ideal of a set of people bound by nothing other than their freely-entered-into contracts. It aims to show that freedom is necessarily coextensive with (at least) objective well-being and some form of ethical life, thereby supporting a view of the free society as one of socially embedded individuals reinforcing and constituting one another's freedom through mutual flourishing. Drawing on the rich legacy of the meta-ethical version, especially the work of Hegel and other politically oriented rationalists (such as Spinoza), this version of the project takes off in the wake of the Industrial Revolution and is developed primarily by socialists, anti-imperialists, and left-liberals of the nineteenth and twentieth centuries.

Although the two versions have different philosophical aims, they're united in their commitment to evaluative unification. What's more, both draw on a shared pool of intellectual resources in order to establish that unification. Four basic argumentative strategies are particularly important, which I label as the *rational order strategy*, the *reflective consciousness strategy*, the *recognition strategy*, and the *social nature strategy*. In the next two sections, I sketch the historical trajectories of the two versions of the unification project, and I also outline these four basic strategies for securing the unification. Before embarking on this history, however, I make two preliminary points about its intended scope.

The first is that my topic here is the nature of freedom itself, i.e., *what freedom is*. We should recognize, however, that not everyone who's had something important and original to say about freedom has been concerned with its finer conceptual details, or has occupied themselves with advancing our strictly philosophical understanding of its fundamental nature. Many have focused instead on other pressing questions about freedom, such as how it's to be obtained, how it's to be preserved, or how it's curtailed in practice. This is true, for instance, of much Marxist theory: from Marx's immediate successors, Friedrich Engels and Karl Kautsky, to intellectual revolutionaries such as Rosa Luxemburg,

Vladimir Lenin, Leon Trotsky, Mao Zedong, and Fidel Castro, to "Western Marxists" such as György Lukács, Karl Korsch, Antonio Gramsci, Antonio Negri, Max Horkheimer, Theodor Adorno, and Herbert Marcuse, to Marxist anticolonial theorists such as M. N. Roy, José Carlos Mariátegui, and C. L. R. James, theoretical attention has tended to focus more on the *hows* of freedom than on the *what* of freedom. That is, discussions of how exactly capitalism defeats human freedom, of how capitalist and state structures operate to shut off opportunities for freedom by myriad and subtle means (including ideological means), of how this can be meaningfully and successfully opposed in practice, of what a socialist society ought to look like – such discussions typically just take for granted something like Marx's conception of freedom as creative and cooperative self-realization (though see Cohen 1983 for a prominent exception). Such a conception forms part of the common political orientation that enables such theorists to debate other, more pressing questions within a shared conceptual framework. But these further questions aren't my topic here.

The second is this. It's that there's a difference between holding, say, a theory of self-realization, and holding a theory of *freedom as* self-realization. One can theorize self-realization in detail, and regard it as a concept of great importance, without identifying it with freedom. Hence one might have a theory of self-realization but define freedom negatively (as did J. S. Mill 1981 [1824]: 296; MacGilvray 2011: 159); or one might have a theory of self-realization and take no explicit view on the nature of freedom at all. One cannot be said, in these cases, to have a positive view of freedom. Of course, if *we* subscribe to the view that freedom is self-realization (or collective self-determination, or social recognition, or any of the other things commonly identified with positive freedom), then, from our point of view, any theorist of these things is thereby a theorist of freedom – a freedom theorist *de re*, as it were. But there's no reason (yet) to ascribe to *that theorist* any thesis about freedom at all. The tradition of positive freedom, as I here understand it, isn't a tradition of theorizing *these things*; it's a tradition of theorizing *freedom* by identifying or connecting it with these things. My focus in what follows is, therefore, the development of explicit ideas about the concept of freedom itself.

1.2 Evaluative Unification as a Meta-ethical Project

Although freedom was by no means a central concept in classical Greek philosophy, our story nevertheless begins in the fourth century BCE with

Plato's attempt to secure morality against skeptical challenges. Plato addresses a family of skeptical positions (voiced by Callicles in the *Gorgias* and Thrasymachus and Glaucon in the *Republic*), but the basic challenge can be characterized in terms of three central themes. The first is the idea that those who do good willingly are *irrational*: they're fools, duped to serve the interests of others at their own expense, whereas those who understand the true nature of the world see through morality's fog and pursue their own advantage with clear eyes. The second is the idea that morality requires us to act *against our self-interest*: morality commands us to be honorable and honest, and thus to forgo opportunities for self-advancement. The third is the idea that morality is *oppressive*: both a constraint on our agency (as Glaucon puts it, "no man is just of his own free will, but only under compulsion" [*Republic* 360c]), and an illegitimate mode of social control, a way for others to "subdue" us "into slavery" (*Gorgias* 484a).

In response, Plato mounts the strongest possible counterargument. Focusing on the charges of irrationality and disadvantage, he aims not only to *reject* these claims but to *invert* them. Thus, he argues that virtue stems not from a misunderstanding of the true nature of the world but from the greatest possible insight into the nature of reality (specifically, rational understanding of the Form of the Good). At the same time, he argues that justice isn't a restraint on one's ability to pursue one's interests but a constitutive condition of psychological well-being (since only a just soul can be internally well-ordered). So, morality, reason, and well-being necessarily coincide, and morality is thereby secured from skeptical challenge.

By contrast with reason and well-being, Plato has little to say about freedom, and he doesn't respond to the third strand of the skeptical challenge directly. Nevertheless, it's clear what he would need to argue were he to wish to extend the strategy: that moral virtue isn't oppressive, but liberating. Indeed, such an idea was already implicit in much of Plato's work (Stalley 1998), and was increasingly brought to the surface by later theorists as they sought to shore up and extend his anti-skeptical arguments. In this way, it eventually became common to include freedom as an additional target of unification (as well as oneness with God, a theme of Plato's later works).

We see this most prominently with the Stoics. From the third century BCE to the second century CE, Stoic thinkers advanced exactly such a comprehensive version of the evaluative unification doctrine. Moreover, they developed a highly influential set of arguments in favor of it.

According to Stoic doctrine, the world is a fully deterministic system providentially ordered by God in accordance with reason, such that everything occurs by both causal and rational necessity (Cooper 2003). As we become more rational, and achieve greater insight into the workings of the world, our rational purposes come into alignment with God's, and with the operation of the universe itself. Hence rationality entails oneness with God. Moreover, since everything that happens is rationally necessary, the truly rational person desires all and only what's actual, and is therefore guaranteed always to get what they want. Hence rationality entails well-being. What's more, insofar as we desire all and only what's actual, we can never be prevented or constrained from getting what we want. Hence rationality entails freedom. Finally, a rational order is one that treats all of its parts appropriately, and a rational person will be motivated accordingly. Hence reason entails morality. As the first-century Stoic Epictetus puts it, when the capacity for reason is rightly exercised "there is freedom, serenity, cheerfulness, constancy, and there is justice, too, and law, and self-control, and virtue in its entirety" (*Discourses*, F4).

Call this the *rational order strategy*. It relies on the key metaphysical premise that everything unfolds by rational necessity. Its basic idea, that reason, virtue, freedom, happiness, and oneness with God are necessarily bound together by an underlying rational order, and that this grounds the authority of morality, was the common intellectual currency for many centuries: important variations on the theme can be found, for instance, in the works of Ibn Sina (970–1037), Thomas Aquinas (1225–1274), and Gersonides (1288–1344) among others. However, the view was also subject to increasing pressure, not from moral skepticism but from a rival view about the ultimate ground of moral authority. This was theological voluntarism: the view that the ultimate ground of morality is just God's arbitrary will.

Theological voluntarism has ancient roots; Plato himself famously saw fit to try to refute it in the *Euthyphro*, and it was debated forcefully throughout the medieval period. Yet the rise of Protestantism in the sixteenth and seventeenth centuries put it increasingly on the front foot. The view challenges every part of the evaluative unification doctrine. It holds that the ultimate justification of the moral law is rationally inscrutable, breaking the connection between virtue and reason. It makes God an external lawgiver located outside our moral community, breaking the connection between virtue and oneness with God. It denies that piety must be in our earthly interests, breaking the connection between virtue and well-being (that is, the *constitutive* connection: virtue and happiness remain instrumentally connected by means of divine reward and punishment). And it treats obedience to the moral law as a form of submission to God's arbitrary will, breaking the connection between virtue and freedom.

Some aspects of this voluntarist position can be found in the moral systems of philosophers as otherwise diverse as Hugo Grotius, Thomas Hobbes, René Descartes, Samuel von Pufendorf, and John Locke (Schneewind 1998). To some other philosophers of the sixteenth and seventeenth centuries, however, theological voluntarism was unacceptable in its entirety. If moral terms are definable only with reference to God's arbitrary will, then the idea of the moral goodness of God is emptied of content. What's more, if it's only God's brute power, and not His goodness, that supplies our reason for doing as He wishes, then God seems reduced to an amoral tyrant whose decrees we must subserviently obey. Thus Leibniz, for instance, inveighed against those who took the view that God could "cause sins to be committed, simply at his will and pleasure," complaining that they "liken us to earthworms which men crush without heeding as they walk" (*Theodicy*, Preface).

Partly influenced by the Stoic revival of the late fifteenth century, several philosophers, therefore, attempted to beat back the threat of theological voluntarism by defending evaluative unification. Once again, they looked to the rational order strategy as a means of securing unification. Spinoza (1632–1677), Leibniz (1646–1716), and Christian Wolff (1679–1754) all developed speculative metaphysical systems aimed precisely at establishing the key premise of rational order, that the world unfolds by rational necessity. This enabled them to argue that the ultimate authority of moral rules lies not in God's arbitrary will but in reason itself; that virtue requires not self-abnegation but the full realization of one's own good; that reason and understanding bring us closer to God; and, most importantly for our purposes, that compliance with moral and rational principles is not a form of subjugation, but true freedom. As Spinoza puts it in his *Ethics*, therefore, "virtue itself, and the service of God" is "happiness itself, and the greatest freedom" (II, P.49, Schol.4a).

However, a persistent difficulty with the rational order strategy was its seeming commitment to causal determinism. If every event is rationally necessitated by prior events, then every event is predetermined. This idea, fundamental to the strategy, is one that many were unable to accept due to its apparent incompatibility with free will and moral responsibility. Indeed, Spinozism was widely condemned on these grounds, and Leibniz's disciple, Wolff, was banished from the University of Halle by theologians alarmed by the determinism seemingly inherent in Leibniz's Principle of Sufficient Reason.

It was in this context that Immanuel Kant (1724–1804) sought a new way of grounding the authority of moral imperatives. He, too, regarded the rational order strategy's commitment to determinism as morally unacceptable. Yet he also rejected theological voluntarism, holding that the ultimate ground of morality lies in our own capacity for reason and not in external commands. His task, therefore, was to find a way of grounding morality in human reason without presupposing a rational order. Part of his solution, famously sketched in his *Groundwork of the Metaphysics of Morals* (1785), was to try to uncover necessary conceptual connections between freedom, reason, and morality simply within the structure of reflective consciousness itself.

The basic idea is this. In deciding what to do, one could choose simply to act on the basis of some externally given principle, such as a natural inclination, an internalized norm, or a command. Yet any such externally given principle stands in need of further justification, and in failing to consider its further justification one abdicates one's powers of reason. Simultaneously, one forfeits one's freedom, since one allows oneself to be subject to an external principle. So, *both* freedom *and* reason demand that one step back from externally given principles of action and seek further justification for their authority; in this way, freedom and reason necessarily coincide in the search for self-given principles of action. Moreover, both necessarily coincide with morality too, since once one has stepped back from all contingently given principles, the only rational principles that remain are lawlike and universal in form, such that they must be binding on all rational beings. Hence freedom, reason, and morality necessarily coincide.

Call this the *reflective consciousness strategy*. It offers a pared-down version of the doctrine of evaluative unification, linking only morality, freedom, and reason. Its central idea, that both freedom and reason inhere in the very structure of reflective consciousness, is foundational to Kant's critical project. For many members of the influential generation of German philosophers who came up in the immediate aftermath of Kant, too, this served as the fundamental philosophical insight from which their systems were to be constructed (Henrich 2008). Moreover, some of these philosophers came also to accept the claim, initially associated with Friedrich Jacobi, that any fully coherent rationalist philosophy must be Spinozist, and so to seek a reconciliation of Spinoza with what they took to be the fundamental insights of Kant. This "Spinozism of freedom," a rational order derived from the structure of reflective consciousness, was to constitute a synthesis of the two strategies for evaluative unification.

This, in short, is the task that Hegel (1770–1831) aimed to complete. In doing so, he also developed a sophisticated analysis of the inherently social dimensions of individual freedom that would prove highly influential. I note just two important features of his approach. First, part of what Hegel purports to find within the structure of reflective consciousness itself is the fact that free agents are rationally bound to protect and promote their own subjective capacity for freedom (Patten 1999). Yet, he holds, this subjective capacity is itself constitutively dependent on a certain form of life supported by particular social and political institutions. To protect and promote one's capacity for freedom, therefore, is necessarily to protect and promote the freedom-sustaining culture in which one finds oneself, and the social and political institutions that support it.

Second, Hegel brought to the fore a new argument designed to secure a version of the evaluative unification doctrine: the *recognition strategy*. The central idea is that in order to be a genuinely free or autonomous agent, and for your projects to have meaning and worth, your agency and autonomy must be acknowledged and recognized by others. Put differently: eternal solitude would eventually render all of your projects pointless, thereby undermining your capacity for autonomous agency. What's more, your agency and autonomy must be *freely* recognized by others. Coerced or brainwashed "recognition" is meaningless. In this way, the freedom of each is necessarily bound up with the freedom of all: free beings have reason to care about the freedom of others, since this is necessary for their lives to be worthwhile. Thus freedom, well-being (understood as self-realization or meaningfulness), and ethical concern necessarily coincide.

For most of its history, the meta-ethical version of the evaluative unification project looked predominantly to versions of the rational order strategy as a way of securing the desired unification. Yet in the nineteenth and twentieth centuries, waning religious belief made it increasingly difficult to substantiate the key premise of rational order on which that strategy relies. As a result, philosophers came to focus more on alternative routes to evaluative unification, and both the reflective consciousness and recognition strategies became increasingly influential. Indeed the central question, for neo-Kantian and neo-Hegelian moral philosophers respectively, came to be whether sufficiently naturalized versions of these arguments could be extracted from the metaphysical systems in which they were originally embedded and be vindicated on their own terms. Attempts at affirmative answers to this question continue to this day: the meta-ethical version of the evaluative unification project has been, without doubt, one of the most stable and long-lasting research projects in human history.

1.3 Evaluative Unification as a Political Project

If evaluative unification could be established, however, its significance would not be restricted to meta-ethics alone. The original project was to defend morality by showing its necessary connections with reason, well-being, freedom, and oneness with God. But this same set of necessary connections, once in place, can be put to work in different ways. To take one set of examples: some early modern scientists sought to defend their work by arguing that by increasing our rational understanding of the world they were thereby increasing our virtue and freedom, and bringing us closer to God (Shapin 1996), and in the late seventeenth century Mary Astell (1666–1731) argued (in her *A Serious Proposal to the Ladies* [1694]) in favor of the education of women partly on the grounds that to develop women's powers of reason is also necessarily to increase their virtue, freedom, well-being, and Godliness. Such arguments draw on the same inferential connections as the meta-ethical project but put them into reverse; that is, instead of seeking to defend virtue by appeal to its necessary connections with reason (and other values), they seek to defend reason by appeal to its necessary connections with virtue (and other values).

I turn now to another such redeployment of the unification doctrine. Its aim was to articulate an alternative to the rhetorically potent conception of market freedom that had emerged during the eighteenth century, and continued to develop and grow in political importance throughout the nineteenth and twentieth centuries. By "market freedom" I mean, roughly, the idea that open markets are essential to individual freedom (MacGilvray 2011). Prior to the Industrial Revolution, this was a predominantly republican idea, aimed at dismantling the monopoly power wielded by large landowners and guilds and eliminating the "servile dependency" they engendered. The eighteenth-century republican vision – as found, for instance, in the work of Adam Smith – was of a society of independent tradesmen, yeomen, and small-scale proprietors dealing with each other on equal terms, no longer vulnerable to the arbitrary whims of the local Lord or Baron. In the nineteenth century, however, industrialization and the vast economies of scale it permitted radically changed the nature of economic production. As firms grew, new social hierarchies and new relations of domination and dependence arose within them. Market freedom ceased to be an unalloyed republican good (Anderson 2017). Indeed, republican ideas came to be influentially turned *against* the goal of unfettered markets, and a new "labor republican" movement, rooted in the working class, argued that propertyless wage laborers were subject to the domination of employers and therefore were unfree (Gourevitch 2013).

Partly for these reasons, the ideal of market freedom came to be defended by appeal to a thinner, negative conception of freedom. This conception, associated in this period most closely with Jeremy Bentham but descended ultimately from Hobbes, takes political freedom to consist primarily in "the silence of the laws," that is, in noninterference by the state or others in one's actions. It's controversial exactly to what extent the idea of negative freedom does in fact succeed in helping to support the ideal of market freedom (see, e.g., Cohen 2011b). However, what concerns us here isn't negative freedom in its strict philosophical form, but its rhetorical form: that (somewhat vague) ideal of noninterference typically invoked by politicians and polemicists in defense of small-state, *laissez-faire* capitalism. This is the idea to which positive theorists are best taken to be reacting.

Such a conception may be characterized, for current purposes, in terms of two key features. First, it's a conception of freedom as *social noninterference*: freedom is fundamentally a matter of other people getting out of your way. (What exactly it means for someone to be "in your way" in the relevant sense is a matter of some delicacy, the most common interpretations being physical prevention, coercion, and rights violation.) The second feature, which follows from the first, is a commitment to *preference neutrality*: a person's degree of freedom has nothing to do with the content of their preferences. Individuals may therefore be treated as black boxes from the point of view of freedom with no need to interrogate the nature or origin of their desires. Taken together, these features yield a view of freedom that appears at least *prima facie* conducive to the following, classically liberal picture of the free society: one of atomic individuals bound by nothing other than their own freely-entered-into contracts.

Many opposed this vision: from reformist, left-liberals to revolutionary socialists, this constituted a broad swathe of political opinion. Some, such as J. S. Mill, L. T. Hobhouse and Isaiah Berlin, accepted the negative account and opposed unrestricted market capitalism on the basis of values they took to be distinct from freedom, such as equality or self-development. However, others, such as Karl Marx (1818–1883), Thomas Hill Green (1836–1882), John Dewey (1859–1952), Hannah Arendt (1906–1975), and Simone de Beauvoir (1908–1986), sought to reject the negative conception. Instead, they argued that freedom is necessarily coextensive with active participation in some form of social and ethical life, and in doing so they drew on the rich legacy of the meta-ethical version of the evaluative unification project. Moreover, in addition to reworking the old strategies for establishing the unity of freedom with other values, some of them also turned to a newer one: the social nature strategy.

We see the continuing influence of the old strategies most clearly in the work of thinkers like Green. A key figure in the dissemination of German idealism within anglophone philosophy, Green deploys recognizably Kantian and Hegelian versions of the reflective consciousness and rational order strategies to demonstrate the necessary coincidence of freedom, reason, virtue, happiness, and oneness with (a somewhat naturalized) God. On the one hand, this evaluative unification offers him a traditional solution to the old problem of securing the moral order, here presented in Victorian guise as the problem of finding space for Christian conceptions of moral community within an increasingly scientifically disenchanted world. On the other hand, however, it also offers a solution to a newer problem, increasingly pressing for those of Green's political leanings: that of developing a philosophical critique of laissez-faire capitalism grounded in an alternative vision of liberalism (Simhony 1993; Dimova-Cookson 2003; see also Simhony's and Dimova-Cookson's essays in this volume).

In particular, it enables him to define political freedom, not as non-interference, but as "the liberation of the powers of all men equally for contributions to a common good" (Green 1986a: 200). This, in turn, allows him to move away from the wholehearted commitment to freedom of contract familiar from natural-rights-based forms of classical liberalism, and to mount a freedom-based argument for restrictions on trade and employment. Thus, for Green, one doesn't limit a person's freedom by preventing them from getting drunk, or taking an exploitative job: to the contrary, one keeps open a space in which they might come to attain freedom. Similarly, one doesn't limit a person's freedom by preventing them from selling alcohol, or exploiting others: one helps them to contribute to the common good, and so to realize their freedom. This is, for instance, the basis of the philosophical case that Green developed in favor of the legislative program of the reforming Liberal government of 1868 to 1874.

However, not everyone was so amenable to the underlying idealist metaphysics that Green used to secure these conclusions. For less spiritually minded thinkers, the *social nature strategy* suggested a promising way forward. Drawn from Aristotelian ideas, its key premise is that we're naturally social beings, and that we can realize our natures only through certain forms of (at least minimally ethical) social relationships. Since to realize one's essential human nature is to flourish as a human being, this connects objective well-being with participation in social and ethical life. Moreover, inasmuch as freedom requires that we be determined to action not by alien forces but by our own essential natures, this individual and collective flourishing also necessarily coincides with individual freedom. Thus freedom is necessarily coextensive both with objective well-being and with participation in social and ethical life.

We find something like this line of thought, for instance, in Marx's early works (such as his *Economic and Philosophic Manuscripts of 1844*). For Marx, our essential human nature – what he calls our "species being" – consists in both doing and understanding ourselves as doing creative labor for the sake of the community. When we realize our essential human nature in this way, we flourish, and we experience our lives as meaningful and worthwhile. By contrast, when we're alienated from our own humanity, as Marx believes most people necessarily are under capitalism, we're reduced to a bestial existence, we experience our lives as meaningless (or we seek meaning in comforting illusions, like religion), and we're unfree (Wood 1981; see also Michael Quante's essay, Chapter 2, in this volume). True freedom and human flourishing, therefore, necessarily coincide.

So too do freedom and ethical life. If we're inherently social beings, and if freedom consists in the realization of our human nature, then freedom requires that we act from an understanding of our proper role within society. It requires, for instance, that we work in concert to meet our shared needs, and that we exercise collective control over our jointly held productive powers. Someone who seeks to exploit or to dominate others is therefore necessarily unfree, since such a person is failing to act from consciousness of their true nature as an inherently social being. Thus true human emancipation, according to Marx, can be achieved only when each person "has become a *species-being* in his empirical life, his individual work and his individual relationships, only when man has recognized and organized his own forces as *social forces* so that social force is no longer separated from him" (Marx 1975: 234).

Though elaborated in different ways, the idea that human beings are inherently social, such that our individual and collective flourishing is always ultimately in alignment, is one that's common to many different ethical traditions (including, among others, ancient Greek ethics, Ubuntu ethics, and Confucianism). However, not all such traditions explicitly identify this socially oriented form of individual flourishing with *freedom* or, indeed, treat freedom as a central moral value at all. However, as capitalism came to be exported and imposed around the world with increasing force throughout the nineteenth and twentieth centuries, many of its anti-imperial opponents turned to versions of the social nature thesis in order to articulate what they saw as the incompatibility between such traditional philosophical ideals of collective ethical life, on the one hand, and the ideal of market freedom, on the other. In some cases, as with Kwame Nkrumah (1909–1972) in Ghana and Julius Nyerere (1922–1999) in Tanzania, this involved connecting Marx's deployment of the social nature strategy with existing versions of the social nature thesis; in other cases, as with Mohandas Gandhi (1869–1948) in India, local versions of the thesis were harnessed in service of anti-imperialist ends without any general commitment to Marxism (Bilgrami 2014).

Some non-Marxist liberals, too, looked to the social nature strategy as a promising basis for rejecting unfettered market capitalism. Dewey, for instance, took the negative conception of freedom to be the lynchpin of a dangerously atomized, overly individualistic form of liberalism that he wished to reject. Drawing from Hegel, he argued that human beings are necessarily constituted by their cultures and their social institutions, and that this inherent sociality renders mere noninterference a questionable ideal. Instead, a true concern for freedom requires that we look to the nature of our institutions, and that we aim to create and maintain a culture that permits the full development of individual potential. Thus liberty is "that secure release and fulfilment of personal potentialities which take place only in rich and manifold association with others" (Dewey 1927b: 150), and it's possible only within a substantively democratic culture in which people exercise collective deliberative control over the full range of social and economic institutions by which they're constituted.

Similarly, Beauvoir deployed a version of the social nature strategy with Hegelian elements, though hers is a distinctively existentialist rendering of that idea. For her, as for other existentialists, human beings are fundamentally, ontologically free; this is something we can either deny, by living alienated lives bound by external rules and norms, or realize, by living authentically and taking ultimate responsibility for our choices. But only in the latter case do we achieve a second, higher form of freedom – authenticity – and only then are our lives and projects truly meaningful. In this sense, failure to realize one's own freedom as authenticity is self-destructive; it's also irrational, inasmuch as freely pursuing unfreedom can be taken to involve a kind of practical contradiction. These lines of thought connect freedom, flourishing, and reason. Yet a common criticism of existentialism as developed in the mid-twentieth century was that its strict denial of the bindingness of external values and norms committed it to a form of moral nihilism. Beauvoir did more than anyone else to rebut this charge (primarily in her *The Ethics of Ambiguity* [1976]), and she did so in a way that also enabled her to reject socially atomistic forms of liberalism in favor of more democratic and egalitarian social and political institutions.

Beauvoir seeks a middle path between a conception of human beings as pure, free, reflective consciousnesses and one of them as materially embodied and causally determined. Hence consciousness is fundamentally free – humanity is freedom – but it's also, essentially, constrained by the world around it: the natural world, and the world as shaped by our past and current actions, including the social meanings with which we've imbued it (Morgan 2008). This tension between our "transcendence" and "immanence" is, for her, the fundamental ambiguity at the heart of the human condition. It means that our freedom, although primary, is vulnerable to the world, and especially to the social world. Insofar as we value our own freedom, then, we must value the freedom of others, and we must act together to protect and promote our freedom over time by developing democratic institutions capable of respecting both our individual freedom and our social embeddedness (Pettersen 2015). Thus freedom, flourishing, reason, and morality all necessarily coincide in the fully authentic life: this is an existentialist rendering of the classic doctrine of evaluative unification.

1.4 Positive Freedom: Its Shape

I've argued that "positive freedom" names a particular intellectual tradition. This tradition, I've suggested, is unified by a concern with evaluative unification, but disunified with respect to the overall programmatic aims of that unification. Whereas some positive theorists have sought unification in order to supply an ultimate ground for moral authority, others have done so in order to support a non-individualistic conception of the free society, and still others have done so for both purposes at once. Nevertheless, what constitutes the positive tradition as a unified whole is its endorsement of conceptions of freedom that permit the unification of freedom with *some or all* of reason, virtue, well-being, and oneness with God. A positive conception of freedom, therefore, may be profitably characterized as any conception of freedom primarily designed to facilitate such a unification.

This approach offers a more promising way of making sense of the idea of positive freedom than one that seeks to analyze it in terms of its underlying conceptual form. Positive accounts needn't share a single underlying conceptual form. For instance, it's often been pointed out that a standard negative account, on which freedom is construed as an absence of external constraints, can be transformed into a positive one simply by expanding what's meant by "constraints" (MacCallum 1967; Nelson 2005). If "constraints" are taken to include internal constraints, and – more to the point – if irrational, immoral, or self-destructive motivations are taken to be necessarily constraining, then we'll have arrived at what is, in effect, a positive view. Some have taken this to show that there's no deep distinction to be drawn between positive and negative accounts. Yet what makes a view positive isn't its attitude towards the idea of constraint, but its taking freedom to be necessarily coextensive with rationality, virtue, well-being, or oneness with God – a doctrine that's compatible with a variety of different positions regarding the nature of constraints.

Epictetus, for example, starts from a definition of freedom as the absence of all possible constraints to the satisfaction of actual desires (*Discourses*, D4.1). As a view of the relationship between freedom and constraint, that's a difficult position to categorize. It shares with modern republican accounts the idea, rejected by negative ones, that *merely possible* constraints are sufficient to compromise freedom; but it departs from both in focusing only on possible constraints to actual desires. Nevertheless, it *becomes* a positive account when combined with the Stoic version of the rational order doctrine to yield the view that freedom, so defined, is necessarily coextensive with reason, virtue, well-being, and oneness with God.

By contrast, Spinoza defines freedom as that "which exists from the necessity of its nature alone, and is determined to act by itself alone," and unfreedom as that which is "determined by another to exist and produce an effect in a determinate way" (*Ethics* I, def. VII). This definition doesn't depend on any meaningful conception of constraint at all; instead, it focuses on the causes of one's activity. What justifies us in ascribing a positive account of freedom to Spinoza isn't any purely logical feature of this definition, but the fact that he deploys it in concert with a broader metaphysical system designed to secure evaluative unification. Positive freedom isn't positive by virtue of having a certain canonical underlying logical form; it's positive by virtue of being designed to facilitate such a unification.

Nevertheless, positive accounts do typically share certain general features, and this way of characterizing them with reference to their historical point allows for a satisfying and unified explanation of them. Four such features are particularly important. They are, first, the idea that freedom has *specific content*; second, the idea that freedom is an *exercise concept*; third, a focus on *inner freedom*; and, fourth, a tendency towards *split views of the self*. Taken together, these give the general shape of any traditional positive approach, and all four can be explained in terms of the imperatives of evaluative unification.

I start with specific content. On a negative approach, removing constraints frees people regardless of what they choose to do with that freedom. Republican accounts, too, typically take freedom to be preference-neutral, insofar as they tend not to place principled limits on what undominated people might choose to do. By contrast, positive accounts traditionally require that free people act in certain ways, or on the basis of certain motivations. According to Kant, for instance, you're autonomous only insofar as you're acting from pure principles of practical reason; according to Green, similarly, you're free only insofar as you're acting out of concern for the common good. Different positive accounts may set broader or narrower prescriptions regarding this specific content. But it's a common commitment of traditional positive accounts that those who act, say, immorally, or irrationally, or self-destructively, are *thereby* unfree. This follows trivially from evaluative unification.

Moreover, this idea that freedom has specific content entails that merely having a range of options is insufficient for freedom. In Charles Taylor's (1979) terms, therefore, positive freedom is an "exercise" concept. If freedom requires you to choose or act in certain ways – that is, if freedom has specific content – then options aren't enough: you have to choose or act in the specified ways. Thus Marx, for instance, doesn't take freedom merely to require that one have the *option* of engaging in unalienated labor. One must actually do so, and someone who "chooses" to engage in alienated labor instead isn't free. In this sense, positive accounts treat freedom as a particular mode of agency (Christman 2005a). This also follows from evaluative unification. That's because rationality, virtue, and well-being are all exercise concepts: you don't qualify as rational or virtuous or flourishing just on account of having the *options* of acting in rational or virtuous or flourishing ways – you actually have to exercise those options. And if freedom is to be necessarily coextensive with one or more of these exercise concepts, then it must be treated as an exercise concept too.

What's more, if freedom is an exercise concept – a particular mode of agency – then it must also be, at least in part, an internal or psychological matter. Unlike negative and republican accounts, which traditionally focus mainly on external enemies of freedom, positive accounts are centrally concerned with questions of motivation and consciousness. Thus the Roman Stoics famously held that even someone with maximal external freedom, such as an Emperor, could nevertheless lack true freedom by having a slavish mentality (and that, contrariwise, even a slave could be truly free). Other positive conceptions, such as Kantian moral autonomy, are realizable in the absence of external freedom too. Moreover, this focus on the psychological aspects of freedom is also a direct upshot of evaluative unification. Rationality and virtue are internal properties, at least in part; throughout much of the tradition well-being, too, was conceived as something wholly internal, such as *ataraxia* or calmness of mind. Thus, if freedom is necessarily coextensive with rationality, virtue, and well-being, and if rationality, virtue, and well-being are internal properties, then freedom must also be an internal property.

Of course, not all positive theorists do take freedom to be a wholly internal matter. Yet this, too, can be explained with reference to the imperatives of evaluative unification. For not all positive theorists take rationality, virtue, and well-being to be wholly internal properties either. Instead, some argue that their full realization in fact requires participation in certain kinds of social relationships. Thus Hegel, for instance, sees reason itself as subject to historical development, such that certain modes of practical rationality are available only within particular historical and cultural contexts. True rationality is therefore an inherently social, and so partly "external," achievement. More obviously, proponents of the social nature strategy take *well-being* to be a partly "external" achievement, such that one can truly flourish only in the right kinds of relationship with others. Despite a common concern with the internal aspects of freedom, then, positive conceptions are often intimately concerned with its external aspects too.

Finally, this general concern with internal freedom brings with it a standing tendency towards split views of the self. The connection is this. Everyone is susceptible to irrational, immoral, and self-destructive ideas and dispositions. If freedom requires rationality, virtue, and flourishing, then such wayward inner forces are obstacles to freedom. Insofar as you're subject to them, that is, you're unfree; freedom requires you to rise above them and to liberate yourself from their grip. This holds regardless of their phenomenal aspects; it simply follows from evaluative unification that irrational or immoral or self-destructive internal forces are blockages on the path to true freedom. From here it's then a short step (though not, strictly, a necessary one [Garnett 2017]) to the idea that these motivations are *internal constraints* and so *external* or *alien* to one's true self. This yields a view of the self as always fundamentally split between these alien forces, on the one hand, and the "true" self of reason or virtue or flourishing, on the other (Berlin 1969).

Variations on this "split self" theme occur throughout the tradition. However, the form it takes differs greatly depending on whether the task of overcoming self-alienation is conceived primarily in individual or in social terms. For the Stoics, for example, liberation is primarily a matter of learning to control your own irrational impulses: in Plato's famous metaphor from the *Phaedrus*, you must tame the unruly horse of irrational desire and prevent it from dragging your chariot off course. For Hegel and Marx, by contrast, there are limits to what any individual can achieve in this regard, and freedom instead requires the creation and maintenance of non-alienating societies. For Marx, for instance, people can't fully realize themselves as species beings while treating others instrumentally as means to profit, but capitalism's structure of material incentives works specifically to force people to do this. Only by overcoming the alienating features of our social system, therefore, can we overcome the alienation within ourselves.

All four common features of traditional positive accounts can be explained, therefore, in terms of the historical *point* of this approach in securing evaluative unification. I submit that understanding the tradition of positive freedom in terms of its commitment to the project of evaluative unification, as this chapter has argued we should, allows for a clear view of its general shape, its strengths and its weaknesses and, most importantly, its further theoretical possibilities.

CHAPTER 2

Positive Liberty as Realizing the Essence of Man

Michael Quante

2.1 Introduction

In this chapter, I will explore the question of whether the philosophical foundations of Karl Marx's thought can be explained as developing a specific variant of an ethics of positive freedom. This variant is specific in a double sense: On the one hand, Marx develops his conception of positive freedom as a component of a perfectionist ethics that is inserted into his philosophical anthropology of species being. On the other hand, Marx identifies the institutional setting necessary for the realization of human species-being, and, thus, for the realization of positive human freedom within the framework of his critique of political economy. In other words, positive freedom consists in the unrestricted realization of a person's own essential traits. The institutional and material conditions necessary for this realization are determined by Marx through a critique of capitalism by way of a set of "negations," as I will explain.

The question raised with this examination brings on a hornet's nest of conflicting interpretations of Marx's philosophy which have been the focus of numerous exegetical disputes within Marxism. Its answer requires premises that cannot be justified in this chapter, and it also calls into view follow-up questions and systematic problems that also cannot be dealt with here. These disputes go beyond interpretive subtleties of individual Marxian conceptions, theorems, or argumentations, and concern the most fundamental aspects of Marxian thought. Disagreement about them is still a defining feature of the debate about Marx, and the many disputes within (or between the different types of) Marxism. While my diagnosis cuts across these great plains of Marx and Marxism studies, it is at the same time incompatible with many of the positions to be found in them. For this reason, I will focus exclusively on Marx and on my central question here, if only to contribute to a multilayered interpretive terrain.

Because of the complex nature of this debate, I will, in the first part of this chapter, reveal my assumptions, my goals, and the procedure by which I want to achieve them (Section 2.2). I then present the philosophical anthropology that Marx developed in the mid-1840s interpreted as presenting a specific version of positive freedom (Section 2.3). In the third step, I turn to *Capital*, and thus to Marx's research program of a critique of political economy. I will also explicate this critique, which Marx developed in his theoretical writings beginning in the 1850s, as a component of his conception of positive freedom (Section 2.4). In the conclusion, I will point to exegetical and systematic questions or problems raised by my proposal for other questions of interpretation (Section 2.5). My major goal, however, is to understand Marx as a representative of a conception of positive freedom that is founded in philosophical anthropology.

2.2 Prerequisites, Procedure, and Goals

1. At the outset, our central question must be formulated explicitly: Does Marx's philosophical anthropology, possibly including his critique of political economy, develop a version of positive freedom? In view of the many research contributions that have presented an analysis of Marx's ethics, it is important to clarify three points about my analysis: First, my chapter is concerned exclusively with what Marx himself thought; the question of what ethics as part of Marxism would be (whatever version of Marxism that is) is not posed. Secondly, in my analysis, I explicitly do not pursue the goal of identifying Marx's ethics as a version of metaethics that I myself, for systematic reasons, favor. In other words, I would like to clarify whether we can understand Marx's thoughts as a representative of a conception of positive freedom, regardless of whether that is a plausible or even systematically attractive theoretical option from a metaethical point of view. Moreover, and thirdly, my contribution does not aim at developing a reconstruction of Marx's critique of political economy which can be regarded as a systematically plausible conception for us today. Of course, one can and must interpret Marx's texts and be allowed to pursue independent systematic interests. But this contribution is explicitly limited to an immanent explication.

2. In order to proceed, the textual basis on which my interpretive proposal is based must be defined, which will thereby indicate the passages against which my proposal must be measured. The bases of my interpretation include all Marx's philosophical texts from 1843 onwards, i.e., both

those belonging to philosophical anthropology, including his left-Hegelian discussions, as well as those texts in which Marx develops the conceptual foundations of his research program of a critique of political economy. For the sake of simplicity, I will refer in this chapter to the *Economic and Philosophic Manuscripts of 1844* (including the so-called *Mill Excerpts*) for the former, and to the first volume of *Capital*, including the first two editions of the German edition, for the latter. Decisive for my interpretational demands is the text stock in the critical edition, the so-called $MEGA^2$.[1]

3. Four points that are central to my argument should be made clear: I start (i) from what is commonly known as the continuity thesis, namely that Marx's philosophical work and his critique of political economy form one coherent conception; (ii) I take both his anthropology and the research program of a critique of political economy as *philosophical* projects. Furthermore, (iii) I assume that the critical social philosophy developed with the latter by Marx *presupposes* the former conceptually (and in this sense is not an independent philosophical project of his). Finally, (iv) I understand philosophical anthropology as a conception that is consistently and indelibly organized in an *evaluative* manner; it follows from this (in conjunction with my third premise) that his critique of political economy also has an irreducibly evaluative dimension.

A further point that is central to my aims here is whether Marx's theory, especially his critique of political economy, has an ethical dimension inscribed in it at all? The question of the ethical dimensions of Marxian thought lies at right angles to the opposition of the continuity and discontinuity thesis. On the one hand, one can (assuming the continuity thesis) take the position that Marx developed an essentialist anthropology and philosophy of history, which is a philosophy free of an ethical dimension. On the other hand, one can (assuming the discontinuity thesis in its weaker form) locate a break between the early and the later conceptions of philosophy and at the same time assert that these are two different

[1] In view of the extremely complex, sometimes confused editions in which Marx's central writings were published after his death and throughout the entire twentieth century, and which were mostly guided by the editors' and publishers' interests, this is indispensable as a basis for solid Marx exegesis. Also, Marx wrote texts of very different types having very different degrees of elaboration. The chronological sequence of their posthumous publication does not coincide in many cases with the chronological sequence of their creation (or sometimes multiple revisions), and this is systematically relevant especially for the texts belonging to the critique of political economy. Furthermore, a distinction must be made between the various projects that Marx pursued as a journalist, as a politician, and as a theorist. This has to be taken into account in the interpretation of the texts and the use of his arguments to be found there.

ethical concepts. For many adherents of the discontinuity thesis (in both its strong and weak form), however, it is precisely the loss of the ethical dimension that is the central aspect of the presumed change of theory.

4. For sure, Marx's striking criticism of deontological moral concepts on the one hand and social institutions such as law and the state on the other is well known. In view of the immoralism and scientism of Marx's thought, which seems to follow inevitably from this, the question of this chapter is relevant: If Marx's critique is limited to certain types of ethics and certain conceptions of freedom, then it may be possible to identify, by means of a conception of positive freedom, an ethical foundation of Marx's philosophy that is also inscribed in his critique of political economy. This is at least the ultimate aim of the question that guides my reflections here, whether Marx's conception of self-realization of species being represents a variant of positive freedom.

5. With this in mind, the central goal of my contribution here can be stated, namely to address the question of whether Marx developed an ethical conception of positive freedom in his work, given the constraints on interpretation I just described. As a further product of this investigation, I also want to make visible other problems and ambiguities found in Marx's work. As an independent contribution to our general understanding of these topics, I would also hope to use Marx's ideas to point to the ethical and metaethical value that such a conception of freedom might offer.

2.3 Marx's Conception of Species Being as a Variant of Positive Freedom

In his writings of 1844, which I will use as a basis for my text here, Marx developed a philosophical anthropology, the center of which is his conception of species being. I will answer the question of whether this conception can be understood as a version of positive freedom in two steps: First, I will briefly present the central elements of Marx's conception of a philosophical anthropology (Section 2.3.1); then I will discuss three alternative interpretations of this conception of objective species being as well as three systematic problems raised by the version of positive freedom Marx develops (Section 2.3.2).

2.3.1 The Conception of Self-Objectifying Species Being

Few terms have attracted as much attention in Marx's research as the concept of alienation. The approximately ten pages that Marx wrote on the subject, which are the only systematically developed treatment of this concept in his writings, appeared for the first time in 1932 in the posthumously published *Economic and Philosophic Manuscripts of 1844*. If one analyzes this concept, one finds that it can only be explained if one adds two further Marxian ideas to it, namely, his objectification theory of action and his philosophical anthropology, of which the term "species being" is the central expression. A deeper analysis of Marx's overall concept then shows that "alienation" contains two contrasting concepts, that of appropriation and that of recognition. For this reason, in addition to the concept of alienation found in the *Economic and Philosophic Manuscripts of 1844*, one must also add the idea of recognition outlined by Marx in his *Mill Excerpts*. These three conceptions (alienation, appropriation, and recognition) form the central components through which Marx unfolds his concept of positive freedom.

The conception of the representational species being is based on the assumption that human beings have bodily needs and are acting beings who can be philosophically characterized as "self-objectifying." This last phrase can be understood in a threefold sense: (i) human beings can be understood as instantiating both consciousness and self-consciousness according to the subject-object model; (ii) they are themselves objects as organisms in the sense of spatiotemporally existing individual things; and (iii) they realize their intentions and thereby their essence through objectification. At the same time, human beings are "generic beings," which can also be explained philosophically in a threefold sense: (i) they are individuals of a species; (ii) as self-consciously thinking beings, they make the essence (the species being) of things (including their own) their conceptual object in their thinking; and (iii) as genuinely social beings, they can only realize their individual essence and their basic nature with the help of other human individuals through interaction and within the framework of suitable social institutions.

The human species is oriented toward realizing its essential powers by acting through objectification, which – here Marx adopts historical–philosophical and educational–theoretical models of German idealism – is only possible through a historical process of self-realization and self-education. The goal of this development is the perfecting realization of species being in the form of individually successful lives within reasonable social (including economic) institutions. This historical process, however, does not run in a straight line, but rather through ever-sharpening conflicts and stages of alienation. Only at the end of this development, which according to Marx represents the prehistory of human species-being, is the dissolution of alienation and thus the adequate realization of species being achieved.

In order to understand how Marx can deduce the necessity of alienation from these premises, one must add an epistemological premise resulting from the combination of the objectification model and the subject/object model of self-consciousness: Self-knowledge is only possible if "man" reifies his essential powers in action (intentionally, but also in unintentional form). The produced object (which can be a material object or simply a fact) then exhibits characteristics and abilities that are actually those of the generic being itself. They are externalized to an object and, insofar as this context of objectification is not understood, they are also alienated. Self-knowledge is only possible when a subject recognizes the qualities and abilities given to an object reified in this way as his own and appropriates them practically and theoretically. As a thinking being, man can only acquire his species being when he theoretically recognizes all forms of social coexistence, including his interaction with nature, as the realization of his species-being-related powers and when he succeeds in acquiring them practically through social change. Since self-knowledge belongs to species beings, however, it must be realized, which can only happen by means of expression. In contrast to an infinite self-awareness that does not exist in space-time, man, as a finite being bound by space-time, can only gradually see through and learn to master this expression. From this arises the necessity of alienation as a step that cannot be skipped in the self-realization process of the human species on the way to the realization of its positive freedom.

The more people, in their social interaction, objectify their individual and generic characteristics in an alienated way, the more their generic nature is realized as a reified and dominating world of social constraints. In capitalism, according to Marx, this alienation has progressed to the extreme. The essential powers of species being are completely released in alienated form and must now, as the last step of self-realization, be consciously appropriated. From this, the new social formation then emerges as a conscious and vivid realization of the species being, which forms the conclusion of the perfection of that being. In this, according to Marx, all human individuals can unfold freely and together realize their species being in the right social forms. To this final state belongs the historical experience and the knowledge of the possibility of alienation; for this reason, the prealienated state, here Marx again follows Hegel's dialectic of the negation of the negation, is not to be equated with that of sublated alienation. The final state itself remains fragile and for this reason, too, requires the memory of prehistory in order to consciously prevent relapses. At the same time, according to Marx, it does not come about with a certainty guaranteed by the philosophy of history: This realization of positive freedom can fail, according to Marx, and therefore the perfection of species being can fail, too. In this case, the historical development toward the final state to be achieved would start all over again.

The historical–philosophical dynamic conception of species being thus outlined qualifies as a version of positive freedom. It is inscribed with a perfectionist ethics in the sense of the appropriate formation of social (including economic) institutions as well as the appropriate ethical attitudes (i.e., recognition) of individuals among each other. The goal of development is the complete (perfect) unfolding of all the essential powers of the species being, which includes freedom from obstacles, but at the same time requires positive aspects. This perfection is conceived as self-realization and objectification of one's own abilities, not as the implementation of an external standard or plan. Moreover, according to Marx, the final state to be achieved guarantees not only the free development of all the powers of the person's species being, but also the free development of the species being of all individuals. The goal of this development is the perfect exercise and realization of theoretical and practical self-determination within the necessary social institutions and evaluative forms of human interaction with one another. This goal, according to my interpretive proposal, represents a conception of positive freedom specific to Marx.

2.3.2 *Three Alternative Interpretations and Three Systematic Problems*

It is not my aim to discuss the plausibility or systematic attractiveness of this conception by Marx. Instead, I will briefly point out three possible alternatives to this interpretation, followed by three systematic problems that might be raised about it.

The evaluative dimension of this picture of a conception of positive freedom can in principle be explicated in another way within the framework of essentialist premises of a philosophical anthropology. This brings us to the first alternative interpretation, which is that the normativity that arises here rests in the target of a being's development defined as its essence. However, without further assumptions, such as that the realization of one's essence is ethically necessary or ethically good, no conception of ethics can be diagnosed on the basis of an essentialism of species being alone. This applies even if the target state is the perfect realization of positive freedom. As long as this goal is not itself formulated as an ethical good or its (maximal) realization as an ethical imperative, one can remain within the framework of what could be called an ethics-free essentialism.

A second interpretive alternative consists in explicating the evaluative dimension through a purely metaphysically interpreted philosophy of history, that is, to understand the necessary state to be achieved through the lens of a historically based teleology. However, this strategy can only be successful if evaluative concepts such as that of progress can be eliminated. Whether this is possible at all is already questionable. In any case, it is more than unlikely that one would come up with a plausible interpretive hypothesis along these lines for Marx's texts.

As a third alternative, one could mention the strategy of dissolving Marx's essentialist premises via an empirical (mostly scientistic) reduction. The reorientation undertaken by Marx and Friedrich Engels in reaction to Max Stirner's fundamental criticism can provide some nourishment for this interpretation.[2] However, it will not only be difficult to translate Marx's strong modal statements in a reductionist manner of the sort this reading would require, the historical–philosophical foundations of Marx's broader views would also serve as a significant obstacle to such a reductionism.

This brings me to three systematic problems with the view of positive freedom that emerges from this reading. One difficulty is the danger of undue paternalistic intervention based on essentialist demands. The imposition of such external standards for individual self-determination would violate a commitment to the value of autonomy. However, by setting autonomy itself as a good to be perfected (and not merely being counted within a utilitarian maximization strategy), Marx avoids this danger, at least on the principal or categorical level. But even under this condition, a first systematic difficulty remains: Should this essentialist presupposition, as it is inscribed in Marx's conception of species being, be understood as an external standard of evaluation and critique for our social practices, or as an (albeit implicit) internal standard?

A second systematic problem is revealed in the conception of Marx's position as not only metaethical, but also as quite practically extremely

[2] In his *The Ego and Its Own* (Stirner 1995), Max Stirner has analyzed and rejected all modal claims as variants of "the Holy" or philosophical idealism. This poses a problem for Marx and Engels: Both religious and idealistic thinking are unacceptable for Marx and Engels on the one hand, and they agree with Stirner's diagnosis on the other hand. Therefore, they try to get rid of the essentialism of their anthropological conception to meet Stirner's objections (cf. Quante 2015 for a detailed analysis of Stirner's critique).

urgent: Whose autonomy is at stake in the perfection, that of species being generally or that of each individual? Without entering into a detailed discussion here, it must be said that little attention was paid to the problems arising from this question regarding the variant of positive freedom developed by Marx. His idea of perfection seems to be oriented toward a harmony of individuals that is established according to the prehistory of mankind, in which there is no need for social institutions to protect individual claims or to regulate conflicting interests in a normatively appropriate manner. (For this, however, he believes that a specific arrangement of economic institutions is definitely needed.) Whether Marx adhered to such an idea can be left open here. However, a sensitive gap in his overall picture must be noted, in that he did not comment on the social institutions needed to solve the questions related to the second issue.

A third systematic problem that an account of positive freedom in the Marxian register raises can be referred to as "overstraining." If perfection is not conceptualized as an infinite, never completable process toward an ontological target (an ought-to-be) or conceived as a moral demand that can never be fulfilled by finite beings, i.e., transformed into a moral target, does not this perfection set a standard for real social institutions and human actions that they can never meet? In other words, is the ideal of universal and conflict-free recognition between individuals and the complete elimination of alienation a standard that human societies cannot meet in principle? What would a concept of positive freedom look like that would take this danger of overstraining seriously and take it into account in theory formation? As we will see in the next section, Marx at least guessed in his later writings that he would have to take this difficulty into account in his critique of political economy.

2.4 The Critique of Political Economy: A Contribution to Positive Freedom?

One of the central points of contention in Marx and Marxism studies alike revolves around the question of whether the critique of political economy, in terms of its theoretical type, can be understood as a philosophical project at all. That is, it can either be assigned to a single scientific discipline such as economics, political science, or sociology, or one can take the position that Marx developed a completely new type of theory in *Capital* (which is then characterized, for example, as "historical" or "dialectical" materialism, occasionally also as a "scientific worldview"). It is certainly not unreasonable to claim that apart from proclamatory statements or programmatic announcements there are no substantiated research results that can be termed scientific that support the view that Marx succeeded in developing such a new type of scientific theory. Nor can it be denied that the research program of a critique of political economy includes extensive source studies and the inclusion of research results from various individual disciplines as well as arguments and theorems that can be understood as theoretical features within these various individual disciplines. In other words: *Capital* contains both Marx's assertions which can be falsified (or supported) by individual scientific findings and theses and justifications which can easily be understood as arguments within the various individual disciplines.

As I have already stated at the beginning of this article, I start from the premise that Marx's theoretical work, including both his early writings of the 1840s and the texts belonging to the research program of a critique of political economy, can be interpreted as a contribution to philosophy. Marx's critical departure from philosophy was always aimed at Hegelian philosophy and the various left-wing Hegelian versions of it. It does not necessarily follow from his critique of philosophy in this narrow sense that the critique of political economy cannot also be a philosophical project in a broader sense.

Closely related to this central bone of contention in the study of Marx and Marxism is the dissent regarding the question of whether there is an – epistemological or methodological – rupture between the theoretical works of the 1840s, which are more or less undisputedly considered philosophy, and the writing from the 1850s onwards, which can be regarded as contributions to his critique of political economy. However, these are two questions that must be distinguished. For on the one hand, Marx could have pursued a philosophical project even after this "break" (for example, by "breaking" with left-wing Hegelian philosophy but not with philosophy in general). On the other hand, the turn toward a research project that can no longer be understood as philosophy could also be conceived as a reorientation that does not include a "break." This would be the case, for example, if Marx used his philosophical premises and theorems from the 1840s as a basis but for other purposes.

As I explained above, in this chapter I assume both that *Capital* is a contribution to philosophy, more precisely to critical social philosophy, and that at the fundamental level of theory-building, between the writings of the 1840s and the work from 1850 onwards concerning the critique of political economy there is no break in Marx's thinking. This clears the way for the question of whether *Capital* can also be counted as a contribution to Marx's conception of positive freedom. This remains an open question since it would also be conceivable that the philosophical anthropology of the 1840s, but not the critical social philosophy that Marx developed in *Capital*, could be understood in this way.

Some good reasons can be given for such a skeptical assumption. First, Marx does not conduct his analysis at the level of individual actors but explicitly refers to functional structures that are realized behind (and on) the backs of the actors. According to Marx, these can be philosophically explained as the realization of the unintended consequences of collective interactions. Secondly, Marx orients himself to Hegel's *Science of Logic*; thus, a theory is at play that likewise does not move on the level of the explication of concrete actors of speech, but rather the explication of the functional structure of categories. In addition, Hegel's logic introduces a claim to seclusion and totality into Marx's theory formation, which, at least prima facie, does not seem to be very compatible with the idea of an anthropologically founded conception of positive freedom. Finally, as a third reason, Marx explicitly rejects an interpretation of his critique of capitalism as moral. This, too, does not fit well with the type of perfectionist theory that I propose here as a conception of positive freedom.

Despite these important objections, I claim that *Capital* (and the research program of a critique of political economy as a whole) can also be understood as part of the version of positive freedom specific to Marx. As I have argued in Section 2.3, such an interpretation presupposes that Marx's philosophical anthropology can be understood as a variant of ethical perfectionism. For only then can it be made plausible that his critique of political economy also fits into it (despite the three concerns just formulated), because it inherits this trait from the conception of species being. If this succeeds, the way is thus also clear for Marx's critique of political economy to be read simultaneously as a contribution to his conception of positive freedom. In other words: Marx's proof that capitalism necessarily causes the attempts of people to realize their freedom to fail would thus at the same time be a negative reference to the positive conditions under which the positive freedom of species being can be realized.

In order for the interpretation proposed here to succeed, it must therefore be assumed, first, that the conceptual foundations that Marx developed in his philosophical anthropology are also (at least part of) the basis of his critique of political economy. There is a great deal of evidence to support this assumption: for example, the model of objectification in *Capital* continues to be based on a general theory of action. His conception of action as objectification is not only still central to Marx's concept of labor, but is also a necessary component of his value analysis and thus the conceptual basis of the entire theory. This analysis is also based on the thesis that human beings must acquire their generic characteristics by means of reifying expression. The fact that Marx allows commodities themselves to appear as actors, makes systematic sense because on this functional level the alienated intentions of the interacting subjects can be philosophically explained. Secondly, the talk of capital as an autonomic subject, and the entire metaphorical field of zombies, vampires, living vs. dead labor, or the sucking out of living labor by capital that Marx presents, can also be seamlessly integrated into this basic model of objectification. The fact that this alienation qua species being is realized through the antagonism of capitalist and worker and is at the same time determined by the antagonism of nature and capital also fits the basic concept of species being: because it is an alienated objectification, species being (on an individual and collective level) finds itself in a contradiction between its natural and social dimension. This fundamental contradiction manifests itself also in the social relations between people (on the individual and collective level), something which is a central theorem in Marx's concept of alienation. That Marx conceived the capitalist form of production as a double antagonism (between capital and labor and between capital and nature) cannot be denied. This finding fits seamlessly into his conception of species being. The same applies to the positive dimension of the conscious appropriation of these species being characteristics, which have been objectified in alienated form. In the few places in *Capital* where Marx even addresses the overcoming of the capitalist form of production, he not only uses Hegel's concept of a "negation of the negation," but also presents this process as one of reconciliation with nature and as appropriation by the workers. The latter is at the same time the expropriation of the capitalists; the former, unlike what is said in the *Economic and Philosophic Manuscripts of 1844*, is no longer conceived as the completed naturalization of man and humanization of nature. In *Capital*, the emphasis on reconciliation found in the early writings gives way to a more realistic version that implicitly corrects (or clarifies) the standards inscribed in its conception of positive freedom that has been called for in philosophical anthropology. By abolishing alienation, work does not become like a game and the sphere of material production remains constitutively determined by necessities that can be rationally shaped but can never be a frictionless realization of unlimited and undisturbed human freedom.

One more condition needed for the success of my proposed interpretation is to identify the evaluative dimension in Marx's picture. Without this step, the critique of the political economy might well be a critical social philosophy compatible with Marx's concept of positive freedom, but then it would not itself be a component of his ethical perfectionism, nor would the institutional critique to be found in it be a component of his conception of positive freedom. First of all, it must be conceded that the normativity of a standard of critique can be spelled out without reference to a substantive evaluative standard (based on an axiological or deontological ethics, for example), and still be properly called "critique." For instance, one could reconstruct Marx's philosophy of history as resting on a metaphysical essentialism without any internal evaluative dimension; this would amount in principle to a purely modal-logical normativity in the sense of pointing to the "ought" of realizing an essence. However, as indicated in Section 2.3 of this chapter, this is neither a systematically attractive option nor a plausible one in terms of interpretation. If, on the other hand, Marx's analysis of the capitalist formation of society is inserted into his philosophical anthropology, a coherent overall picture emerges: Capitalism is that stage in the historical course of the self-realization of species being that is characterized by the most complete and radical form of alienation and hence by the maximum distance from the realization of positive freedom. Thus, for the first time, all species being powers are objectified and thus accessible to appropriation in principle for the very first time. At the same time, under the domination of capital as an automatic subject, such powers are present in alienated form, i.e., in social structures that are not transparent to the real actors. According to Marx, the appropriation of these generic powers should then be made permanent through rational control (planning) and the creation of transparent social institutions (transparency) as well as the elimination of the alienating effects of the unilateral division of labor and the reduction of the working time to be used for reproduction. This would then have to be developed further in a conception of positive freedom suitable for political philosophy, because Marx describes the social changes associated with this as the expropriation of the capitalists, which is at the same time to be understood as the appropriation of the generic powers by the workers, and he does this without going into the political shaping of these processes in more detail. Indissolubly linked to this appropriation is the elimination of the ideological distortions through which people deceive themselves about their roles and live together in alienated social relationships. It is important to understand that this abolition must not only be understood as the elimination of ideological deceptions (i.e., as mere negation) regarding the conception of positive freedom, but as a process of experience and learning (so also as preservation) of that conception.

This is because, as we found in Section 2.3, the correct evaluative attitude toward each other as Marx describes is also an essential internal component of the realization of species being, not only an external evaluative dimension which is simply added to his overall view. As I mentioned, this must at the same time also be understood as a process of experience and learning, so in this sense, one could speak of an educational history of positive freedom in Marx's work.

On the whole, Marx presents capitalism in *Capital* as a failing formation of the human form of life. His critique through representation is methodologically oriented toward Hegel's *Phenomenology of Spirit* and *Science of Logic* in equal measure: Under the condition of philosophical anthropology (including the philosophy of history inscribed in it and its evaluative dimension in the form of positive freedom), Marx can measure capitalism by a standard inherent in human beings (qua species being). This is true even though the standards it entails are only known to the actors in the prehistory of humanity – i.e., that part of history in which alienation hasn't been overcome – in a distorted form or are even only implicitly inscribed in their actions.

Marx's assertion that he does not criticize capitalism any more than individual capitalists (or their actions) is morally compatible with this: On the one hand, as already mentioned, Marx equates morality with an a priori deontological conception of the type found in Kant or Fichte, which applies an ahistorical, abstract and thus external standard to its object. In this sense, Marx's critique does not in fact represent a moral philosophy.

On the other hand, Marx organizes the evaluative dimension of his critique by depicting alienation taking place, without classifying it as inappropriate even by means of such an ethical category. Marx wants his evaluative critique to show itself without having to explicitly express it. The yardstick of this critique, on which Marx bases his philosophical conception as a whole, can, according to the proposal made here, be developed as a specific form of ethical perfectionism. On my view, Marx is claiming that throughout history and the stages of alienation associated with it, man realizes his essential traits and thus his freedom. This is a historical development that can be philosophically explicated as positive freedom, which is designed to optimize the development of all its generic characteristics. This complete realization, according to Marx, is the development of freedom from the powers of nature and social alienation. At the same time, it creates the framework within which every human being can also unfold his or her individual characteristics and abilities. The complete unfolding of species being that is no longer alienated is then at the same time the full realization of its positive freedom.

2.5 A Short but Complex Conclusion

It comes as no surprise when the work of a historical author does not fit seamlessly into a philosophical framework elaborated 150 years later. As the argumentation in this contribution has shown, the question pursued here nevertheless yields a double philosophical product: On the one hand, our perspective reveals systematic fuzziness in Marx's philosophy. On the other hand, our findings also give rise to follow-up questions and developmental tasks for the further systematic explication of a concept of positive freedom within the framework of ethical perfectionism.

2.5.1 *First Fuzziness: Individual or Species Being?*

The first blurry point, which can be found explicitly in Marx, but also implicitly in other representatives of ethical perfectionism, is encountered when one asks whose (positive) freedom this perfectionism is about. Marx's philosophical anthropology is characterized by the talk of species being and the human being. After the reaction to the intervention of Stirner, who criticized Marx's reference to the human being or species being as a specific form of the "sacred," Marx admittedly begins to give his conception an empirical foundation. But the fuzziness in his talk of the human remains unresolved: Is it about the single individual and his (positive) freedom? Or does the perfection of positive freedom primarily and ultimately aim at the realization and unfolding of the potentials of species being more generally? Even in the works that belong to his project of a critique of political economy, the idea of developing and unfolding the productive powers of (general) species beings remains central for Marx.

In the first volume of *Capital*, Marx analyses the social structures of capitalism at the level of reified relations between commodities. The individual actors are taken into account here only as bearers of intentions for action ("character masks"), insofar as functional intentions attributable to them by the capitalist system of production can be assigned to them. These intentions need not be known by the individual actor as his own. Moreover, Marx's critical social philosophy is geared toward analyzing the systemic effects of capitalism that can be explicated as the realization of unintended consequences of collective cooperation. Both of these lead to the fact that in his theoretical program of a critique of political economy, the connection between the system level and individual action on the one hand and unintended consequences of collective cooperation and individual actions on the other is not explained. However, such a theoretical component is indispensable in order to determine the relationship between the realization of the productive powers of species being and the realization of the potentials of the individual members of this species being. Otherwise, there is a danger that the realization of the positive freedom of species-being, in general, might be bought at the price of ethically unjustifiable limitations of the freedom of individuals.

The action theoretical and methodological questions associated with the absence of this theoretical building block have not received much attention in Marx's research to date. The general normative register in which this complex of problems plays out is somewhat better off. In the debate about the metaethical status of Marx's theory in general and his program of a critique of political economy in particular, the question of the relationship between individual freedom, self-realization of the individual and self-realization of species being has been discussed. However, since this debate has downplayed the action theoretical foundations at work in Marx's picture, the question has mostly been reduced to whether his theory can be understood as an evaluative conception at all. Those who give an affirmative answer to this question then discuss whether this is a deontological, consequentialist, or perfectionist conception. To my mind, what is more relevant, however, and I would like to plead for this at this point, is to clarify which safeguards of individual self-determination can be developed within Marx's view and in particular in utilizing the concept of positive freedom developed there.

As stated in Section 2.2, I make no attempt to answer this question concerning how Marx imagined the relationship between individual self-realization and the realization of the powers of species being. In order to be able to pose this question in a meaningful way at all, one needs in Marx's theory a programmatic account of how individual action and systemic functions are related to each other. To be able to pose this question in a normatively adequate manner, one must take into account that Marx, in his concept of alienation of the 1840s, rejected all institutional mediations designed to deal with conflicts between the individual and general claims as inadequate (and symptoms of alienation). Thus, he was committed to the ideal of an immediate resolution of opposites and conflicts. The question of what effects the deflation of the concept of alienation observed in *Capital* must have on the systematic foundation of the theoretical program of a critique of political economy is complex, and Marx himself contributed little to answer it. But systematic answers to this question are not an answer to the other question of how Marx normatively imagined the relationship between individual and species being in cases of conflict. Answers to these two questions, which aim at clarifying his conception of positive freedom, will probably not be able to be developed completely independently of each other. But the two different questions nevertheless remain. What they do have in common, however, is that the texts that Marx has written as part of his research program of a critique of political economy contain no explicit and very few indirect answers to them.

2.5.2 *Second Blurriness: Ethical Perfectionism and the Ambivalence of Positive Freedom*

If one accepts the finding developed here that Marx's conception of positive freedom can be understood as a variant of ethical perfectionism, then the critical discussion of his conception will reveal questions and problems that systematic further development of these ideas must face. Not only the question of whose freedom is actually at stake (individual or species being), but the question of what exactly is meant by positive freedom must also be answered. In the tradition of Hegel and Marx, it is not a principle to be explained deontologically, which is to be understood formally as the capacity for self-determination and normatively as the right to it. If, on the other hand, it is a value to be spelled out within the framework of an axiology, then it would have to be clarified whether this is the only currency of such ethics, whether this value can be quantified, and whether the perfection of positive freedom can thus be understood as something to be maximized (which would result in a utilitarian conception). Does positive freedom aim at the abilities of man, which, analogous to conceptions in virtue ethics, would have to be unfolded as an ethics of enabling and empowering?

The concept of positive freedom that can be identified in Marx's work shows aspects of the free self-realization of species being, and it allows for divergent metaethical interpretations and different specifications. It is up to us to use this openness in his conception as an opportunity for our own systematic efforts regarding our own theoretical and practical needs.

CHAPTER 3

Moral and Personal Positive Freedom

Maria Dimova-Cookson

In liberal societies, people routinely have to engage in a balancing exercise between morality and freedom. On the one hand, there is a moral imperative to become a better person by contributing more effectively to the "common good" of family, friends, work community, nation, or humankind – the multiple overlapping social groups that make up the fabric of our lives. On the other hand, our capacity for self-determination and personal development is compromised if we are unable to resist moral exhortation to do more than our fair share or to bend ourselves to the will of others.

We are pulled in two directions: moral development enjoins us to serve the common good while personal development requires us to resist the impact of moral narratives that allow others to exploit us.[1] Importantly, both moral and personal development can be seen as advancements of liberty. Commitment to moral action has been conceptualized in terms of moral freedom (see Green 1986c: 228–229), but if anything, freedom has been more readily associated with the second pull, that is, with the capacity to discern, interpret, and resist the moral pressures we are under. Most contemporary theorists of liberty emphasize the latter category and distance themselves from the former. Exploitation, manipulation, and indoctrination, dressed up in moral rhetoric, are recognized as significant impediments to liberty. Contemporary political theory has managed to escape this moral tension at the heart of liberty by downplaying the moral concept of freedom. Even those who commit to positive freedom distance their theories from a purely moral concept. Here, however, I would like to show that a concept of moral freedom is extremely important for a

I am indebted to Richard Cookson, Avital Simhony and Stephen Welch for their substantive and editorial feedback.

[1] See Darby's discussion about the "moralizing" of "oppressive social and legal arrangements" as one of the mechanisms of legitimizing these arrangements (Darby 2009: 75–77).

comprehensive understanding of liberty that takes matters of morality, opportunity, autonomy, and the capacity to resist domination, seriously.

I argue that the moral tension at the heart of liberty has to remain in conceptual focus and that key insights from Berlin's dual conceptualization of liberty have to be built into contemporary liberal theories. These key insights apply even though, currently, most debates on the nature of liberty have migrated to a positive freedom platform. In fact, as will be argued in Section 3.1, this transferring of the theorization of freedom onto a positive liberty platform is to some extent a consequence of Berlin's analysis of the ways moral authorities affect the human agency. I argue that, if we take moral freedom seriously, we will have to reinstate the dual conception of liberty by acknowledging two positive freedom concepts. I will refer to these as moral positive freedom and personal positive freedom. Moral positive freedom is the classical positive freedom which I base on reconstruction and defense of T. H. Green's concept of moral freedom understood as the acquisition of moral agency and attainment of excellence in a recognized field.[2] Under the category of personal positive freedom, I put together a broad range of contemporary approaches to positive freedom with characteristics including the agent's capacities to engage with valued activities, capacities to act morally (as opposed to already having attained moral agency), and the provision of the material, legal and social resources which allow one to exercise control over one's well-being. Concepts of freedom as autonomy, freedom as based on recognition, and freedom as non-domination[3] would fall under this broader, personal positive freedom category.

I argue that a better understanding of moral positive freedom leads to a more comprehensive grasp of personal positive freedom. First, we can see that the narrative behind Green's moral freedom reveals a new understanding of personal freedom as the capacity to maintain continuous development. That is, in order to be free, it is not enough that one is able to fulfill a desirable objective: one needs to be able to do so continually (Sections 3.2–3.4). Second, the lens of moral positive freedom allows us to expose some of the deficiencies of existing conceptions of personal positive freedom, including their limited account of the moral dimension of

[2] See my discussion on what constitutes a recognized field and why the attainment of excellence or perfection should be seen as an aspect of positive freedom (Dimova-Cookson 2020: 159–162).

[3] The concept of non-dominations rests on a socioeconomic analysis which is superfluous to a negative concept of freedom as noninterference. Also, Pettit's discussion of freedom as "antipower" brings in an element of personal capacity as constitutive of the exercise of freedom. See Pettit (1996: 591–592).

freedom (seeing this component purely in terms of moral constraints) and their failure to appreciate the role of satisfaction and personal well-being as some of the key parameters of personal freedom (Section 3.5). The chapter challenges the deep-seated assumption that freedom should be associated with opportunities and not with achievements and it shows how exactly opportunities lead to freedom. It helps develop a better understanding of the dynamics of opportunity and achievement in the context of freedom. It shows that the process of choosing values, which is at the heart of personal positive freedom, has a similar structure to the process of attaining moral agency, which is the essence of moral positive freedom.

3.1 The Widening of the Positive Freedom Platform and the New Conceptual Duality

The complex and controversial role which moral authorities (moral ideals and the normative underpinnings of social institutions) play in the constitution of liberty has been captured most eloquently by Berlin's two concepts of liberty. He argues that positive freedom reflects, among other things, the insights of those like Kant and Green who saw freedom as moral freedom. His negative concept of freedom, on the other hand, aims to protect a zone of privacy from external interventions, and most of all, from moral interventions (see Dimova-Cookson 2020: chapters 4 and 5). But what Berlin's conceptualization achieved, unwittingly, was to transfer the analysis of freedom onto the terrain of positive freedom altogether. This is because Berlin's analysis revealed the centrality of moral motivation and moral authorities in the exercise of liberty. His significant insight into how rationalistic doctrines and totalitarian regimes threaten freedom led to the realization that freedom depends on a process of understanding and shaping one's priorities and values.[4] Ultimately both of his concepts rest on a vision of authentic agency and legitimate political interventions. Rainer Forst makes a similar observation when he argues that "there is no question that negative freedom implies a certain conception of autonomy of a person as 'a being with life of his own to live' – that is, as having the capacity of reflection and meaningful choice between options in his or her life. One can even say that securing this type of autonomy is the point of negative freedom" (2005: 228).

[4] George Crowder argues "that a case for personal autonomy is central to liberalism follows from Berlin's deepest commitments, in particular his commitment to pluralism" (Crowder 2004: 86).

The distinction between personal and moral autonomy, as advanced by thinkers like Joseph Raz, Harry Frankfurt, Gerald Dworkin, and Jeremy Waldron,[5] conveys some of the essences of Berlin's negative/positive freedom duality. While all these thinkers are convinced that a moral concept of freedom (moral autonomy) is legitimate, they all see the need for an alternative concept of freedom (personal autonomy) which guards against moral authorities when they threaten to undermine individuals' independence.

But if we accept that the duality between personal and moral autonomy is a more sophisticated version of the negative/positive freedom distinction, we have to admit that the entire duality of freedom has been transferred on the terrain of positive liberty. Most concepts of liberty in contemporary political theory are in some way positive, even if their authors are wary of the dangers of moral freedom. To some extent, precisely the undesirable ramifications of moral positive freedom led to a negative freedom which is positive-freedom-savvy. Thus, most contemporary concepts of liberty are imbued with some positive freedom contents, whether they accept the legitimacy of moral freedom or not: they have to build in an understanding of value formation and some, even if minimal, moral component, among other things. However, if we believe in the legitimacy of moral freedom, *and* take the ambivalent positioning of moral authorities in the formation of liberty, then we need two concepts of positive freedom: a moral positive and a personal positive one.

Most liberty concepts that contemporary political theorists endorse would fall under the personal positive freedom category.[6] Such concepts include Simhony's understanding of liberty as "the coming together of opportunities (external ability) and capacities (internal ability)," (1991: 361) Gould's freedom as "a capacity for self-transformation or self-development as a process over time," (2013: 108) Anderson and Honneth's conception of autonomy as "capacity that exists only in the context of social relations" (2005: 129), Christman's autonomy as "minimal cognitive competence and hypothetical self-endorsement" (2005b: 345), Philip Pettit's freedom as "antipower" which includes "the capacity to demand non-interference" (1996: 589) Sen's freedom "seen in the form of individual capabilities to do things that a person has reason to value" (1999: 56), Raz's personal autonomy as "the ideal of free and conscious

[5] For discussion of these views, see Waldron (2005: 314–320).

[6] The pure negative freedom concepts as developed by Hillel Steiner (1983), Ian Carter (1999) and Matthew Kramer (2003) are an obvious exception to this.

self-creation" (1986: 390), and my concept of negative freedom as "advancement of one's own well-being" in a fashion which keeps open the possibility for the moral agency (2020: 7), among others. All these concepts contain a moral component and commitment to valuable activities, and most of them refer to the need for a social environment that can curtail practices of domination. What most of them lack is (1) the understanding of freedom as the capacity to stay in a process of development, and, with the exception of Raz, (2) a more comprehensive vision of how the moral component works in the context of personal positive freedom. These accounts also do not acknowledge sufficiently (3) the role of satisfaction and the centrality of personal well-being in the concept of personal freedom. This chapter shows how we can start to make up for these omissions.

3.2 Moral Positive Freedom and the Process of Development Which Lies behind It

I have argued elsewhere that Green has two viable concepts of freedom (Dimova-Cookson 2020: chapters 2 and 3). The first is moral positive freedom understood as acquisition of moral agency and the attainment of personal perfection. This is the kind of freedom he refers to as "true" or "real" freedom in his moral philosophy lecture "The Different Senses of Freedom." In this context "true" freedom is the highest among several forms of freedom. Green also has a broader, more open-ended, concept of freedom, developed in "Lecture on Liberal Legislation," which is based on the individual's capacity to pursue worthwhile activities and make the best of themselves in a fashion that is fair to all. It is this freedom he calls freedom in the "positive sense." Green and his critics view these freedoms as interrelated, or as representative of the same concept: Green refers to both as "true" freedom and critics refer to both of them as "positive" freedom.[7] It will not be difficult to show that these concepts differ, as we will shortly see and that the difference between them can help us explain the nature of the second concept better.

For the sake of uniformity of terminology in this chapter, I will refer to Green's freedom from "The Different Senses of Freedom" as moral positive freedom, and to his freedom from "Lecture on Liberal Legislation" as personal positive freedom. It is widely acknowledged that the discussions of the accounts of freedom in these two lectures are based on two separate

[7] See Nicholson (1990: 115), and Tyler (2010: 116).

contexts and fulfill distinct explanatory purposes.[8] I will say something about each and then try to connect the two accounts in a new fashion – a fashion that gives more credibility to both.

Green's moral positive freedom is the ultimate form of freedom on an upward sliding scale of partially good freedoms: hence the adjectives "true" and "real." Two other freedoms are discussed in "The Different Senses of Freedom" – formal freedom and juristic freedom – and they both precede moral positive freedom. Formal freedom reflects the capacity of the will to be directed toward objects that bring satisfaction. Human will is free by default, that is, formally free, because the will is our capacity to be directed toward chosen objects; it is our capacity for purposive action. Human beings live in a freedom mode, so to say, as they are always directed toward things, wanting things, doing things; in this respect, they are formally free. Juristic freedom has an additional feature: lack of impediments placed by others. Green's juristic freedom reminds us strongly of Berlin's concept of negative freedom as noninterference. Juristic freedom is also defined as "power to do what [one] wills or prefers" (Green 1986c: 234) and thus supersedes formal freedom: in addition to being free through willing, individuals are able to fulfill their desires by overcoming or by not having hindrances from others. Green acknowledges that most would be inclined to think that juristic freedom should be the paradigm understanding of freedom, but he insists that it is not true or real freedom. This is because its exercise brings only a temporary sense of satisfaction. Once the obstacles placed by others have been removed and one's desire fulfilled, the sense of achievement dissipates fast – possibly a more desirable objective appears and therefore new obstacles have to be overcome. Freedom is not only about getting what we want despite the hindrances placed by others: Green believes that real freedom would be found only when a lasting sense of satisfaction is achieved. This is possible only when one achieves what is most desirable, that is when one lives up to her duties and develops her capacities to perfection (1986c: 228–229). Green's moral positive freedom is the ultimate form of freedom, and some argue the most comprehensive form of freedom as it contains the other freedoms and adds what is missing in them (Nicholson 1990: 119–120). Shortly I will comment on why this is a viable sense of freedom and how it throws additional light on the other positive freedom he discusses.

[8] See the editorial notes by Paul Harris and John Morrow on the two lectures in Green (1986b: 343, 352).

In "Lecture on Liberal Legislation," Green questions and radically redefines the prevailing understanding of freedom as a lack of "restraint or compulsion" (1986c: 199): in this fashion what Green is doing is not dissimilar to what he did in the previous lecture. But here he focuses much less on how the nature of human agency affects the constitution of freedom, and much more on how freedom should be understood so that it is effectively protected by the state. Green argues that the safeguarding of freedom necessitates legal reform because the existing institution of free contract, despite appearances, violates freedom. For those with no bargaining power the free contract, which aims to regulate the conditions of employment and land tenancy, secures only bad deals. It does not protect workers' or tenant farmers' freedom – quite the opposite. It brings exploitation, poor health, and low morale.[9] The institution of free contract does not teach habits of independence and self-reliance, as its proponents insist. When freedom has to be defined for the purpose of agreeing on political action and legal reform, it should be understood in terms of individuals' capacity to do worthwhile things, capacity to contribute to the common good, and doing so in a fashion fair to all (Green 1986b: 199).

Although the freedom discussed here, like the freedom discussed in "The Different Senses of Freedom" is also directed toward the common good and personal perfection, it is a different freedom to the extent that it focuses on the capacity to achieve valuable things rather than on their actual achievement. If a new law helped workers and tenant farmers to secure better contracts which permitted them to work sensible hours and earn enough to enable them and their families to live well, if their work-life allowed them to do the things they found worthwhile, and if they had a sense of belonging to a community and thus a sense of duty, they would be free in the personal positive sense defined by Green. They would be free even before they developed moral agency and reached personal perfection. So, which is the true positive freedom? The one experienced at the point of full success or the one experienced when you know that what you value and aim at is within the range of what is possible for you?

A lot is to be said in favor of the concept of personal positive freedom discussed in "Lecture on Liberal Legislation." It conveys the idea that freedom is about real opportunities: "freedom which consists in *an open field* for all men to make the best of themselves" (1986a: 206). This concept combines factors reflecting free agency ("doing or enjoying something worth doing or enjoying") and the need for the adequate social

[9] For a discussion of the exploitative nature of free contract see Simhony (2019: 125–127).

environment ("and that, too, is something that we do enjoy in common with others") (1986a: 199). The concept is pluralistic as it does not specify how one should make "the best of themselves," nor whether one has to go the whole way to doing so. The concept also conveys a clear commitment to personal well-being. My argument, however, is that this vision of personal positive freedom is impossible and incomplete without a viable concept of moral positive freedom.

Green's idea of moral positive freedom is a viable concept of freedom because Green tells a story that one can understand and connect to. This story has persuaded many that moral freedom exists and it helps us see what the broader exercise of freedom – personal positive freedom –actually is. I would like to show that personal positive freedom is about, in addition to the things mentioned above, the capacity to sustain a developmental process. And this developmental process is defined by moral positive freedom. Moral positive freedom marks its destination, its final point. But it also explains the dynamics of the journey. It shows in what circumstances personal development becomes freedom. We change in various ways and follow different developmental curves – not all of them make us free.

3.3 The Liberating Dynamics of Achieving a Goal

Green's moral positive freedom has features that have raised concerns among many liberals. These include the implied certainty in the contents of the moral ideal, the commitment to perfection understood as the full development of one's capabilities, and the focus on the inner self. It has long been said that one of the main worries about positive freedom is the way that it may allow undue imposition of a narrow conception of moral value on citizens in the name of its promotion. Also, some believe that the positive conceptions reduce the value of freedom to "the value of the specific possible achievements for which it is a necessary condition" (Carter 1999: 57). Green's moral positive freedom has also been criticized by Colin Tyler for being based on a "spiritual determinist theory." "The spiritual determinist approach establishes that one's motives and therefore one's will are essentially self-determined" (Tyler 2010: 124, 132). Simhony observes that when positive freedom is associated with "a condition of the inner self," it is critiqued for tending "to ignore, or at any rate, to marginalize, the externality of freedom" (Simhony 2019: 128). On these grounds, one could say that the "real satisfaction" aspect of Green's moral freedom is subjective and spiritualist, and that it fails to acknowledge the role of material and social realities. I argue that once we see how these controversial features actually invigorate moral positive freedom, we will be able to discern their role in shaping the nature of personal positive freedom.

The argument in support of moral freedom is complex and I will not be able to do full justice to it here. But let me offer an interpretative summary of Green's theory. There are three key ingredients that in their various interactions produce the dynamics of freedom: the *purposiveness* of human action, *satisfaction* as a signal that a goal is achieved, and the personal assessment of the *value* of our goal. The first two are captured by what Green calls formal freedom and the last by his moral freedom. Notably, juristic freedom – the freedom of not having obstacles – does not add an essential ingredient. This is because what stands behind our aversion to obstacles is our purposiveness, our default "forward" mode of wanting things and doing things. We are mistaken if we associate our thirst for freedom exclusively with our dislike for obstacles: we dislike obstacles because they prevent us from getting what we want. In this sense, the logic of purposiveness and satisfaction, precedes the logic of aversion to obstacles. Obstacles hinder freedom only in proportion to how desirable the objective we pursue is.[10] In fact, the habit of seeking freedom by making sure there are no external impediments on one's way is counterproductive. Juristic freedom leads to temporary satisfaction only.

The big breakthrough in the pursuit of freedom – breakthrough in the sense that one finds out how to be free on a consistent basis – is when one understands that one's satisfaction does not increase in proportion to how far one succeeds in blocking the interference of others, but in proportion to how successful one is in collaborating with them. The demand for juristic freedom increases the rift between oneself and others, and decreases the possibility of long-term satisfaction. A more lasting satisfaction and, indeed, increased powers will be achieved by finding ways of seeing personal well-being as connected to that of others. By choosing their objective more carefully, people create a chance for themselves to find deeper satisfaction. Finding the correct objective (one that enhances collaboration, not confrontation) also means identifying the correct obstacles to fight. Internal obstacles could be as hard or harder to overcome than external obstacles: hence overcoming the former can be more liberating.

When we understand this link between freedom and quality of satisfaction, we can see that freedom is experienced at a particular turning

[10] See my discussion of the progressive nature of satisfaction in Dimova-Cookson (2020: 74–78).

point: at the point when a valuable objective is achieved. Only at this point has the obstacle been overcome. So, the experience of freedom does not reflect a state of affairs where obstacles do not exist: it comes at the point when our goal is attained. In this sense, freedom is understood better as *overcoming* obstacles rather than not having them. But more importantly, the *process* of doing what it takes to reach your objective is not accompanied by a feeling of satisfaction or the joy of liberation – these feelings come in place only when the task is accomplished.

Green's account of moral positive freedom makes us question a widely shared assumption that freedom is about an opportunity, that the benefits of freedom are given by having something available in potential. If anything, the argument in "The Different Senses of Freedom" shows the opposite – that being able to do something but not having done it, is frustrating. This makes us think about the circumstances in which this happens. What are the scenarios where only the achievement of a goal brings satisfaction, and where the mere capacity to achieve this goal but not yet having done so, is deeply frustrating? If we look more carefully at Green's examples, we can discern two ways in which this might happen. First, this would be the case when our goal is very hard to accomplish. Second, this would happen when we are trying to achieve our goal by taking the wrong steps.

The first scenario is exemplified well by the pursuit of self-improvement. Green comments on "the feeling of oppression, which always goes along with the consciousness of unfulfilled possibilities" implicating the hardship of the process and the scale of satisfaction achieved in the end (1986c: 242).

We can add other examples here. Students often say that they feel freest after an exam that they believe has gone well. They would not feel free the night before the exam even though they have the opportunity, the capability, and the likelihood of passing the exam – the satisfaction and the sense of freedom come after the exam is taken. Now turning to Green's own paradigm example: arguably, the acquisition of moral agency is one of the hardest things of all. A moral agent subordinates her personal good to the common good. This can be experienced as satisfying only if one has cultivated a disposition whereby the common good becomes more desirable than otherwise cherished personal goods. Before such a disposition has been developed, duty is experienced as hardship.

The second scenario of finding freedom only "in the end" is where one has a challenging goal but is not doing what is needed to achieve it. This comes close to the essence of Green's argument about the different senses of freedom: the pursuit of juristic freedom might be misguided – it might be taking us further from, not closer to, freedom. As Green has argued, true freedom, and accordingly real satisfaction, can be found in the acquisition of moral agency: when one lives up to one's duties. Moral action is about service to the common good and this typically implies some form of suspension of the pursuit of exclusively personal objectives. One needs to stop doing what is habitual, namely, advancing personal well-being, often not mindfully enough of others, in order to be able to find moral positive freedom.

Green's moral positive freedom shows very well how the three key aspects of freedom (purposiveness, satisfaction, and a valued objective) connect. One's understanding of duty is a valued objective. Green believes we carry the knowledge of what we must do and this knowledge is compelling. The satisfaction in fulfilling our duty is real and lasting, both because we want to fulfill it and because it is hard to do so. Achievement brings satisfaction. Now we can see why the three controversial features of moral positive freedom, discussed at the beginning of this section, play a key role in the account of how it works as a form of freedom. The clarity and specificity of the moral ideal are essential for its motivational function. The requirement for achieving perfection has a more symbolic function: it implies that the objective is fulfilled only "in the end," that the process is complex and it has to go in the right way. The real satisfaction experienced when duty is fulfilled, or the good deed is done, is the evidence that this is an experience of freedom. The satisfaction marks the turning point when hardship is over (the obstacle has been overcome), and the valuable objective has been accomplished: the point at which the experience of freedom starts.

Fulfilling our moral duty is liberating because we know what our duty is, we feel compelled to live up to it, and succeeding in doing so is one of the hardest and most satisfying things we can do. This clashes with the general intuition that freedom is about not being told what to do and not being told what is right. Yet when you know what is right, freedom is about achieving it. When you know what you want, freedom is about getting it. Potentiality is frustrating, only the reality is liberating.

3.4 How a "Possibility" Can Be Liberating

Up to this point, I have challenged the general wisdom that freedom is about opportunity and potentiality. Now I would like to return to this shared intuition and lend it some support but from the vantage point of having seen the structure of moral positive freedom. Let me now turn to one of Green's explanations about why the liberty given to us through the "possibility" of something is not a real one. In the following passage, Green comments on what it is that makes juristic freedom lacking. The problem with juristic freedom is that

> [i]t is a form of self-enjoyment, however, which consists essentially in the feeling by the subject of a possibility rather than a reality, of what it has in itself to become, not of what it actually is. To a captive on first winning his liberty, as to a child in the early experience of power over his limbs and through them over material things, this feeling of boundless possibility of becoming may give real joy; but gradually the sense of what it is not – of the very little that it amounts to – must predominate over the sense of the actual good as attained in it. (1986c: 241).

This is a rich, controversial, and telling passage and a lot depends on its interpretation. I would like to take two things from it and put them together. The first is the message Green wants to convey: that real freedom is to be found only when we have achieved something absolutely desirable, like the moral ideal or personal perfection. This is the rationale of moral positive freedom and I have defended it so far. But there is also something else here, which Green does not explicitly pursue. Even though juristic freedom is deficient, it is a step toward real freedom. It has some of the characteristics of real freedom – it brings "self-enjoyment" and it is a form of achievement, in its own right. Also, the claim that juristic freedom brings a "feeling of boundless possibility of becoming" makes it hard for us to agree with Green that it is not a real sense of freedom.

The way to bring these two messages together is to accept – as I have already done – that there are cases when a "possibility" is not related to freedom. But at the same time, we are now in a position to define more precisely the possibilities which *are* representative of freedom. This transition between experiences and different senses of freedom which Green describes in his lecture shows something which he does not spell out well. Green depicts a process of development – a process embedded both in the nature of human agency and in the dynamism of a changing world – and it is this process that explains best what freedom is. If we go back to the passage, we will see that the juristic freedom of the released prisoner and the walking toddler has lost its "freedom" value because their lives have moved on. They have gotten accustomed to their new powers and now they have seen new possibilities which are already beyond these powers; they now need new powers no longer available to them. The possibilities they had only seemed to be boundless. If they are to stay free, they need to keep up with a developmental curve – the curve of their new desires, the new capabilities they need, and the new obstacles they face. Staying free is sustaining one's power in a changing environment; it is having the capacity to maintain development.

Freedom can be about possibility as well, but it has to be the correct type of possibility – one that keeps what one wants within one's reach. We can also observe that achievements open up possibilities. Shortly after the prisoner was released and the toddler learned to walk the possibilities to do valued things were significant. Without new achievements, these possibilities have been hollowed out. If one manages to reach important landmarks of achievement, one will keep possibilities open. Taylor makes a similar point when he discusses negative freedom concepts that internalize the self-realization view. He comments that in such cases freedom cannot be seen purely in terms of an opportunity concept. For the opportunity to be genuine, it has to internalize some level of "exercise" characteristic of positive freedom.[11] What I add here is that achievements do not guarantee freedom for an indefinite period: new achievements are needed for one to stay free.

But then we are faced with another question. Is the real positive freedom about the one big achievement accomplished in the context of moral positive freedom or is it about our capacity to sustain a process of development, a process made of many achievements each opening a new possibility leading to a new achievement? Is freedom about one big achievement or many little ones? If the concept of moral positive freedom helped us discover the understanding of freedom as sustaining the capacity to keep developing, has not this concept fulfilled its function and made itself redundant?

3.5 The Morality of Personal Positive Freedom

The short answer is no. Moral positive freedom is valid in its own right: it does open space for another freedom that is sufficiently different as to warrant a second concept. The difference at stake is not merely the difference between open possibility and actual completion. Moral positive freedom does not simply open space for another freedom, it also threatens certain exercises of personal positive freedom. Berlin is one of the most articulate observers of this: When ideals are too demanding they could

[11] Taylor argues "that with the freedom of self-realization, having the opportunity to be free requires that I already be exercising freedom" (2006: 144).

cause inner torment, loss of satisfaction, and loss of motivation (2002: 181–183). Also, the trade-offs between personal and common good that are part and parcel of the process of developing one's motivation to act dutifully may lead to a loss of personal goods of genuine value. Green saw how the personal good could be enhanced by the engagement with the common good but he did not allow for a genuine conflict between the personal and the common good.[12] It is the possibility of this conflict that is at the heart of a meaningful distinction between two concepts of freedom.[13] Most contemporary scholars who see freedom as positive avoid having to endorse two concepts by effectively dismissing moral positive freedom, believing that its important features have been reaccommodated in a single but broader concept.

But the dismissal of the narrative behind moral positive freedom has led to some deficiencies in the existing accounts of personal positive freedom. The previous three sections theorized personal positive liberty as the capacity to sustain a process of development. Both the direction and the dynamic of this development can be understood only through the lens of moral positive freedom. Here I will look at two further ways in which contemporary accounts of personal positive freedom could be enriched. First, with the exception of Raz, scholars have not explained well the moral component of personal positive liberty. Morality features in their accounts in the form of moral constraints, while it has a more direct function in the shaping of personal objectives and personal powers. Second, contemporary accounts of personal positive freedom do not sufficiently acknowledge the role of satisfaction as a key component of freedom. As a result, there is not enough appreciation of the centrality of personal well-being in the context of personal positive freedom.

In order to illustrate my first point, I will turn to some of the most perceptive and comprehensive accounts of personal positive freedom: those of Simhony, Waldron, and Raz. All three distinguish their account of freedom from a moral concept of freedom even if they all emphasize the need for a moral component of liberty. In the case of Simhony and Waldron, morality functions as a form of *moral constraint* to the exercise of liberty. Both scholars use John Rawls's approach to the relationship of the right and the good in order to explain how freedom – associated with the pursuit of the good – has to work within the parameters of morality or justice – associated with the right.

[12] See Green's discussion in 1890: 354–356, § 324.

[13] See Dimova-Cookson (2020: 7–12, 224–229).

Simhony defends Green's idea of freedom as self-realization and reconstructs the concept along the lines of the freedom perspective from "Lecture on Liberal Legislation." She argues that freedom should be understood as "a complex conception that consists of entwining together of distinctive human capacities (inner/internal) and just social institutions (outer/external)" (2019: 101). Freedom as self-realization is ethically perfectionist – habitual pleasure-seeking is not self-realizing – but it is not politically perfectionist because nobody can provide self-realization for others. Most importantly such freedom relies on the existence of just social institutions as they provide the necessary conditions, the right framework. "*Within the boundaries* of non-selfishness and non-exploitation, any active long-term project counts as self-realising" (2019: 105 emphases added). Seeing the moral element of freedom in terms of moral constraints allows Simhony to maintain a pluralistic conception of freedom.

Waldron's analysis of the relation between personal autonomy and moral autonomy is highly relevant to the discussion here. Waldron sees the need for such a distinction, yet he is keen to keep the two concepts fairly close together and in particular to "consider how far something approximating Kantian moral autonomy is implicated in modern liberal conceptions of personal autonomy" (2005: 314). His answer is that indeed it is, not least because both types of autonomy depend on "an achievement of critical distance" toward one's objectives. No matter whether one seeks moral or personal autonomy, one has to make sure that at some stage "desire is checked or spontaneous inclination subjected to scrutiny" (2005: 317). Yet when it comes to explaining how exactly moral considerations impact upon personal visions of good life, Waldron offers his preferred interpretation of Rawls's relation between the right and the good:

> [T]he priority of the right over the good may be understood as a claim about the relation between individual aspirations and the social demands of morality. People have their own individual conceptions of the good, but these are subject to the demands of right conceived as a system of morally reconciling individual ends. (2005: 322)

Approaches that explain the moral component of personal freedom as a moral constraint or as a characteristic of the social setting do not sufficiently acknowledge the role moral ideals play in the actual shaping of personal objectives. Their role is evident when our objective is to achieve a higher landmark on the path of self-realization. In this context, the better we align the personal and the common good, the more recognition and success we are likely to achieve. The role of moral ideals is also evident when the advancement of our personal well-being depends on our effective resistance to exploitative moral pressures. In such instances, we would be unable to deal adequately with the challenges we faced without the capacity to understand and assess moral codes. Simply being resentful toward or critical of our social setting is not enough to protect our personal interest: we still need to express our interest in terms of the common good if any recognition is to be received, if any external support is to be secured. Our personal freedom depends on our moral competence, on our capacity to find and internalize the moral norms that *do not* undermine our personal well-being.

In this sense, the process of envisaging our personal objectives is more dramatic than choosing between options. We do not choose our significant goals and then work hard to attain them. Our goals are shaped in a process of exploring what is possible. These goals are always a mixture of personal and common goods and as such, some motivational adjustment is always called for. Our values are unique because the mixture which is best for us is unique: This is how I believe we should interpret "the post-Romantic idea that each person's form of self-realization is original to him/her, and can only be worked out independently" (Taylor 2006: 142). Our capacity to produce the mixture best suited to us of personal and common goods depends on existing viable and already recognized moral ideals. Options are open in a very particular manner. They are open in the sense that they are not available ready-made. They are open to trial and error; they are open for us to do the work of completion. Since we work within pre-existing parameters – existing institutions, existing moral ideals, our own natural endowments – the available possibilities are not countless.

One of the authors who comes closest to seeing how deeply embedded morality is in the constitution of personal freedom is Raz. His depiction of personal autonomy as "the ideal of free and conscious self-creation" (1986: 390) conveys this understanding that freedom is achieved as a result of a process of constructing values. Here is a powerful and telling passage:

> In embracing goals and commitments, in coming to care about one thing or another, one progressively gives shape to one's life, determining what would count as successful life and what would be a failure. One creates values, generates, through one's developing commitments and pursuits, reasons which transcend the reasons one had for undertaking one's commitments and pursuits. In that way a person's life is (in part) of his own making. It is a normative creation, a creation of new values and reasons. (1986: 387)

Raz's vision of the role of morality in the shaping of personal ideals rehearses key components of Green's argument for moral positive freedom. Gaining personal autonomy is an outcome of a process at the end of which one is not the same person. There is also a clear direction: the moral nature of one's objective is mandatory: "Autonomy requires a choice of goods. A choice between good and evil is not enough" (1986: 379). However, in the context of personal autonomy, the agent is not restricted to a single moral option: it is the availability of options that is crucial in seeing this as freedom. "The autonomous person's life is marked not only by what it is but also by what it might have been and by the way it became what it is. A person is autonomous only if he has a variety of acceptable options available to him to choose from, and his life became as it is through his choice of some of these options" (1986: 204, see also 371). So the actual process of finding one's objective is also very important.

Now let us pause and look more carefully into this process of how one became what one is. Why does the availability of choice expand one's freedom? Raz would have difficulty answering this question on the basis of his own account. Despite what he says about the process, the end result is crucial for his vision of personal autonomy: "When judging a person's well-being one is judging the success or failure of his life, not the means for that success or failure." (1986: 289). Creation implies completion. Waldron also observes that Raz's account of personal autonomy is so morally rich that the distinction between moral autonomy and personal autonomy which he otherwise upholds becomes questionable (Waldron 2005: 321–332).

I believe that the availability of choice between several moral ideals helps advance personal positive freedom because this allows one a greater chance of finding a moral objective that best accommodates one's personal idiosyncrasies and preferences. People vary in their natural endowments of morally relevant personal traits, including the degree of sociability or energy levels. A greater variety of morally viable ways of life would allow one to find an objective that advances the common good but is also more satisfying. The process of moral development which leads to the acquisition of moral agency and moral positive freedom shares a major similarity with the process of personal development within which one creates one's own values: motivational adjustment. The role of motivational adjustment is more obvious in the context of moral positive freedom as there we have a distinct moral ideal and the challenging task is to develop the disposition from which its exercise is satisfying. The motivational adjustment is also a part of the process of value exploration pertaining to personal autonomy. There the search for values and the motivational adjustment needed to embrace these values go hand in hand.

This brings me to my second critique of existing accounts of personal positive freedom: The lack of sufficient acknowledgment of the role of satisfaction in the experience of freedom, resulting in limited attention to personal well-being as a key aspect of that freedom. Waldron's account of personal autonomy, in line with those of Frankfurt and Dworkin, emphasizes the rationalist dimension of the process through which one finds worthwhile objectives. It concentrates on "capacity to stand back from one's occurrent volitions, to consider whether one wants to be influenced by them, and to act at least some of the time on the basis of these 'second-order desires'," on "specific capacities of rational deliberation and self-control," and "critical distance" (2005: 316, 307, 317). This commitment to rule out first-order desires as relevant to personal autonomy leads to underappreciation of the role played by emotions in the experience of freedom.

Berlin's ethical attack on positive freedom – as opposed to his political attack on its totalitarian implications – is motivated by his concern that the pursuit of high ideals can be damaging to personal integrity, including personal well-being. Berlin shows how in response to unreachable ideals we could "retreat to the inner citadel," we could give up on existing desires, ambitions, and personal attachments (2002: 181–182). Adjusting our desires to what is possible, rational, or desirable may lead to losing what is most essential, what is most authentically human. To put this in the terminology I have used so far, Berlin would argue that there are limits to the value of motivational adjustment, or of cultivating the right desires and dispositions. Our uncultivated, "empirical," desires have a value of their own. In his attack on the spiritualism of the moral concept of liberty and its focus on inner satisfaction, Berlin misses the opportunity to associate negative freedom more directly with validatory personal emotions, like the experience of pleasure, happiness, enjoyment, or satisfaction. Benjamin Constant whom Berlin celebrates as a champion of negative liberty, does exactly this: he defines modern liberty in terms of "peaceful enjoyment of private independence" (Constant 1988: 316). Contemporary concepts of personal positive liberty seem to have lost the appreciation of satisfaction which has played a significant role in the articulation of modern liberty.[14]

I believe satisfaction plays an important role both in the moral and the personal positive concepts. An appreciation of this role in the first sheds light on how it will work in the second. Depending on our objectives, satisfaction marks the achievement of different types of balance. The motivational adjustment could take different directions: it could go toward a higher level of serving the common good, up to the point of moral

[14] See my discussion of the role satisfaction plays in Constant's analysis of liberty (2020: 50–52).

agency, but also toward accommodating a greater share of personal goods, if this is what was needed for one's personal well-being.

3.6 Conclusion

One of Berlin's significant legacies is that most contemporary liberal theories preclude commitment to specific moral ideals in order to protect people's capacity for value exploration, and also their capacity to resist the moral narratives underpinning practices of domination. Yet Berlin has also influenced a decline in the conceptualization of moral freedom. One of the undesirable consequences of this has been the absence of more constructive accounts about how morality shapes personal freedom. Raz has been an exception in offering a dedicated explanation of the morality of personal freedom. But Raz has not appreciated fully why an independent concept of moral freedom is of great benefit here.

Seeing freedom in terms of opportunity, as most liberal scholars do, diverts attention from the cases where opportunities are not leading to anything desirable or where they are significantly short of what one aims to achieve. In this chapter, I looked at the instances where one's goals have been hard to achieve and where one is judging wrongly what needs doing for one's objective to be fulfilled. We could add more scenarios of deficient opportunities. Some opportunities may be false as they could be concealing a genuine obstacle, as illustrated by the metaphor of the glass ceiling. Opportunities could entail obligations that we may not be ready to fulfill. Ample opportunities could also distract us from our duties. The wrong opportunities could undermine either of the two positive freedoms. The argument in this chapter aimed to show that the concept of moral positive freedom helps us understand in what sense achievement or completion leads to freedom. Once we appreciate this, we can see that it also applies to personal positive freedom. Personal positive freedom obtains when opportunities keep desirable objectives within one's reach. I have argued that opportunities remain viable if they are reinvigorated through regular achievements.

Personal positive freedom replicates moral positive freedom in a minuscule and repetitive fashion. Moral positive freedom carries the archetype of one big achievement – arguably the most valuable and the hardest – that of acquiring moral agency. Personal positive freedom is based on a continuous developmental process made of many small achievements. Each of these small achievements is a synthesis of personal and common goods and each is based on some degree of motivational adjustment. Although the two freedoms are motivated by different objectives – moral positive freedom by the common good and personal positive freedom by personal well-being – there are similarities in the mechanism through which they are obtained.

Berlin associated negative freedom with our natural aversion toward obstacles placed by others.[15] Here I have tried to associate both moral and personal positive freedom with our natural disposition to seek success, excellence, or perfection, all these being representative of the value of completing an important task. Personal positive freedom depends on completing, among other things, the task of value formation. Liberty requires one to understand, adjust, and respond effectively to the surrounding world. This learning, adjusting, and finding responses is a permanent process. One needs to be able and willing to learn new lessons. Our appetite for success is a vital source for doing this.

[15] He quotes Rousseau approvingly: "The nature of things does not madden us, only ill will does" (2002: 170).

CHAPTER 4

Positive Freedom and Freedom of Contract

Fairness, Faring Well, and Freedom

Avital Simhony

4.1 Introduction

In the face of the widespread poverty that beset society in late nineteenth-century Britain, social liberals, led by T. H. Hill Green, forged a conceptual–normative alliance between freedom of self-realization (self-development) and fairness. By so connecting self-development with fairness, well-being with well-doing, well-fare with faring well, social liberals rendered social justice an internal element of freedom of self-development, and thereby fashioned a new conception of positive freedom. Green worked out this new conceptualization by criticizing the classical liberal model of freedom of contract and advocating placing restrictions on it. His conception of positive freedom, I argue in this chapter, was of great importance as a normative vehicle for ensuring effective membership in the society for disadvantaged and excluded groups such as working people. The relevance of positive freedom as a tool for the inclusion of excluded groups as sharers in the benefits of full social membership is still with us.

The positive freedom–social justice alliance faces two challenges. The first was raised by Isaiah Berlin's classic 1958 essay, *Two Concepts of Liberty*. He holds that positive freedom amalgamates in one single concept of various ideals – liberty, equality, justice – that should be kept conceptually apart. As he famously puts it "everything is what it is, liberty is liberty, not equality, or fairness, or justice" (Berlin 2002: 39). Berlin is not alone. This has become a standard criticism of Green's conception of positive freedom. The main charge here is that Green's conception of freedom is confusing. By connecting freedom with fairness (social justice), Green fails to convey "what we ordinarily mean" by the term liberty. Among others, W. L. Weinstein, William Parent, David Miller, all level

My thanks to Abisi Sharakiya, Maria Dimova-Cookson, and John Christman for very helpful comments.

some version of that criticism against Green's conception of positive freedom (Weinstein 1966: 146, 150, 152–153; Parent 1974: 166; Miller 2006: 10–12). Rather than illuminating and elucidating the meaning of liberty, Green, so the criticism goes, under the disguise of a definition, recommends social ideals and principles such as social justice. This charge receives support from a second challenge to positive freedom. On this challenge, the claims of negative freedom are capable of defending social legislation, the welfare state, and socialism (e.g., Waldron 2006). That such a defense is not inconsistent testifies to the complexity of the normative political argument.

The validity of these two challenges is not the focus of my concern. I argue, instead, that these challenges overlook the important interplay between context, conceptual mutability, and conceptual relationality in the construction of normative political arguments. Green's conceptualization of positive freedom unveils just such an interplay. Herein lies also my response to the second challenge that positive freedom confuses freedom with other ideals such as social justice. My response avoids engaging in pure conceptual analysis. (There is, however, a sense in which a conceptual analysis of freedom entails an inclusion of essential aspects of positive freedom. The argument pursued by Stanley Benn and Weinstein is a case in point [Benn and Weinstein 1973; see also Dimova-Cookson 2019: 86–90]). Rather, I turn to a particular dominant argument in the late nineteenth century (and early twentieth century) about positive freedom to show how the link between freedom of self-development and fairness (just institutions) was made without incoherence. Put differently, I argue that the second and third challenges miss the mark not least because they are a-historical. They cut off the important interplay between social–economic crises (as well as cultural and political ones) and conceptual–normative change. A context-sensitive approach to the conception of freedom reveals that negative freedom failed to adequately meet the social–economic problem of the widespread poverty that stemmed from the consequences of the industrial revolution. I stress "conceptual–normative" in order to divorce the discussion of positive freedom from a mere definitional account of the meaning of freedom. A "conceptual–normative" approach views concepts as the normative building blocks of political arguments. Accordingly, this approach stresses, first, the language of conceptions, following John Rawls's distinction between *concept* (formal) and *conception* (a particular substantive interpretation of a *concept* [Rawls 1971: 5–6, 9–11]), second, the mutability of concepts (as against understanding them as fixed and frozen), and third, the relational nature of conceptual boundaries (in contrast with keeping them rigid).

The chapter comprises three sections. Section 4.3 introduces briefly the essential features of the individualist model of freedom of contract: negative freedom, its default formal–abstract nature, and its grounding in a stark distinction between the private and public spheres. So understood, freedom of contract rules out distributive concerns and substantive rules of fairness. Section 4.4 explores Green's argument for restricting freedom of contract between employers and workers as well as between landlords and Irish tenant farmers. Far from securing freedom, Green argues, the individualist model of freedom of contract is, in fact, an instrument of disguised oppression and exploitation. Green's argument proceeds in two steps, all of which are required and justified by real freedom of self-development. *First*, he rejects coercion (and fraud) as the only legitimate obstacle to freedom, insisting that exploitation is a major obstacle also. In doing so, he challenges the formal–abstract nature of freedom of contract as a legal fiction that fails to take into consideration the concrete inequalities of capitalist markets. *Second*, in claiming that the unfreedom suffered by the weaker parties to contract is not merely a private matter, he dissolves the stark private-public distinction. Section 4.5 ties the various threads that makeup Section 4.4 into a single narrative. It focuses on Green's claim that just institutions are internal to freedom of self-development (positive freedom) and essential to its realization. Justice institutionalizes mutual recognition as the external dimension of positive freedom necessary for the exercise and development of distinctive human capacities, the internality of positive freedom. First, however, two preliminaries: a word about why Green (Section 4.2.1) and his conception of positive freedom (Section 4.2.2).

4.2 Two Preliminaries

4.2.1 Why Green?

Green is important here, primarily because he introduced positive freedom to liberalism. His normative conceptualization of positive freedom via his criticism of the classical liberal conception of freedom of contract, from within liberalism itself, has, importantly, opened a new era of social liberalism (as both a challenge and an alternative to classical/neoclassical liberalism) which led "to transform a tract such as Green's *Liberal Legislation and Freedom of Contract* of 1881 into a policy document such as the *Beveridge Report* of 1942" (Freeden 2005: 5). Though Green's positive freedom lies at the center of my analysis, its relevance extends to social liberalism as a whole. Not only did Green's argument launch the new phase of social liberalism, it clearly influenced the main critical approach to freedom of contract both in the United Kingdom and in the progressive movement in the United States. Indeed, his distinctive conceptualization of positive freedom as a relational conception anticipates a clear contemporary strand that forges a close link between freedom of contract and social justice and freedom of contract or unconscionable contracts. Moreover, Green's argument is valuable in that it introduces to social liberalism the argument from the commodification of labor. I focus mainly on Green's "Lecture on Liberal Legislation and Freedom of Contract" since it is the *locus classicus* for his conceptualization of positive freedom (Green 1986a: 194–212).

4.2.2 Green's Conception of Positive Freedom

Green conceptualizes positive freedom as freedom of self-realization (or, interchangeably, self-development). It consists in the entwining together of the exercise and development of distinctive human capacities (inner/internal) and enabling social institutions (outer/external). (Simhony 2019: 116–119: see also Section 4.5). Self-realization is the necessary function of both internality and externality; either one alone will not do. Internality alone is insufficient: slaves, to use Green's example, possess distinctive human capacities. The social organization in which they live, however, blocks the chances necessary to realize these capacities. A slave, to use Green's own example, possesses "powers that are his own to make the best of ... [that find] a stimulus to its inward development, though *no opportunity for outward exercise*" (Green 1986b: §114; emphasis added.) Conversely, one may have external enabling conditions but still cannot make use of them because one lacks the capacities (one is mentally disabled) or is internally impeded from exercising them (e.g., one is a habitual drunkard [Green 1986a: §18]) and hence would be unfree. Both capacities and enabling conditions have to obtain for one to be free. Hence Green speaks of "'really free,' in the sense of *being enabled to make the most of their capabilities*" (Green 1986b: §248).

Green's conception of positive freedom, entwines together, then, internal positive freedom – the exercise of distinctive human capacities – and external positive freedom – the availability of enabling social institutions. In this way, and following Hegel, Green – joined by few others, e.g., John Christman, Carol Gould, and C. B. Macpherson (Macpherson 1973; Gould 1995; Christman 2012) – links into a single integrative account two distinct strands that are discernible in the tradition of positive freedom. One strand identifies positive freedom as a condition of the inner self. This is largely associated with the idealist tradition. With Kant, in particular, this argument tends to ignore, or at any rate marginalizes, the externality of freedom. The second strand considers positive freedom in terms of the availability of resources or enabling conditions (Crocker 1980). This is largely associated with the socialist and egalitarian liberal traditions, and sometimes rejects inner positive freedom as metaphysically unsound and even problematic (Flikschuh 2012: 567, 571).

4.3 The Individualist Model of Freedom of Contract

To fully appreciate Green's conception of positive freedom it is essential to get a good handle on the nature of the liberal concept of contract to which Green critically responded. While contractual freedom lies at the heart of laissez-faire capitalism, the rationale of the liberal concept of contract is not, as such, market-oriented (Gutmann 2013: 39–40; Dimova-Cookson 2019: 112–120). Green's criticism of freedom of contract is, therefore, not only criticism of unhindered capitalism but also of individualist liberalism as a whole.

The classical liberal model of freedom of contract is one of liberal individualism. It holds that a contract is a reciprocal bargain entirely dependent upon the will of the parties, with the parties entirely free to pursue their own interests, and that the general law should intervene as little as possible with the freedom of the parties to contract. Three features make up this individualist model: The primacy of negative freedom, its default formal–abstract nature, and its grounding in a stark distinction between the private and public spheres. First, the "freedom" in "freedom of contract" is essentially negative freedom. To be sure, some contemporary scholars conceptualize freedom of contract in terms of individual autonomy (e.g., Gutmann 2013: 40–41), and the language of autonomy is employed by some scholars discussing the nineteenth-century doctrine of freedom of contract (Rosenberg 2013: 167). However, the language of autonomy, expressed in terms of legal formalism, is not inconsistent with the language of negative freedom. For one thing, negative freedom is not bereft of the idea of agency (Dimova-Cookson, Chapter 3, this volume). For another, the only obstacle to such a default idea of autonomy is limited to coercion (and fraud) as is the case with negative freedom. Moreover, in nineteenth-century political discourse, "freedom" in "freedom of contract" is usually connected with negative freedom (e.g., Sidgwick 1897: 85–91; Mensch 1980–1981: 763–764).

The pride of place that individualist liberals assign to freedom of contract illustrates their claim that absence of coercion means freedom (Goodwin 1985: 32–34). As Benn and Weinstein put it, "Action under coercion or threat is, for the liberal, the very paradigm of unfreedom; the incompatibility of freedom and coercion is, after all, what classical liberalism is all about" (Benn and Weinstein 1973: 318). Negative freedom is bound up with the formal nature of the individualist model of freedom of contract.

Formalism is the second feature of the individualist model of freedom of contract. As much as default autonomy shares the formal nature of negative freedom, similarly with the conception of juridical equality which must regard "its addressees not in all their particularity, but as *identical abstract beings*" (Mensch 1980–1981: 763; DiMatteo 1998–1999: 884; Gutmann 2013: 40–41, original emphases). Stressing the legal formalism of freedom of contract, Roscoe Pound, chief advocate of "sociological jurisprudence," identified legal formalism – "mechanical jurisprudence" – as a major defining feature of the individualist model of freedom of contract (Pound 1909: 462).

Negative freedom and formalism are bound up with the third feature of the individualist model of freedom of contract: A stark distinction between the private and the public. The former is the sphere of private property and contract rights, requiring protection from legislative interference. The individualist liberal theory of freedom of contract conceives of "of contract law as a legal institution that, in general, recognizes and respects the power of private individuals to effect changes in their legal relations *inter se*" (Gutmann 2013: 40). Essentially, proponents of the individualist model of freedom of contract insist on the private nature of contracts in order to argue that contracts concern parties' rights, not their welfare (e.g., Hevia 2007).

4.4 Positive Freedom and Fair Freedom of Contract

4.4.1 The Problem of Unfair Contracts

The controversy over restricting freedom of contract began in the 1880s, focusing on the wisdom of efforts to ensure fundamental fairness for individual contracting parties by protective and distributive legislation. It was fueled by the gap between classical contract theory's vision of the institution of contract and the realities of the marketplace where strong parties took advantage of those who were vulnerable to unfair overreaching. Such unfairness exposed freedom of contract as a legal fiction characteristic of individualist thinking that flies in the face of actual social-economic facts. Put differently, the individualist doctrine of freedom of contract could provide only formal protection at the expense of actual protection. Only purely procedural grounds were available to individualist liberalism: coercion and fraud.

The legal formalism of freedom of contract excludes any serious consideration of the actual circumstances of concrete individuals. As Pound put it: "Decisions regarding freedom of contract draw on rigorous logical deduction from a predetermined conception in disregard to, and even contrary to, actual facts" (Pound 1909: 462). Thus, as Lester Ward, considered by some the father of American sociology, put it: "Much of the discussion about 'equal rights' is utterly hollow. All the ado made over the system of contract is surcharged with fallacy" (quoted in Pound 1909: 454). A contemporary scholar articulates the fairness problem of individualist freedom of contract in a fashion that fits well into Green's frame of argument: "The norms of justice and fairness are seen as competitors to the formalistic use of contract rules to promote certainty in contractual transactions. The latter is individualistic in its perspective and incorporates notions of freedom, security, and efficiency. The former is communitarian centered in its focus" (DiMatteo 1998–1999: 884). The choice for Green was not between freedom that demands state restraint and fairness that limits the exercise of freedom of contract. The choice was, rather, of forging an alliance between freedom and fairness in order to secure effective freedom of self-development to the vulnerable parties in overwhelmingly one-sided contracts that are in favor of the party who has the superior bargaining power. To that end, Green employed the normative tool of positive freedom to justify restricting freedom of contract.

4.4.2 *Positive Freedom and Restricting Freedom of Contract*

But, how, exactly? For Green and other social liberals (e.g., L. T. Hobhouse and John Hobson) thickening "freedom" – in the shape of positive freedom – is the conceptual–normative vehicle for connecting self-development with fairness, well-being with well-doing, and well-fare with faring well. Thickening freedom into positive freedom, in turn, required revising the concept of equality by ridding it of its formal character and dissolving the stark private-public distinction. This reconfiguration, ultimately, rendered just institutions internal to, and essential to, the exercising of developmental capacities.

It is not uncommon, however, to reject positive freedom as an adequate justification for restricting freedom of contract. One objection is leveled at Green directly. Though explained and quoted at length, his conception of positive freedom is briefly dismissed, following Berlin, as politically dangerous because of its potential for totalitarianism (Spector 2006: 1122–1124). This charge, I have argued elsewhere, is without foundation (Simhony 1991).

The second objection seeks to disqualify positive freedom because of its perfectionist nature. Autonomy is a formal notion of free agency and is "independent of … *ideal* conceptions of autonomous personhood or positive liberty" (Gutmann 2013: 40–41, original emphasis). Relatedly, freedom of contract is consistent only with the priority of the right over the good. Nineteenth-century liberals shared an ethical vision that is grounded in a rich conception of the human good which, in turn, yielded a commitment to securing good-enabling institutions. That commitment was compatible with both consequentialist and non-consequentialist justifications. It is indisputable that Green assigns priority to the good of self-development over the right. His prioritization of the good, however, does not come at the expense of instrumentalizing it. Rather, the "right" – a just system of rights – is both constitutive of everyone's freedom of self-development and is essential to its realization. If the self-development of all is, for Green, the ethical common good, then a just system of rights – internal to it and is essential to its realization – fits the bill of a political common good. Moreover, Green's perfectionism is neither consistent with paternalism, nor does it require political perfectionism. Self-realization requires the self-effort of the individual; it is an achievement of individual active effort, something that could not be given to one by another (Green 1924: §332). Hence, paternalism is unacceptable. Nor is political perfectionism defended. Self-realization is ethically perfectionist since it denies that certain pursuits, such as habitual pleasure-seeking and more generally, habitual selfishness, could provide self-realizing satisfaction. However, ethical perfectionism is not political since no one could convey self-realization to another. Political and social institutions function as enabling conditions, not as deliverers of self-realization. For the purposes of state action, restricting freedom of contract concerns only the external dimension of positive freedom which can be properly described as "effective freedom" (Hobhouse 1994: 40, 44), or, as Green has it, "real freedom"

(Green 1986a: 203). Finally, ethical self-realization is pluralistic, not monistic; it is *one* in form – developing distinctive human capacities – but *many* in content (Green 1924: §283). Within the boundaries of non-selfishness and nonexploitation, any active long-term project counts as self-realizing.

A third charge holds that positive freedom is too vacuous to provide a determinate action guide for either the individual or the state. Though famously made by Henry Sidgwick, and not in the context of freedom of contract, this critique is still relevant in this context given the alleged failure of positive freedom to provide an action guide (Sidgwick 1884: 170) While Sidgwick has a point, his criticism also misses the mark to the extent that Green does provide a clear action guide in terms of social justice as a principle of moral rightness (Section 4.5).

How, then, does Green's conception of positive freedom justify restricting freedom of contract? First, challenging coercion and fraud as the only legitimate obstacles to freedom of contract, he establishes exploitation as also an essential obstacle. In doing so, Green targets the formal nature of the individualist model of freedom of contract. A significant result of such an argument is to show that protecting the weak party to contracts is not necessarily paternalistic. Second, insisting on the essential sociability of self-realization, Green rejects the private–public distinction that is closely bound up with freedom of contract. Taking each justification in turn, Green's argument proceeds in two steps.

4.4.2.1 Step 1: From Coercion to Exploitation

Using concrete cases of the "starving laborer" and the Irish tenant farmer, Green argues that not only coercion, but, importantly, exploitation constitutes a legitimate obstacle to freedom of self-development. To be sure, some social liberals (and American progressives) sought to expand the conception of coercion to include economic need (Ely 1902: 65; Fried 2009: 18). Green's argument, however, keeps coercion and exploitation apart. Though lack of self-development can stem from coercion, it can also result, in the absence of coercion, from the presence of exploitation.

Two forms of exploitation are relevant to Green's argument: "*bargaining exploitation*" and "*corporeal exploitation*" (Hodgson 2015: 354, original emphases). *Bargaining exploitation* arises from asymmetries of bargaining power between agents in the sphere of exchange. *Corporeal exploitation* concerns the inseparability of the workers and their labor power.

Bargaining Exploitation Bargaining exploitation indicates unfair or unconscionable contracts:

> If a contract is unfair or oppressive to one party in a way that suggests abuses during its formation, a court may find it unconscionable and refuse to enforce it. *A contract is most likely to be found unconscionable if both unfair bargaining and unfair substantive terms are shown. An absence of meaningful choice by the disadvantaged party is often used to prove unfair bargaining.* (www.law.cornell.edu/wex/unconscionability, emphases added).

Note that unfair contracts comprise two related elements of exploitation: unfair bargaining and unfair substantive terms. An "absence of meaningful choice by the disadvantaged party" indicates "unfair bargaining" that, in turn, results in unfair substantive terms.

Green employs two concrete examples in support of bargaining exploitation: Irish tenant farmers and the "starving laborer" (Green 1986a: 208). Both lack meaningful choices. Thus, "in many parts of Ireland eviction means starvation to the evicted tenant . . . [because] the hiring of land to till presents itself as a necessity of life" (Green 1986a: 208). Moreover: "The only alternative is emigration, and during the recent years of depression in America that alternative was to a great extent closed" (Green 1986a: 208). The conclusion is inevitable: "Under such conditions" – absence of meaningful choice – "freedom of contract is little more than a name. The peasant farmer is scarcely more free to contract with his landlord than is a starving laborer to bargain good wages with a master who offers him work" (Green 1986a: 208). Exploitation of the Irish tenant farmer by his landowner and the "starving laborer" by his employer is evidenced by "unfair substantive terms" – the second element of unfair exploitative contracts. Examples are low "starvation" wages, unsafe working conditions and the like. Moreover, exploitation is further enabled by "long habits of domination on the one side and dependence on the other" (Green 1986a: 208). The concrete reality of helplessness entrenched in habitual dependence inevitably disables the weaker party to a contract from making the best of his own interests.

Green's conclusion establishes the urgent need for justice for the vulnerable: "To uphold the sanctity of contracts is doubtless a prime business of government, *but it is no less its job* to provide against contracts being made, which, from the helplessness of one of the parties to them, instead of being a security for freedom, becomes an instrument of disguised oppression" (Green 1986a: 209; emphasis added).

Freedom of self-development entails, therefore, a thicker conception of equality. As Hobhouse puts it: "In the matter of contract true freedom postulates substantial equality between the parties" (Hobhouse 1994: 40).

The movement toward thicker equality illustrates my claim that conceptualizing freedom in terms of self-development is conceptually normatively associated with rethinking other relevant conceptions, such as equality. A normative movement for positive freedom of self-development is also a movement for "positive opportunity for self-development" as David George Ritchie puts it (Ritchie 1895: 139–140) or for "real opportunity of self-development," as Green puts it (Green 1924: §245).

This new alignment of freedom of self-development with real opportunity was central to the political argument of social liberalism beginning in the 1880s with Green and stretching into the twentieth century, as evidenced by Hobson's "inquiry into the nature of the fuller and more positive liberty to which the Liberalism of the future must devote itself" (Hobson 1974: 97). This inquiry, he holds, should provide an answer to the following question: "What are the equal opportunities which every Englishmen requires to-day in order to secure real liberty of self-development?" (Hobson 1974: 92–94, 99, 113, 164, 171–172, 174).

The gap between hollow equality and substantial equality helps reveal the problem social liberals have with paternalism as justifying either the rejection or embrace of restrictions on freedom of contract. First, however, completing the discussion of exploitation is in order.

Whereas bargaining exploitation is widely, though not always explicitly, recognized in the literature on Green and social liberalism, corporeal exploitation constitutes an innovative move, which, though crucial to his argument, is little noticed.

Corporeal Exploitation Corporeal exploitation is a consequence of the inseparability of the workers and their labor power. "The peculiarity that labor power, unlike other factors of production, is inseparable from its owner was noted by Green (1888), Alfred Marshall (1920), and John A. Hobson (1929)" (Hodgson 2015: 355–356). Hodgson explains that the inseparability of labor power from the owner of it (the worker) confers disadvantage on the laborer compared with the owner of other factors of production (the employer), resulting in exploitation.

For Green, the essential point regarding corporeal exploitation relates to the inseparability of labor power from the developing capacities of the personhood of the laborer. He focuses on the inseparability of labor power from the powers of human development. His core claim recalls a similar argument by a contemporary scholar: If self-development is vital to positive freedom, "then inalienability, needed to foster that development, will be seen as freedom-enhancing rather than as an imposition of unwanted restraint on our desires to transact in the market" (Radin 1987: 1910–1911).

This claim challenges a neoclassical and libertarian argument according to which labor should be free from unwanted restraint on an individual's wish to transact in the market. Such commodification of labor poses a clear and present danger to "the free development of the human faculties" (Green 1986a: 203). As Green puts it: The power of labor "attaches in a peculiar manner to the person of man" such that exploiting (unfair) conditions of labor renders it impossible for the person selling it to freely develop his distinctive human capacities. This is especially so because, as the examples of the "starving laborer" and the Irish peasant farmers illustrate, the worse off in society are subject to bargaining exploitation as was established earlier. Because the worker's labor power is inseparable from his human powers of self-development, the sale of labor power in unfair contracts hinders self-realization. Workers are unfree if their distinctive human capacities are unfulfilled because blocked. Hence, restraints that are placed on unfair contracts are self-realization-enabling. Interference with an unfair contract in the areas of "labor, and education, and health, involving as it does manifold interference with freedom of contract, is justified on the ground that it is the business of the state … to maintain the conditions *without which the free exercise of human faculties is impossible*" (Green 1986a: 200–201, emphases added). These enabling conditions, importantly, become definitive of freedom of self-realization.

To return to the issue of paternalism. The gap between hollow equality and substantial equality helps reveal that social legislation restricting freedom of contract in order to protect the well-being interests of workers and tenant farmers does not have to be paternalistic.

4.4.3 Freedom of Contract and Paternalism

"Paternalism is the interference of a state or an individual with another person, against their will, and defended or motivated by a claim that the person interfered with will be better off or protected from harm" (Dworkin, G. 2020). Paternalism was used by late-nineteenth-century classical liberals both to reject and justify protective legislation. Green's fairness justification for restricting freedom of contract reveals a possible rejection of the paternalist argument, however it is used. If working people or the Irish tenant farmers are indeed the weaker parties to contract, as he clearly established, and if he can show that restriction of freedom of contract is not against their own will, but rather that such legislative interference is in accord with their will, then his case against paternalism would be on solid ground. Such a route, put forward by Russell Hardin, is available to Green. Green advocates legislative restriction of freedom of contract, Hardin holds, in "defending the defenseless in order that they might eventually become autonomous developed persons" (Hardin 1986: 62). But how can we know what were the views of "the defenseless" who were protected by the allegedly (apparently) paternalist legislation? Though such knowledge is beyond our ability, Hardin proposes that "the defenseless" could plausibly express their will collectively by voting rather than by individually entering their separate contracts. By voting, they "would have overwhelmingly have chosen to restrict themselves as the legislation eventually did" (Hardin 1986: 62). If so, then legislative action could not be adequately described as paternalistic since it improved the conditions of "the defenseless," not against their will and judgment, "but rather in support of their judgment of their interests" (Hardin 1986: 62).

Ample support for such an argument can be found in Green's views. To begin with, he stresses that recent protective legislation (the 1870s and 1880/1) begins, in the main, with the more democratic parliament of 1868 (Green 1986a: 197). He also claims that the effort made by Parliament to apply the earlier factory acts "to every kind of factory and workshop" was carried out "only alongside of the second reform act of 1867" (Green 1986a: 197). Moreover, his concern with restricting freedom of contract did not aim at protecting this or that individual, but rather "the suffering classes," and "the degraded population" (Green 1986a: 202). Whereas in the past, governmental action liberated another class by defending it against "close privileged corporations" and "against monopolies" (Green 1986a: 196), late nineteenth-century "work of liberation" (Green 1986a: 197) required defending working-class and tenant farmers against those who wish to maintain the status quo. Throughout, Green is concerned with advancing the "cause of social interest against class interests" (Green 1986a: 196). This, he claims, has always been the liberal cause. More directly relevant evidence, still, is provided by Thomas Marshall's analysis of the working-class struggle to gain decent conditions and wages in the late nineteenth century and ultimately to campaign, with the support of the Liberal Party and then the Labor Party, for social rights in the twentieth century (Marshall 1950: 1–85). For social liberals, the cause of social interest is bound up with linking individual and public responsibility.

4.4.3.1 Step 2: Positive Freedom and Dissolving the Stark Private-Public Distinction

Positive freedom cuts across the stark private–public division that underpins the individualist model of freedom of contract. The "private" is the sphere of private property and contract rights, requiring protection from legislative interference. But, as Pound argued, public interest inheres in seemingly private contracts. "The currency in juristic thought of an individualist conception of justice, which exaggerates the importance of property and of contract, exaggerates private right at the expense of public right" (Pound 1909: 457). Then and now, proponents of the individualist model of freedom of contract insist on the private nature of contracts in order to argue that contracts concern parties' rights, not their welfare (e.g., Hevia 2007). Appreciating the pernicious role of economic power underlying the fictitious freedom of contract, social liberals, however, insisted on the non-individualistic, relational element of rights which could not exclude considerations of social justice. This motivated Green's unique rejection of the stark private-public distinction.

Green holds that injury to the health of the contracting individual is a public injury. This claim stems from, and is justified by, his relational conceptualization of self-development. Individuals, he holds, cannot achieve self-development in separation, only through mutual interdependence on which I discuss more later. Contracts, then, should not be only a matter of private relations, excluding consideration of welfare rights.

4.5 Positive Freedom, Social Justice, and Mutual Recognition

Establishing exploitation as an important obstacle to free self-development and denying the exclusive private nature of contracts, Green aligns self-development with social justice as the essential institutional dimension of positive freedom. This alignment lays bare Green's account of positive freedom in terms of the interrelation between its inner and outer facets.

A careful reading of Green's famous conceptualization of "freedom, rightly understood" reveals that just institutions are internal to, and essential to, the realization of self-realization as a joint achievement of all.

It comprises three elements; each is stated both negatively and positively:

> We do not mean merely freedom from restraint or compulsion. We do not mean merely freedom to do as we like irrespectively of what it is that we like. We do not mean *a freedom that can be enjoyed by one man or one set of men at the cost of a loss of freedom to others*. When we speak of freedom as something to be so highly prized, we mean a positive power or capacity of doing or enjoying something worth doing, and that, too, something that we do or enjoy *in common with others*. (Green 1986a: 199)

Rightly understood, freedom comprises three elements, each is stated both negatively and positively. First, the capacity to do – freedom involves the capacity to do things, not the mere absence of restraint; second, the value element – freedom means realizing distinctive human capacities, doing something valuable, not merely doing something we like; third, the social element – realizing one's distinctive human capacities should benefit others, and not be "founded on a refusal of the same opportunity to other" individuals (Green 1986a: 199). Rightly understood, then, freedom results jointly from the absence of restraint and the presence of a positive capacity to do or enjoy self-realization in common with others.

Of interest, here is the third component since it is the locus of justice. Social justice is the external institutional constituent of freedom of self-realization. As Green puts it: "'The just' equals that complex of social conditions which for each individual is necessary to enable him to realize his capacity of contribution to social good," by which Green means self-realization of all (Green 1986b: §187, n. 1). Green was keenly aware that liberals of the late nineteenth century had to deal with "this great problem of social justice," namely, that everyone "should have a fair chance of making the best and most of himself" (Nicholson 1997: 385). Negatively stated, social justice is a principle of nonexploitation: Freedom cannot "be enjoyed *by one man or one set of men at the cost of a loss of freedom to others.*" Positively put, justice takes the shape of a principle of "real opportunity of self-development" (Green 1924: §245). Unhappily, Green puts it here negatively. Speaking of "true freedom" as "the full exercise of the faculties with which man is endowed," he hastens to add: "But we rightly refuse to recognize the highest development on the part of an exceptional individual or exceptional class, as an advance toward the true freedom of man, if it is founded on a refusal of the same opportunity to other men" (Green 1924: §§176, 273–274, 354; 1986a: 199). "Same opportunity" requires securing a "real opportunity of self-development" to "the worse off in society" (Green 1924: §245). Unless it is secured, pursuing or enjoying self-realization "in common with others" – and therefore effecting the ideal of a "society of men really free" (Green 1986b: §248) – remains a mere possibility, lacking in reality. Both principles of social justice are integral to, and are required for effecting, freedom of self-realization as "something that we do or enjoy in common with others."

The importance of just institutions to enabling free self-development for all cannot be overestimated. For one thing, it sheds light on the innovative element in Green's conceptualization of freedom, drawing on Hegel: Freedom is relational and requires a particular set of institutions. Robert Pippin argues that the real uniqueness of Hegel's conception of freedom falls on the objective side. Realizing freedom, as Pippin explains, requires both reciprocal relations and a certain set of institutions (Pippin 2008: 151–155). They are closely connected for while intersubjective recognition is essential to being free, it is embodied in the institutions of ethical life. Green does not follow Hegel's specific vision of the institutions of ethical life. The essential point for Green is this: Since intersubjective (mutual) recognition is essential to being positively free, securing it must take effective shape in just institutions. Social justice institutionalizes mutual recognition as the external dimension of positive freedom.

Whereas exploitation separates and divides by securing "a freedom that can be enjoyed by one man or one set of men at the cost of a loss of freedom to others" (Green 1986a: 199), justice creates a civic bond by ensuring that self-development is a cooperative achievement of all members of society. As a cooperative, self-realization is both mutual and complementary. Though these two adjectives are closely related, they serve to highlight the distinctive facets of relational self-realization which forge the cooperative nature of the common good society. The good of self-realization is mutual. No one can achieve self-realization in separation from and independence of others; one's development is dependent on and is reciprocal with others'. As Hobhouse – who not for the first time injects clarity to Green's ideas to which he largely subscribes – puts it: "The development that each man can achieve is conditioned in kind and degree by the development of others" (Hobhouse 1921: 90). This claim presupposes a view of shared social life "in which . . . all men, shall participate" (Green 1924: §370, §288). The good of self-realization is complementary. Anticipating Rawls, Green would agree with Rawls that no one can become a complete exemplar of humanity; for "we are by ourselves but parts of what we might be" (Rawls 1971: 529). We need each other to complete our humanity. Hence, it is only in a social union that "the members of a community participate in one another's nature . . . the self is realized in the activities of many selves" (Rawls 1971: 565). Green could not agree more (Green 1924: §§269, 273–274, 279, 288, 360, 370). We complete ourselves in shared institutions that satisfy and express our most fundamental ends. We are this way as participants in shared ways of life, institutions, that enable us to exercise and develop our capacities through reciprocal relations with others.

How do, then, the principles of justice give institutional effect to mutual and complementary self-realization? Briefly put, by securing equal rights to all, such that no one gains at the expense of another (Green 1986b: §132), and by securing "real opportunity of self-development" for all with a special emphasis on "the less favored members of society" (Green 1924: §245). The core claim here is not simply that all are secured effective opportunities which allow them to pursue their own life plans uninterrupted by and independently of others, provided they do not infringe on the freedom of any other individual. This would be to regard freedom of self-realization as a private good achieved "in separation," as is illustrated, for example, by Herbert Spencer's formula of justice. The core claim of justice is, rather, that our own realization is mutual and complementary. This is why, for Green, poor health and bad contracts are not just individuals' private disasters but public ones. Speaking of the case of an individual who "bargains to work under conditions fatal to health, e.g., in an unventilated factory," Green claims, as we saw earlier that every injury to the health of the individual is a public injury because it hinders the accomplishment of cooperative social life by reducing the power of individuals, as members of society, to make the best of themselves. The principles of nonexploitation and fair chance are the institutional enabling conditions that are internal to cooperative social life and essential to its achievement.

A just system of rights provides an institutional effect to Green's important conception of mutual recognition. It challenges and replaces the thin formal legal mutual recognition associated with individualist freedom of contract because of its failure to provide actual protection against exploitative relations. Institutionalized in a just system of rights, mutual recognition is essential for securing freedom of self-realization. Why so? Because mutual recognition is the conceptual core of rights. Mutual recognition constitutes rights (Green 1986b: §138). Claiming rights is not and cannot be egoistic or self-centered because claiming rights is mutual. As mutually recognized moral claims for self-development, rights equally emphasize the development of others. To recognize someone is to acknowledge his or her equal status as being an end (rather than means) in itself to view others on a moral par with oneself; to be able to relate to them as "I" and "Thou" and vice versa. It is a form of communication between self-conscious persons who are aware of others as themselves and of their relation to them as part and parcel of their own awareness of themselves as persons with their own ends. Mutual awareness, however, has to result in "practical recognition," that is in the actual practice of "acting and being treated" as equal members of society. A system of equal rights embodies just such practical recognition.

The right not to starve is a concrete application of practical recognition embodied in a just system of equal rights. "Suppose a theft by a starving man . . . the right violated is a primary and essential one; one which, where there are many starving people, is in fact pretty sure to be protected by the most stringent penalties" (Green 1986b: §194). It might be argued that, far from giving reason for a lighter punishment, the hunger of the thief should require heavier punishment in order that the temptation to steal will be neutralized.

Jeremy Bentham made such an argument. He recognizes that "the fact of extreme hunger suggests 'the depravity of a man's disposition is less conclusive' than if the act had been committed by someone in different circumstances, where the temptation was weaker." He, nevertheless, and this is the crucial point, "goes on to argue that the strength of the temptation does not excuse punishment because to do so would provide encouragement to those who may be tempted" (Green 1986b: 337, n. 12). Green could not disagree more. For: "It is not the business of the state to protect one order of rights specially, but all rights equally," that is no one, or a group, gains at the expense of another, or a whole group. This is just what Bentham suggests by connecting the violation of property rights with heavy penalties. Doing so in face of "the fact that many people are on the edge of starvation . . . diverts attention from the true way of protecting the endangered right, which is to prevent people from falling into a state of starvation" (Green 1986b: §194).

4.6 Conclusion

Green's conception of positive freedom entwines together internal positive freedom, the exercise of distinctive human capacities, and external positive freedom – the availability of just social institutions. This innovative conceptualization carries threefold significance. First, appreciating Green's integrative conceptualization of positive freedom enriches our understanding of past and present discourse on the nature of positive freedom. Second, though the alignment of positive freedom and social justice does not meet the pure analytic enterprise of setting rigid conceptual boundaries, if it is situated in its proper context, it is by no means a simple case of confusion. Rather, it reveals the relevance of taking seriously the mutability and relationality of "normative-conceptual" analysis. Third, rightly understood, Green's positive freedom was of great importance as a normative vehicle for ensuring effective membership of the society for disadvantaged and excluded groups such as working people. The relevance of positive freedom as a tool for inclusion of excluded groups as sharers in the benefits of full social membership is still with us.

CHAPTER 5

Recognition and Positive Freedom

David Ingram

5.1 Introduction: Berlin

The concept of *negative* liberty that was famously memorialized by Isaiah Berlin refers to "the ability to do what one wishes," or "to be left to do or be what he is able to do or be, without interference from other persons" (Berlin 1969a: 121–122, 139). The concept of *positive* liberty, by contrast, refers (again citing Berlin) to the "source of control or of interference that can determine someone to do, or be, this rather than that" (Berlin 1969a: 122). Classical examples of positive freedom mentioned by Berlin include *subjective* conditions of agency, such as self-critical reasoning and autonomous willingness. These conditions, he notes, must be realized, in the first instance, from within the will of the lone agent (as Kant described the truly moral self, whose own reason prescribes the universal laws of free action). However, Berlin adds that proponents of positive freedom from Aristotle to the present day have understood that self-determination, however it is conceived, depends on *intersubjective* and *objective* conditions for its *realization*. So understood, positive freedom must also be realized, in the second instance, from within the *collective will* of the political society with whom the individual solidaristically identifies (as Jean-Jacques Rousseau describes the truly free citizen of a democracy, whose identification with his fellow citizens prescribes their common aims and guarantees their harmonious cooperation). Further specifying these intersubjective conditions, and anticipating contemporary theorizing about the multicultural politics of recognition developed most famously by Charles Taylor and Axel Honneth, Berlin observes that, in stark contrast to Kant's subjectivistic understanding of positive freedom, Edmund Burke and post-Kantian philosophers within the German idealist tradition held that:

> I am a social being in a deeper sense than that of interaction with others. For am I not what I am, to some degree, in virtue of what others think and

> feel me to be? ... [S]ome, perhaps all, of my ideas about myself, in particular, my sense of my own moral and social identity, are intelligible only in terms of the social network to which I am (the metaphor must not be pressed too far) an element. The lack of freedom about which men or groups complain amounts, as often as not, to the lack of *proper recognition*. (Berlin 1969a: 155; my stress)

In a footnote, Berlin pointedly observes that this "socialized" version of Kant's doctrine of human freedom is "almost its opposite," in that "Kant's free man needs no public recognition for his inner freedom" (Berlin 1969a: 156n1). Indeed, he remarks that because "I am in my own eyes as others see me ... this is the most heteronomous condition imaginable" (Berlin 1969a: 156n1). For "if I am not so recognized, then I may fail to recognize, I may doubt my own claim to be a fully independent human being" (Berlin 1969a: 157).

Writing at the height of the Cold War, Berlin was keen on showing that the tendency to lump together positive freedom, understood as an individual exercise of rational decision-making, and the psychological need to feel that one's needs, values, and identity are in harmony with society through solicitation of positive affirmation by one's consociates, jeopardized the unique essence of *political* liberty, understood as a natural limit to totalitarian governments. As against the notion that society and state must perfect one's freedom and identity in a social direction, Berlin, again and again, appeals to the common core of negative and positive freedom as *non-domination*, viz., being free to act and control one's train of practical reasoning free from the interference of others. Like George Orwell, he burnishes the scalpel of conceptual analysis to argue that even labeling positive liberty as a kind of solidarity-ensuring social freedom disingenuously amounts to dialectical double-speak in which it becomes permissible to "force someone to be free," to paraphrase Rousseau's famous assertion about the need of all to conform their private wills to the general will or common good ostensibly embodied in the wise legislator's proposals for the democratic referendum (Berlin 1969a: 148). By this route, liberty comes to mean nothing more than allowing oneself to be coerced by public law or public opinion that is judged to be more rational and correct in assessing one's good than one's fallible deliberation.

What interests me about Berlin's perceptive and subtle diagnosis of the dialectic of individual autonomy and socially conditioned identity, about which I shall have more to say later, is his insistence that freedom in both its positive and negative forms reduces to a kind of negative social freedom: non-domination. It is the social domination implicit in totally identifying one's identity in self-sacrificing solidarity with society that leads him to conclude that recognition is "misleadingly – called social freedom" (Berlin 1969a: 158).

> The essence of the notion of liberty, both in the "positive" and "negative" senses, is the holding off of something or someone – of others who trespass on my field or assert their authority over me. . .The desire for recognition is a desire for something different: For union, closer understanding, integration of interests, a life of common dependence, and common sacrifice (Berlin 1969a: 158).

I agree with Berlin that the common essence of freedom is non-domination: The determination of who I am and who we are should not be imposed on me (us) from the outside.[1] However, is Berlin right that the desire for recognition necessarily opposes the idea of freedom as "the holding off of something or someone"? My view is that Berlin is mistaken on this point. Supposing that his understanding of freedom is roughly correct, his identification of recognition with solidarity is not. At the very least, a desire for "closer understanding, integration of interests, and a life of common dependence" can sometimes require political disagreement and non-convergent forms of cultural understanding, non-domination of particular social aims and interests, and independence from particular social institutions. Once we parse recognition into its several modalities, focusing especially on the modern idea of mutual respect for others as free and equal citizens, it becomes apparent that freedom as he understands it depends on *civic solidarity*, or public recognition of the independence of fellow consociates who remain conjoined in democratically shaping their collective identity and freedom.

Berlin himself does not dispute that this kind of publicly acknowledged attachment to a shared democratic ethos comports with freedom. His failure to see the connection between recognition, solidarity, and social freedom might well be attributed to his desire to achieve conceptual clarity at all costs. But even he concedes that "social and political terms are necessarily vague," so that "the attempt to make the vocabulary of politics too precise may render it useless" (Berlin 1969a: 158). Berlin commits this last vice when he opposes the inner and outer sources of volition and identity. Thus, a critic of Berlin might rightly point out that the concept of

[1] Although most contemporary accounts of recognition focus on its contribution to psychological wholeness and well-being, some accounts (Hegel's included) emphasize its objective and, for lack of a better word, *ontological* contribution in constituting *agency* (self-certainty) and intentional, viz., meaningful and purposive, *action.*

positive freedom Berlin deploys presumes that the practical reasoning of individuals mysteriously sprouts up out of nowhere. Such an externally unconditioned source of choice would, however, not be internal, if what is meant by that term is *personal* as opposed to *impersonal* (viz., universal, transcendent, and unchosen). Berlin is too well informed by the facts of socialization to accept this relic of Kantian metaphysics, which in fact obscures the very meaning of individual freedom. Nonetheless, by insisting that "it is important to distinguish between liberty and the conditions of its exercise" (Berlin 1969a: liii) he seems indeed to have rendered the concept of positive liberty rather useless through an all-too-precise abstraction from its social conditions.

This criticism of Berlin is forcefully advanced by Honneth, who today stands among the most eloquent defenders of a recognition-based theory of social freedom. As Honneth observes, Berlin's concept of liberty (in both its negative and positive formulations) is too thin, normatively speaking, to enable it to stand alone as the sole premise supporting Berlin's own defense of political liberalism. Political liberalism, which extols political freedom of thought and action, has a distinctive genealogy that distinguishes it from premodern political ideologies. Its supreme preference for individually exercised negative freedom reflects a cultural preference (something akin, perhaps, to Taylor's notion of a "strong evaluation") that arises not from pure reason but a shared form of life. The liberal form of political life and its presumption of cultural value pluralism both conditions, and is conditioned by, moral positive freedom. Both political pluralism and positive moral freedom presuppose a prior acceptance of a more basic principle of social recognition: Each person should recognize the right of plural cultures to exist free from external *social domination* by other groups, and more specifically, the right of any person to participate in cultural groups wherein their values and identities are nurtured and affirmed by the groups in question. Honneth sums up this argument in the following pithy formulation:

> [Y]ou can't defend a radical, far-reaching notion of negative freedom on the one hand and emphasize the right of the individual to live in his or her own culture on the other. The latter practice is only possible on the condition that some people's negative freedom is reduced enough to ensure the continued existence of cultural communities. (Honneth 2007b: 251)

In sum, Berlin's concept of liberty, in both its branches, presupposes for its useful political application liberal constitutional institutions. Such institutions reflect a prior social recognition on the part of citizens of (1) their mutual *individual* legal and moral rights to freedom of thought, action, religion, and association *and* (2) their mutual *social* freedom from societal (group- or institutionally based) domination.

In response to this irrefutable demonstration, a defender of Berlin's view that recognition is not a variety of freedom might still fall back on Berlin's analytic distinction between an abstract concept of freedom and its concrete, real-life conditions. Indeed, in the most recent adumbration of his theory, Honneth himself follows Berlin in distinguishing negative (legal) freedom and positive (moral) freedom – the latter rechristened as reflective freedom – from a recognition-based conception of social freedom. However, deploying a more dialectical terminology, Honneth argues (following Hegel) that neither abstract negative freedom, which finds preeminent expression in the form of *individual* legal rights, nor abstract positive freedom, which finds preeminent expression in *individual* autonomous moral judgments of right and wrong and ethical valuations of authentic and fulfilling existence, are sufficiently meaningful, useful, and rational apart from the concrete *social* interactions and deliberations that serve to critically and consensually determine them. Following this Hegelian method of developing conceptual content by situating abstract terms within progressive conditions for specifying their actual, concrete force and meaning, and keeping in mind the democratic tenor of social life in a modern liberal society, we can tentatively conclude that the concrete, constitutionally institutionalized, critical exchange of opinions among persons who recognize themselves as free and equal, both morally *and* politically, *enables* such persons to become freer in the *positive* sense of the term (Ingram 2018: 47–84).

At this point, it behooves us to recall Berlin's linkage of positive freedom and freedom from domination. Minimally, enjoyment of equal negative freedom from interference by tyrannical democratic majorities must be constitutionally guaranteed in order to secure moral and political freedom for all citizens. But more than civil liberty is required to protect positive freedom, which becomes obvious once we take account of the fact that persons who possess the necessary capabilities to deliberate and make informed choices about legislators and government officers can decide policies that impact the lives of those who lack these prerequisites. The effects of these policies on the politically marginalized are experienced by them as an external imposition, shaping their choices without their input or consent. The poor, the uneducated, the overworked, and the marginalized thus experience a lack of positive freedom in controlling their lives. They might experience social domination of a quasi-personal kind (e.g., the hegemony of this or that class or group with respect to political power), but they invariably experience social domination of an impersonal, *structural* kind.

Recognition theory cannot illuminate this structural injustice as a species of overt discrimination and disrespect, however much of it underscores the invisibility of the socially marginalized, or their lack of recognition *simpliciter* (Bohman 2007). It can explain this injustice indirectly, as a violation of mutually recognized expectations regarding the normal and proper functioning of economic, educational, familial, and political institutions (see Section 5.3). Indeed, the mutual expectation that all persons have opportunities and capabilities to participate as active citizens in the lives of their communities presupposes not only that they have the requisite capabilities and opportunities, but also that they have the freedom to take advantage of these capabilities and opportunities without threat from another kind of structural domination, which might best be described as the tyranny of economic and legal systems over relationships pertaining to familial intimacy and public discussion. Freedom from this kind of domination, I argue, also intersects social recognition of civic solidarity, but in a secondary way, as reconciliation with society as a community of mutually supportive communities (a "social union of social unions," to paraphrase John Rawls).

5.2 Solidarity and the Circularity Problem

I shall have more to say about institutional domination and recognition as social reconciliation later. Suffice it to say, it makes sense to speak of mutual recognition of persons' freedom and equality as a social condition that enhances an individual's positive freedom only if such recognition is extended to all and only those who properly merit this distinction. Racists, sexists, and other intolerant demagogues diminish democratic political life by silencing the critical voice of others. As Honneth himself states the matter in the passage quoted earlier, the large society of liberal democrats has a right and perhaps a duty to suppress or curtail the freedom of illiberal groups.

Here we have an appeal to civic solidarity – to a widely recognized and shared commitment to a set of liberal democratic values and a liberal democratic identity – against the negative freedom and social domination of extreme dissenters to civility itself. What distinguishes this coercive appeal to solidarity from the totalitarian variety of concern to Berlin is not its alleged foundation in higher social freedom. Both totalitarian and liberal democratic forms of solidarity appeal to harmony of wills and identities; in this regard, even liberalism goes beyond "mere respect and tolerance" and includes the realization that "the aims of my own life are something that [others'] abilities have made possible or enriched" through multicultural and multi-perspective dialogue (Honneth 2007c: 257). The difference between illiberal and liberal democratic solidarity lies in the source and structure of the harmony. In traditional communities ordered according to what is commonly perceived to be a necessary and natural social hierarchy, persons may esteem those within their rank, viz., they may regard their accomplishments and values as of approximately equal worth in comparison to their own; however, lower ranks of persons are held in contempt by persons occupying higher stations who possess something like the status of undiminished dignity and nobility.

Secularization, which undermines metaphysical belief in the objective and eternally preordained nature of society by revealing its human-made character, endows all humans with equal dignity as autonomous individual contributors to their society's order – the principle of recognition underwriting egalitarian democracy (Honneth 2007c: 259–261). Modern totalitarianism seeks to restore the kind of objective rank order found in traditional societies based on race, class, or some other ground. Totalitarian solidarity presupposes hegemonic cultural homogeneity and is generated by government's brainwashing or authoritarian familial socialization. This uncritical (heavily scripted) identification of persons with a set of concrete collective goals and their corresponding social role expectations contradicts the critical (free and self-reflective) identification of persons with the liberal, egalitarian goals and social role expectations that define democratic civic solidarity. The latter presupposes cultural value pluralism and is generated and maintained by inclusive communication and critical challenges by others within political fora.

The reference to political fora suggests a further difference between the two contrasting forms of social solidarity, in that the liberal form institutionalizes a distinctively *secondary,* political order of recognition that reflects on the *primary* orders of recognition that compose economic, familial, and civic life. The institutionalization of formal democratic procedures and abstract rights of citizenship undermines dogmatic adherence to rigidly circumscribed goals and social identities, and reflectively provokes reinterpretations of the procedures and rights themselves.

This distinction between liberal democratic solidarity and totalitarian solidarity explains recognition theory's unique solution to the vicious circle alluded to in Berlin's account of solidarity that seems to render solidarity unsuitable as a form of social freedom. Totalitarian solidarity maintains itself through a relatively closed system of mutually reinforcing patterns of familial socialization and social authority. The seamless integration of all aspects of individual and social life guarantees that the scope for individual choice that has not been socially preprogrammed by society will be very limited. In comparison to totalitarian solidarity, liberal democratic solidarity maintains itself through a relatively open network of institutions and associations that possess their own distinctive – simultaneously complementary and conflicting – values and norms. These institutions and associations make competing demands on their individual members, who are then forced to take up a critical "outsider" stance with respect to each of them. These individuals must then switch from playing the institutional role of obedient and loyal insider (good employee, good friend, etc.) to playing the reflective political role of good citizen, social critic. In this instance, their exercise of personal positive freedom breaks out of the circle of institutionally programmed options to include higher level (reflective), secondary, democratic deliberation on how best to politically harmonize them.

5.3 Social Freedom as Reconciliation to Modern Society

Honneth's understanding of how different recognition orders place competing demands on persons' primary exercise of choice that compel higher-level exercises of democratic social freedom illustrates the point I am making. Just as importantly, it recalls a distinctly Hegelian conception of social freedom, understood as social reconciliation, or higher-order political recognition of the harmonious complementarity of different recognition orders.

In earlier formulations of his theory, Honneth distinguished three major valences of recognition that secure general anthropological conditions of individual agency, personal integrity, and fulfillment: *love* (or emotional affirmation of one's personal desires and capabilities), *respect* (cognitive affirmation of one's equal dignity as an autonomous agent), and *solidarity* (affirmation of one's sharing common, culturally shaped identities with others or, in a rather different vein, one's contributing to the cooperative achievement of collective goals through work). Love and solidarity are universal social goods that are necessary for realizing personal agency and fulfillment in any society. By contrast, equal respect for the inherent dignity of each person is a construction of modern liberalism (replacing traditional codes of nobility), which eventually modulates the modern understanding of love and solidarity as well.

In his latest theory of recognition, Honneth moves beyond philosophical anthropology to a genealogy of modern society, whose presupposition is a distinctly liberal democratic conception of social freedom. Hegel's memorable depiction of human history as a "struggle for recognition" that formed the title of Honneth's inaugural treatise on the subject is now drawn more closely to Hegel's characterization of that struggle as a struggle for individual freedom. The argument of *Freedom's Right* (*Das Recht der Freiheit*) hews closely to the argument of Hegel's *Philosophy of Right* (1821): negative freedom from constraint, objectively institutionalized in the form of individual legal rights, and positive (or reflective) freedom, subjectively instituted in individual moral conscience and existential choice, are both conceived as socially undetermined abstractions. The former, which is a product of modern liberalism, and the latter, which is of ancient vintage, find their ground in three recognition-based institutional practices (Hegel's ethical sphere's [*Sittlichkeit*]) that comprise social freedom: intimacy (the uninhibited expression of personality), economic cooperation (the mutual satisfaction of need), and political life (the determination of freedom and the coordination of social functions around common ends).

For the purpose of illustrating the connection between social freedom and reconciliation, the main shift that motivates my interest in Honneth's pivot toward freedom as the defining feature of modern struggles for recognition pertains to the progressive democratization of all spheres of life.[2]

> I wouldn't speak of a formal theory of the good anymore, but rather of a historically informed concept of ethical life (*Sittlichkeit*). I claim that all these spheres of freedom must mesh freely with each other [*zwanglos ineinandergreifen*] as democratized practices to make a realization of ethical life possible. I do not ascribe to the idea that the realization of these dimensions of freedom would automatically enable the unhindered self-realization of the individual. (Honneth 2015b: 266)

For we who live in modern society, freedom has become our most important end – more important than even individual self-realization; and we become free only when the democratic principle of mutual egalitarian recognition is extended into all spheres of life in a manner that affords us a possibility for harmoniously integrating them within our own lives. To

[2] Honneth's penchant for anthropological speculation is evident in his recent claim that the *democratization* of life culminates an archaic need for reasoned justification (Honneth 2015b: 264).

elaborate further on the first point made in the passage cited earlier, in the last fifty years we see a democratic trend within familial relationships insofar as gender-based roles within the family have increasingly broken down, along with the authoritarian patriarchal pattern of decision-making. Not only adult family members but children participate as equals in family planning decisions. Turning to economic relationships, the growth of unions and worker management, coupled with market regulation and social welfare policy, appear to support Honneth's contention that the market has undergone a process of "communitarianization," an emerging awareness of the rights and duties of all stakeholders in the economic life of the nation (Honneth 2015b: 272). Political life, too, has become more inclusive, with disaggregated forms of citizenship that allow legal residents to vote in municipal elections. All of these developments would seem to suggest that "sooner or later an appropriate [democratic] model of the family and of a socialized market has to be accepted" (Honneth 2015b: 281) along with recognizing that "decisions within the nation state are [to be] made under inclusion of the hitherto excluded other" (Honneth 2015b: 278).

As for the second point made in this passage, Honneth appears to acknowledge that democratizing life within each social sphere taken separately is not enough to secure social freedom. Also required is their second-order democratic harmonization. Social freedom can only be achieved under the broader aegis of a political reconciliation of, and political reconciliation to, all spheres of society, taken as a whole. To paraphrase Hegel's definition of reconciliatory social freedom as "being at home with oneself in another," also needed is a higher-order recognition of "a diversification of solidarities, namely everywhere, where freedoms are realizable together as a form of co-existence and socially being for others" (Honneth 2015b: 276).

An example of this kind of mutually transformative, cross-fertilizing democratic harmonization is reflected in Honneth's claim that if "aptitudes and practices of democracy are developed [in the family], then these aptitudes and practices can be "further practiced and developed in other higher forms and in other spheres" (Honneth 2015b: 270). To a certain extent, the family remains the *locus classicus* for collectively deliberating about how best to balance the different demands of work, politics, and intimacy, just as it remains the *locus classicus* for conflict resolution through democratic negotiation. Therefore, it is the micro-laboratory for developing democratic dispositions and aptitudes in advance of developing democratic workspaces and democratic public spheres.

5.4 Unfreedom in Modern Society

As the last point in the passage makes clear, we should not expect that the democratization of subdimensions of social freedom taken separately will automatically lead persons to feel self-fulfilled and socially empowered unless they can also harmonize these subdimensions in their personal lives. The language of reconciliation further suggests that more is involved in being socially free than successfully balancing the demands of work, intimacy, and public life to one's personal satisfaction. Inner harmony cannot be subjectively experienced, let alone willed, if objective reality is discordant. What if the recognitive expectations generated by each dimension of social life clash in a way that makes reconciliation objectively and subjectively impossible? In acknowledging this possibility, Honneth invokes a very different language of *prioritization*.

> which of the various relations of recognition is to be preferred in a case in which they raise conflicting claims cannot in any way be decided in advance ... We are obligated in concrete situations to accord others recognition in a mode that corresponds to the respective kind of social relationship at issue; but in the case of a conflict, we have to decide which of our bonds is to be granted priority. (Honneth 2007a: 141)

Prioritization implies selection; enjoyment of one kind of social freedom will require not enjoying another kind.[3] Taken in the abstract, within a specific kind of recognitive relationship, such as friendship, my freedom to love and be loved in return does not conflict with, say, my freedom to earn a living as an employee of a firm. Taken in the concrete, however, the time I spend enjoying intimate freedom is diminished in proportion to the time I spend in meeting my material needs.[4]

All of this raises a worrisome question about whether or not society's competing recognition orders can be sufficiently reconciled to enable persons to achieve a higher-level reconciliation with society as on the whole socially empowering as distinct from socially oppressive or alienating.

[3] For Honneth, the highest priority must always be accorded to moral relationships enjoining universal respect for "equal rights to autonomy" (Honneth 2007a: 141).

[4] See Marx's contention that the amount of time spent on "necessary labor" requisite for fulfilling human needs – not to mention the time spent on surplus labor requisite for producing profits – would be eliminated (in the latter instance) or reduced (in the former instance) within a fully developed communist society wherein each person would be free to develop his or her powers in an all-around way. For a related discussion, see Chapter 2, this volume.

In modern liberal society conflicts between different parts of one's personal identity are normal rather than exceptional.[5] This raises the problem of one part coming to dominate other parts to the point where persons feel alienated from both themselves and others. Honneth himself gives many examples in which one kind of social relationship crowds out another kind in such a way that the parties involved experience an overall diminution of their freedom. Family law, for instance, has evolved in such a way as to increasingly protect (and thus enhance) the equal freedom of spousal partners with respect to such matters as child-rearing, but an obsessive focus on the family as a contractual relationship, which typically happens during separation and divorce proceedings, can elevate the question of custodianship over children to such a high point that it occludes the parental care of children – as was depicted in exemplary fashion in the film *Kramer vs. Kramer*. Taking Honneth's interpretation of this film at face value (Honneth 2014: 90–91), one gets the impression that the embattled spouses depicted in the film were themselves victims of an overly juridified construction of the family, having no recourse but to submit to the coercive game of threat and counter-threat promoted by their lawyers and abetted by an adversarial legal system. True, a more accurate interpretation might be that the parents themselves simply exercised poor judgment in allowing their legal battle to interfere with their childcare responsibilities. Be that as it may, there can be little doubt that embattled parents in custody cases are caught in a dilemma – or rather multiple dilemmas – endangering their own and their children's freedom. For, aside from the impending dissolution of an intimate relationship, each party to the dispute must weigh the ethical propriety of using their children as expert legal witnesses who might testify on their behalf against someone they love. In the final analysis, each party must decide how far one kind of freedom-enhancing social relationship (enabling the negative legal freedom to enter into and later dissolve marriage/civil contracts) will be allowed to interfere with another kind (such as enabling the positive moral freedom to expressively expand and enrich one's identity in a committed loving relationship or the social freedom to develop one's self-confidence and other agential capabilities as a child).

No doubt, a judicious exercise in our positive freedom is necessary to ensure that the competing demands of public life, work, and intimacy are

[5] I discuss one particular dilemma – the self-subordination/social recognition paradox highlighted by Serene Khader – that women in societies transitioning toward modern economic relations encounter when they access microcredit in Ingram (2020).

in sync with one another, and that healthy respect for one's rights does not come into conflict with one's ethical duties of care, as Carol Gilligan and many other feminists writing on relational autonomy have pointed out. However, the problem of cultivating our social freedom, Honneth reminds us, is at the bottom a social and political problem, not a personal, ethical one. This is illustrated by an enduring trope that critical theory in the Marxist–Hegelian tradition has invoked for almost 200 years: the destructive intrusion of capitalist market relationships into other areas of public and private life. As Honneth remarks, since the advent of the neo-liberal (post-Fordist) era, capitalist market relationships have devolved in a decidedly anti-communitarian, antisocial democratic direction, which in turn has threatened the democratizing tendencies at work in the family and the political sphere.

In all these aspects of sociocultural democratization and the development of democratic ethical life, the family has improved considerably as an institution, while at the same time facing massive socio-economical structural challenges. The massive pressure for mobility and flexibility challenges and to a large extent undermines the practices of freedom and democratization. One might even speak of an invasion of work onto the family, where mothers and fathers are forced to meet such demanding and fatiguing work conditions that they are forced to bring them into the private sphere, and thus lose the ability to fully benefit from the cultural and moral progress of the last fifty years (Honneth 2015b: 271).

5.5 Defending Social Freedom: Recognition and Critical Theory

The question I raised at the outset of this essay is whether the peculiar interpretation of recognition as social freedom can be explained or understood in a way that is not fundamentally question-begging. First, it might be argued that whatever reasons persons have for identifying or not identifying with an enabling social order will be conditioned by that very same order. Persons may feel loved, respected, and esteemed for lack of knowledge about alternative experiences of love, respect, and esteem that might persuade them to think differently.[6] This circularity in conditioning – the absence of an independent ground for reasoning about the

[6] Notice, too, that if they feel misrecognized and disrespected, they might misidentify the reason for their feelings (for example, by blaming persons rather than societal norms). Does the resentment a financially dependent homemaker feels toward the domestic breadwinner clearly evoke the thought that one isn't being properly respected as an independent claimant to entitlements and liberties? Or does it evoke the thought that one isn't being properly esteemed for contributing to the household

freedom-enabling capacity of the social order – makes it impossible to decide whether the social order in question enables/enhances or hinders/ diminishes one's positive freedom. The resulting identity between society and individual will therefore undermines any potential for independent social criticism, thereby reinforcing Berlin's postulation of an essential link between social recognition/solidarity and totalitarianism/domination.

Second, and conversely, it is not clear how, within a nontotalitarian society in which individuals remain free to criticize society, simply relying on experiences of misrecognition or nonrecognition can be a sufficient reason for judging the absence of positive/social freedom. People experience conflict between their personal identities and prevailing societal norms for different reasons. A male white supremacist might feel caged in by a society that has come to celebrate racial equality. Is his experience best described as a lack of social freedom or as a misperception on his part of the limitations of his own personal belief system? Is he in some non-experiential sense socially free because he lives in a non-racist society but ignorant of that fact due to the compulsions of prejudice? Contrast his case with a black woman who feels caged in by a society that in her own experience, and evidenced by objective statistics, has not fully lived up to its anti-racist and anti-sexist ideals. Here, the experience of not having one's situation, perspective, and needs fully recognized reflects a demonstrable lack of social recognition and, therewith, a diminution of one's social freedom (or psychological discomfort in navigating social relationships with police, doctors, service providers, and others).

What these examples suggest is that something like a *normative* theory of social freedom that is less tethered to uncritical interpretations of societal norms and personal experiences will be needed to distinguish reasonable from unreasonable forms of social contentment/discontent. However, short of invoking a discredited notion of transcendent reason, such a theory will invariably find itself enmeshed in some version of the circularity problem noted earlier; whatever norms recognition theory might uphold in condemning racism, sexism, and other forms of privilege will ultimately be ones that a given society recognizes but imperfectly embodies in its historically evolving institutions and membership.

Third, alternatively, if we postulate a more dialectical form of social criticism that avoids the circularity problem, we run the risk of eliminating the second-order recognitive conditions requisite for social freedom in the

economy or that one isn't being properly loved? The latter possibility doesn't necessarily stand as an indictment of social injustice, whereas the former very likely does.

first place. For example, if the different ways in which we seek recognition from (identification with) others occur within social relations that are structured by antagonistic institutions and not the unified totalitarian state system that worried Berlin – a hypothesis that seems especially pertinent to modern, liberal societies – then it might seem that social freedom is simply impossible. Individuals will not possess stable, coherent, or at any rate, fully integrated personal identities and will feel at home with themselves, their society, and the particular social roles they play during only those fleeting moments when playing these roles does not clash with playing their other socially recognized roles. Furthermore, at the macro-societal level, instead of social harmonization among antagonistic institutions being effected through voluntary recognition of the mutual solidarity among persons inhabiting these spheres, social coordination will be mechanically (or coercively) imposed through legal and market systems whose complex functioning will be experienced by some of those subject to them as alien, reifying, and freedom-denying. Here, a functionalist, rather than identitarian, totalitarianism threatens not just social freedom and positive moral freedom, but individual negative freedom and its kindred concept, freedom from social domination.[7]

Fourth, and somewhat paradoxical, critical resistance to social domination will then *seem* to depend upon the postulation of a utopian desire for social freedom that is nowhere to be found within society itself, even in individuals' exercise of positive moral freedom, but only within individuals' pre-social instincts – the solution proposed by the founding members of the Frankfurt School.[8] Even if we replace the Freudian drive theory that informs this utopian social critique with a theory of socialization that is directly premised on some account of social recognition, as Honneth does

[7] Marx's classical account of commodity fetishism in the first volume of *Capital* has often been regarded as the touchstone for this diagnosis of capitalism. Drawing from Max Weber's cultural analysis of conflicting value spheres and Émile Durkheim's functionalist account of contractual bonds in modern society, first-generation critical theorists such as Theodor Adorno and Max Horkheimer proposed that what few genuinely free social relations had once existed among autonomous individuals had long been extinguished by modern forms of totalitarian administration and social conditioning. Something of this pessimistic diagnosis survives in Habermas' later treatment of the "colonization of the lifeworld" by economic and administrative subsystems.

[8] In *Dialectic of Enlightenment* (1944), Adorno and Horkheimer (drawing from Nietzsche and Freud) argue that the iconic Kantian understanding of positive freedom, understood as moral autonomy, or rational suppression of inclination, is itself a product of social domination: the introjection (internalization) of punitive social authority in the form of "individual conscience." They and other critical theorists of their generation (notably Herbert Marcuse) subsequently proposed less self-centered, less reason-dominated modes of aesthetic freedom incorporating mimetic (imaginative) reconciliation with nature in its sensuous particularity.

in drawing from the object relations theories of Donald Winnicott and Jessica Benjamin, it seems that the most perfect and emblematic form of social (recognitive) freedom, and the form that Honneth himself posits as foundational for all other forms[9] – familial love – designates, by Honneth's own account, at best a partial expression of social freedom and one, moreover, that cannot be extended to other domains of social interaction without violating their proper social functioning. Indeed, extending the exclusive form of caring and loving appropriate to intimate relationships to other social groupings rather threatens illiberal forms of patriotism and group loyalty, such as those associated with virulent nationalism and ethnocentrism (Hedrick 2019: 174–176).

The aforementioned catalog of concerns challenging the viability of a recognitive account of social freedom can be accommodated, if not dismissed, by the following rejoinder. In order to parry the first two concerns noted earlier, regarding the circularity charge, I concede Berlin's point that *robust*, recognition-based social freedom is antagonistic to positive moral freedom. However, I maintain that a less robust recognition-based social freedom is at least *theoretically* conceivable. Nontotalitarian, liberal democratic social orders approximate this genuine kind of social freedom better than illiberal, nondemocratic societies because they permit persons, who exercise different social roles within different schemes for coordinating action, to critically evaluate any given social role's limits and possibilities for actualizing social freedom in light of what other social roles promise in this regard. In other words, the forms of solidarity Hegelians defend as most definitive of recognition-based social freedom do not coalesce into the kind of totalitarian identity that worried Berlin. To illustrate my point, we can compare the different ways in which members of families can enhance or hinder each other's freedom through loving/caring relationships with the way members of political society (citizens) can enhance or hinder each other's freedom through democratically negotiated legal relationships. We can ask whether families should embody more democratic freedom or whether political and legal relations should embody more nurturing freedom. We can ask whether one kind of freedom-enabling social relationship has become so pervasive as to endanger other kinds of freedom-enabling social relationships. For instance, we can ask whether

[9] "[W]e can safely assume that all three forms of relation-to-self [self-confidence, self-respect, and self-esteem—D.I.] can develop in unison through the internalization of parental care, and are only experienced later as distinct aspects of one's life by gradually differentiating various partners in interaction" (Honneth 2012: 205).

market transactions mediated by employee/employer or producer/consumer roles have penetrated into other, noneconomic areas of life and then ask whether this is good or bad for actualizing social freedom in our lives as a whole.

This response to the circularity objection, of course, does not explain why the kind of differentiated liberal democratic society extolled by recognition theorists as actualizing social freedom should be so esteemed. Comparative assessments of the progressive nature of this kind of society relative to its predecessors within a particular historical path of development (e.g., European history) are still question-begging (Allen 2017), but similar assessments can be made across global cultures in a provisional way to the extent that tendencies toward widespread resignation to, if not voluntary acceptance of, capitalist economies and liberal democratic institutions can be confirmed.

As for the third and fourth objections, I argue, following second- and third-generation critical theorists, that modern, market-driven, liberal democratic societies are not totally reified administrative economic systems. As I noted earlier, the kinds of social roles and potentials for social freedom embedded in one sphere of action provide a critical standpoint for reflecting on the social roles and potentials for freedom embedded in other spheres in a non-reductive way. We, therefore, do not need to appeal to psychological theories about emancipatory drive potentials in order to explain critical resistance to reifying tendencies. Likewise, a theory of socialization that sensibly emphasizes the importance of social recognition and communication need not privilege one kind of social recognition and social freedom as exemplary for all social action spheres *tout court.* For example, we can insist that competitive market relationships should also live up to standards of social responsibility with regard to protecting a shared environment and guaranteeing a decent income for all – goals associated with mutual caring – without violating standards of social esteem based on competitive success and achievement. In theory, at least, we can conceive a non-reductive *mediation* of social action spheres conducive to harmonious societal functioning. Conversely, we can criticize and resist the dysfunctional *domination* of some institutionally based social relationships over others. More positively, we can advocate for policies that felicitously integrate and harmonize all such social relationships, so that we can come to reconcile ourselves to the entire social order as a recognition-worthy realization of social freedom for all.

Having suggested the *theoretical* possibility of a *modest*, recognition-based account of social freedom, I now conclude by surveying some of the obstacles to actualizing reconciliation in practice. Some of these obstacles were trenchantly discussed by Marx in his critique of capitalism and, more generally, of monetized market societies. For Marx, Hegel's "rational" solution to the conflictual (antagonistic) and atomizing dynamics of civil society – the sphere wherein individuals recognize each other primarily as legal claimants to negative liberty – required that Hegel logically adduce for its solution the idea of mediating institutions, such as corporate political representation of government, land, and occupational groups (the estates), bureaucratic welfare agencies (the *Polizei*), and business associations incorporating employers and employees (the corporations) that would ostensibly promote the common welfare. Marx was a visionary in criticizing the various forms of class domination and alienation that these mediating institutions concealed and rightly debunked the paternalism implicit in Hegel's bureaucratic welfare administration as itself furthering the particular interests of a professional class (Marx 1994a). Ultimately, given the unresolvable problem of unemployment and poverty in a capitalist society, Hegel himself believed that individuals would experience themselves as socially free only when acting in their capacity as citizens who could participate (in however limited and virtual a manner) in political life and representative legislative bodies. With the guidance of politically independent bureaucrats devoted to the national interest, such organically interconnected bodies, he optimistically believed, could conciliate their particular interests in legislating a general will oriented toward harmonizing the particular spheres of social freedom embedded in society.

Marx believed that this political form of emancipation, even when instituted in a liberal democratic constitution, fails to bring about authentic human (i.e., social) emancipation (Marx 1994b). If we reject Marx's revolutionary proposal to abolish capitalism and, more radically, the distinction between a civil society of self-interested, private individuals and a constitutional state of socially interested, public citizens, then a more social-democratic version of Hegel's political solution to effecting reconciliation remains our only alternative. In that case, we must ask how much our competing institutional roles of an active participant in political life, passive recipient of government entitlement, economic producer/provider, consumer, personal caregiver, etc. can be harmonized in a manner conducive to "being at home with ourselves in an other." We must ask, in other words, whether there is reasonable *hope* that the contradictions among competing demands of modern society and the all-too-pervasive domination of economic and legal relationships in our private and public lives can be significantly reduced over time.

My tentative answer to this question is not much. We have too little reason to hope that market systems that distribute recognition based on success, even when buffered by safety nets, can be easily reconciled with democratic political systems that distribute recognition based on citizenship. Faith in the constitution as a collective learning project oriented toward greater inclusion and freedom seems just as unwarranted: equal protection (civil rights) and robust negative freedom (civil liberties) more often than not conflict with each other *and* with the bureaucratic administration of welfare, health, and security (Habermas 1996). Nor does there exist a privileged standpoint within a liberal democratic society for univocally grounding judgments about which policies enhance or hinder social freedom (Hedrick 2019). In the final analysis, advocates of recognition as a form of social freedom are left with the discomfiting thought that the modes of mediated recognition that exist in modern society promise little more than a possibility for *partially* reconciling ourselves to public institutions that *selectively* limit structural domination while never quite reconciling us to our social existence as a whole.

CHAPTER 6

Self-Mastery and the Quality of a Life

Steven Wall

Contemporary discussions of positive liberty should at some point acknowledge a debt to Isaiah Berlin. I will discharge this responsibility upfront. The opening sentences of the section in his celebrated essay that introduce the notion of positive liberty read as follows.

> The "positive" sense of the word "liberty" derives from the wish on the part of the individual to be his own master. I wish my life and decisions to depend on myself, not on external forces of whatever kind. *I wish to be the instrument of my own, not of other men's, acts of will.* I wish to be a subject, not an object; *to be moved by reasons, by conscious purposes, which are my own, not by causes which affect me, as it were, from the outside.* (Berlin 1969b: 135 – italics added)

This passage construes positive liberty in terms of an ideal of self-mastery. This ideal needs to be further characterized and refined,[1] but the passage rightly calls attention to two of its components. The first of these is interpersonal. It is expressed in the first italicized sentence. To achieve self-mastery, I must not be the instrument of the will of others. The second of these components, which is expressed in the second italicized claim, is intrapersonal. To achieve self-mastery, I must be moved by reasons or conscious purposes and not by alien causes which affect me. Both of these components are important and will figure in the account of self-mastery that I will present. In developing this account, I will be guided by considerations that explain the value of positive liberty. These considerations have different sources, but they all contribute to, what I shall term, the quality of a life.

[1] A good characterization of self-mastery will need to draw on theoretical discussions of responsible agency and autonomy. But, as will become apparent in the ensuing discussion, this ideal should not be identified with either of these notions. Self-mastery is an achievement, one that responsible agents, and even fully autonomous responsible agents, can fail to realize fully.

A proper concern for positive liberty on the account that I will present is, accordingly, primarily a function of its contribution to the quality of the lives of those who achieve it. Since one can value liberty, whether positive or negative, for reasons that have nothing to do with the quality of the lives of those who realize it, I will not claim that positive liberty, understood in terms of self-mastery, is the only kind of liberty worth caring about. Nor will I claim that it is the best conception of liberty. Presumably, different conceptions of liberty can be better or worse relative to different theoretical purposes. I will claim, however, that insofar as we care about the contribution that liberty makes to the quality of our lives, positive liberty as self-mastery has a strong claim to our attention.

The argument of this chapter is both constructive and defensive. On the constructive side, I try to show that self-mastery is an attractive ideal and that it fits with and explains many, although certainly not all, intuitions that we have about personal liberty. I do this by characterizing the notion of self-mastery in terms that reveal it to be a distinctive ideal, but one that coheres with other notions that are related to freedom. On the defensive side, I try to show that accepting a conception of liberty as self-mastery does not require us to reject the two ideas that were most central to Berlin's defense of liberal politics – negative liberty and value pluralism. The chapter concludes with a brief discussion of the functions of the liberty-supportive state, on the assumption that self-mastery is indeed a genuine ideal and one that can guide political action.

6.1 Two Conceptions of Self-Mastery

My claim is that self-mastery contributes to the quality of the lives of those who achieve it. Both of these notions need to be clarified, however. I begin with self-mastery. Once this ideal is in focus, it will be easier to appreciate what is meant by the quality of a life.

Self-mastery, as Berlin's discussion of it vividly brings out, can be understood variously. The "self" can refer to an individual's rational powers (his ability to detect and respond to the reasons that apply to him) or to his volitions (his decisions, purposes, and plans). By privileging one of these features of the self over the other, we can generate rival conceptions of self-mastery. We will see that, in the end, an adequate account of self-mastery must be responsive to both features of the self, but it will be useful to begin by comparing the rival conceptions in their pure forms.

As persons move from childhood to adulthood, they develop a conception of themselves – an evaluative stance – and this stance guides them in making decisions about their lives. We can think of this stance as their "standpoint as a practical reasoner" (Watson 2004: 135). For this stance to guide their decisions effectively, it must display a measure of coherence, integrating different commitments both at a time and across time (Hurley 1989: 260–263; Bratman 2000). In theory, an evaluative stance could be complete and fully determinate, representing a kind of "hyper-plan" that addressed every possible contingency (Gibbard 2003). In practice, a person's evaluative stance is always a work in progress. It is revised and extended in the light of new experiences and reflection. Still, the stance guides where it can, and people are in control of their lives to the extent that their beliefs, desires, and choices properly respond to the reasons that they take themselves to have (Owens 2000: 78–80). As one writer expresses the basic idea: "We are ourselves and we lead our own life so long as we see ourselves as rational agents, so long as we conduct our life under the semblance of rationality" (Raz 1999: 19).

This, in brief, is the rational powers conception of self-mastery. It neatly explains familiar failures of the ideal. Consider weakness of will, for example. We desire to do what we judge we have a decisive reason not to do. When we have this desire and act on it, we do not conduct our life under the semblance of rationality. Our conduct and our evaluative stance do not mesh.

An evaluative stance, on this conception of self-mastery, is a perspective on what is true and good. But such a perspective can distort what it represents. To illustrate this possibility, Charles Taylor points to the example of Charles Manson. On Taylor's reading, Manson has an evaluative stance – "a strong sense of some purposes and goals as incomparably more fundamental than others" – but it is a stance that is "shot through with confusion and error" (Taylor 1985a: 227). The example is instructive. Taylor claims that Manson lacks self-mastery in virtue of his "false appreciation" of what is important and worth doing. But why not say instead that Manson, assuming that he does not suffer from mental illness and that his fundamental purposes are ones that he views himself as having sufficient reason to have, realizes self-mastery when he leads his life in accord with this distorted sense of what is important?

The answer to this question is that, on the conception of self-mastery under consideration, our rational powers have a point. Their point is to discriminate the true from the false, the significant and worthwhile from the trivial and base. A rational agent, on this conception of self-mastery, is not indifferent as to whether or not his rational powers function properly. He has, as I will put it, a *background fundamental purpose*, which is a concern to lead a life that is not only guided by what he perceives to be reasons, but what are in actuality reasons. This background fundamental purpose is frustrated to the extent that he conducts his life in light of perceived reasons that are not genuine.

I will have more to say in Section 6.3 about the nature of this background fundamental purpose and the conception of reason that it presupposes.[2] For now, I want to highlight how this sketch of the rational powers conception of self-mastery brings into view three basic ways by which people can fail to achieve the ideal. First, they can fail to have an evaluative stance at all. Their commitments can lack the integration necessary for them to have a guiding standpoint as a practical reasoner. Second, their decisions and actions can fail to mesh with their evaluative stance. Put differently, their evaluative stance can fail to regulate their will. Third, while people may have an evaluative stance that effectively regulates their will, it nonetheless can frustrate their background fundamental purpose as a rational agent. Here they act merely under the semblance of rationality, failing to be governed by reason.

These failures of self-mastery come in degrees. They correspond to different dimensions of self-mastery. It will be helpful to give them names.

Integration
Mesh
Reason-Responsiveness

The rational powers conception of self-mastery does not address the environment in which agents exercise their rational powers. It puts the accent on intrapersonal self-control. A Stoic sage, locked up in a prison cell, can fully achieve self-mastery on this conception (Berlin 1969b: 135–141). For the sage may have a fully integrated evaluative stance that effectively regulates his will and responds well to the reasons that apply to him in his confined circumstances.

To address the environment in which self-mastery is exercised, we need to turn from the rational powers conception to the volition-based conception. This conception affirms the integration and mesh dimensions, but it rejects the reason-responsiveness dimension. Self-mastery is not a matter of

[2] The background fundamental purpose, as I understand it, need not be self-conscious. Nor is it a condition of agency. Agents could lack it altogether. Still, as I explain in Section 6.3, if one does not have it, one's rational control over one's life is diminished.

responding well to the reasons that apply to one independently of one's will, but rather a matter of being guided by one's own basic purposes.[3] To illustrate: imagine that someone has an integrated, reason-responsive evaluative stance, but that it has been implanted in her by another. If this person were to direct her life in accord with this implanted stance, then she would satisfy the three dimensions of self-mastery identified by the rational powers conception. Yet, intuitively, she would not achieve self-mastery. Her life, and the purposes that guide it, would not be her *own*.

The notion of ownership in play here obviously requires analysis. Implanted stances dramatically illustrate how people could be directed by the purposes of others, becoming literally the instruments of their will. But less dramatic cases also illustrate a loss of ownership. Return to the Stoic sage. Given that he cannot pursue those purposes of his that are inconsistent with imprisonment, it might be reasonable for him to adjust these purposes to his circumstances. But suppose now that this adjustment "takes place behind his back" (Elster 1983: 117) and suppose further that this is exactly what his imprisoner intended to induce. Now, the Stoic sage is guided by the purposes of another, even if his response to his situation cannot be faulted on grounds of reason-responsiveness.

These two examples – implantation and conditioned change of purpose – illustrate how ownership of an evaluative stance is compromised by the interference of other agents. They point to a fourth dimension of self-mastery.

Independence

Independence is interpersonal. But self-mastery can be compromised by environmental factors that are not captured by the independence dimension. One's evaluative stance can be altered by one's unconscious adjustment to circumstances, even when the circumstances were not brought about through the manipulative agency of others, or through any kind of agency at all. Our Stoic sage, for instance, may have fallen into a pit,[4] which was not dug by anyone, but functions as a prison.

The issues raised by this kind of case are complex. An agent's evaluative stance is perforce affected by changes in his circumstances. Accordingly, it

[3] Proponents of the volitional conception invoke notions of importance and/or "what we care about" to explain practically significant beliefs and actions. These notions are a matter of the configuration of the will. Reasons and rationality are downstream from them. For an elegant statement of this perspective see Frankfurt (2004).

[4] The example is adapted from Raz (1986: 373–374).

is necessary to distinguish those changes that limit his self-mastery from those that constitute the background against which it is exercised. With this in mind, and following the lead of others, we need to appeal to a counterfactual condition. Assume an agent with an integrated evaluative stance. Now imagine a change in his evaluative stance that has been brought about by nonconscious adjustment to changes in his circumstances. If the agent were to become aware of the change in his evaluative stance, and if he were to approve of it, or not be disposed to resist it, in light of an adequate understanding of how it came about, then the change would not constitute a limit on his self-mastery. By contrast, if he would reject the change were he to become aware of it in light of how it came about, then it would constitute such a limit.

This statement of this counterfactual condition is very rough and stands in need of refinement;[5] but it points toward a fifth dimension of self-mastery, which we can refer to as counterfactual acceptance.

Counterfactual Acceptance

As I indicated, this dimension of self-mastery applies to changes in one's circumstances that do not compromise one's independence. Could the counterfactual condition not be applied to the examples of implantation and conditioned change of purpose? For example, if one became aware of the fact that one's evaluative stance had been implanted in one by another, and if one accepted this in light of this awareness, then would it cease to diminish one's self-mastery? The answer is no. For self-mastery, on the volitional conception, is an ideal that requires that one not be the instrument of other's acts of will.[6] The independence-compromising effects of coercion and manipulation on one's self-mastery are not canceled by one's acceptance of them.

6.2 Self-Mastery in a Postromantic Setting

The two conceptions of self-mastery that I have described part ways over the significance they assign to reason-responsiveness and ownership of an evaluative stance. But an adequate account of self-mastery must find a place for both. A simple proposal combines the dimensions articulated by

[5] For a more careful statement of the kind of counterfactual condition that is needed and a critical discussion of some of the issues that it raises see Christman (2009: 133–163).

[6] Determining the conditions when a person is the instrument of the will of another in a manner that compromises independence obviously requires analysis. Consensual use of another does not compromise independence, for example.

the two conceptions. In this proposal, self-mastery is a function of all five of the dimensions listed earlier. Reason-responsiveness and ownership are not inherently incompatible, after all. Still, this proposal does not help us to resolve the potential tensions between our rational powers and our volitions, and a unified account should have something to say on this matter, even if it cannot provide a blueprint for resolving all the tensions.[7]

An implanted evaluative stance is an easy case.[8] No increase in one's responsiveness to reason could make up for the loss of independence here. Yet less extreme cases are more challenging. Consider two persons, John and Sally. If John defers to Sally on all the important decisions that he needs to make, then John will do better in conforming to the reasons that apply to him than if he makes these decisions himself. Some deference to rational authority is not inconsistent with self-mastery, but the kind of total surrender to another's judgment envisioned in this example presumably is.[9]

John, we need to assume, has an integrated evaluative stance, one that is reason-responsive to an adequate degree. (If it were not reason-responsive to an adequate degree, then John could not realize self-mastery and an appeal to self-mastery could not explain why he should not defer to Sally.) Two variants on the example can be considered. Suppose first that Sally's decisions do not make sense to John. He does not understand why they are good decisions, or he disagrees with them after careful reflection. Then, in deferring to Sally, John will need to do things – take up a career, decide to have a child with his partner, pursue projects, etc. – that do not mesh with his evaluative stance. As these are important matters, this mismatch between his evaluative stance and how he leads his life will undermine his self-mastery. His evaluative stance will fail to regulate his will. Suppose next that Sally's decisions do make sense to John. Upon hearing them he fully agrees that they identify what he ought to do. He appreciates why her decisions are the right decisions for him to make. In deferring to Sally, he can treat her as a wise advisor, and when he follows her advice, he remains in charge of his life. His self-mastery is not compromised.

The mesh and the reason-responsive dimensions are complementary in this respect. For one's evaluative stance to guide one's decisions one must

[7] Looking for blueprints here is probably a mistake. An adequate characterization of self-mastery may do no more than assign rough weights to the dimensions, seeking to establish a reflectively stable balancing of the different dimensions when they conflict.

[8] See McKenna (2013) for some push back on intuitions about manipulation's impact on the agency.

[9] For discussion of challenge to self-governance posed by this kind of case, compare Valdman (2010) with Wall (2016).

act under the semblance of rationality. To achieve self-mastery, one must not only have an integrated evaluative stance, but it must guide one in one's decision-making. Interestingly, the reason-responsiveness dimension can also explain counterfactual acceptance. For when a person would not accept a change to his evaluative stance, if he understood how it came about, then this change is not one he has reason to accept from his standpoint.

Thus self-mastery, on the account that has emerged, is an ideal of independent reason-responsiveness. Still, it might be thought that this account is too rationalistic and that it does not do justice to the role of volition in self-mastery. Our will must be our own in the sense that it cannot be the product of blind submission to authority or the manipulation and coercion of others. But, on this account, it appears to have no further role to play in our self-governance; or, if it has a role to play, its role is to respond to reason. Yet self-mastery, it has seemed to many, is an ideal that requires more than submission to reason. It requires authentic self-expression. To borrow some language from Taylor, on "a post-Romantic conception of the self" there is not one rational pattern of life that fits us all. Each of us has "his own original form of [self-mastery[10]]" (Taylor 1985a: 216). Nor is it the case that there is a unique pattern of life that reason prescribes for each one of us, given our individual temperament and talents. On the contrary, the will is not merely the handmaiden of reason. It has free play to determine who we are and where our good lies. As Taylor explains, there are "a variety of languages of qualitative contrast" (Taylor 1985b: 236) attuned to different combinations of goods and perceived goods; and reason, while it can determine that some of these are false or distorted, cannot provide a comprehensive ranking of their value.

Behind the "post-Romantic conception of the self" that Taylor invokes thus lies the value pluralism that Berlin celebrated. The case for accepting this background picture of value raises very large issues that cannot be taken up here. I will simply proceed on the assumption that there is truth in what unites Taylor and Berlin. An adequate conception of self-mastery, I will assume, must cohere with value pluralism. On these assumptions, we can now delineate a more creative role for the will to play in the account of self-mastery that I have been advancing, one that answers to the thought that self-mastery involves authentic self-expression.

10 Taylor speaks here of "self-realization," but it is clear from the context that this is his term for what I have been calling self-mastery.

Reason requires, but it also permits. It requires us to value goods over bads, worthwhile pursuits over worthless ones. It also permits us to choose between goods, or combinations of goods. When reason does not determine what one must do, there is scope for authentic self-expression. Here the volitional conception of self-mastery with its emphasis on what we care about or what we find to be important in life comes to the fore, supplementing the rational powers conception. Within the space that reason leaves open for self-expression, self-mastery is achieved only if our conduct is guided by purposes that are genuinely our own.

The contribution of authentic self-expression to self-mastery provides further support for the claim that a life in which one deferred to another on all or most important matters would not achieve self-mastery. Sally may be more attentive to John's reasons than John, but John's task, insofar as he values self-mastery, is not merely to make rationally required choices, but also to make choices that express what he cares about; and he, like us, sometimes will discover what is important to him only by choosing to go down one path rather than another (Wall 2016).

Having different paths open to one, and being exposed to different languages of qualitative contrast, are, accordingly, social conditions that facilitate authentic self-expression. That is why Romantic thinkers, such as Wilhelm von Humboldt and John Stuart Mill who followed him, tied living well to being confronted with "a variety of situations" (Humboldt 1854; Mill 1859). These writers spoke of self-development and individuality, but their claims apply equally to self-mastery in a post-Romantic setting. To achieve this ideal, we must not let the world choose our path for us, but must choose it for ourselves. To be sure, our purposes are always a function of the social world in which we live; but if we have few options, there will be less scope for us to express who we are by the choices that we make.

6.3 Objective Goods and Subjective Valuations

I have claimed that self-mastery contributes to the quality of the lives of those who achieve it. But what exactly is meant by the quality of a life? I have two main things in mind, the goods in a person's life and the attitudes that the person has toward these goods.[11] Roughly, we live

[11] The quality of a person's life is affected by his attitudes toward the goods and bads in other people's lives and perhaps also by his attitudes toward impersonal goods and bads. For simplicity's sake, and because they are more tightly bound up with his life, I put the spotlight on the attitudes a person has toward the goods and bads in his life.

well when we realize objective value in our lives and when we respond – cognitively, conatively, and appetitively – in a fitting way to that value.

The quality of a life is related to its well-being, but is not equivalent to it. We lead better lives both for ourselves and for others when we realize objective goods. Still, our achievements and relationships with others can come at the expense of our well-being. People often make genuine sacrifices for the sake of goods that are important to them, and these sacrifices, while they may on balance reduce well-being, can enhance the quality of a life.

The quality of a life could be measured simply by the quantity of the objective goods (and bads) that it contains, goods such as pleasure, friendship, understanding, and achievement (and bads such as pain, isolation, confusion, and failure); but it is plausible to hold that more than this is required if one is to live well. Consider a mundane example. Through years of practice, a person masters the piano, becoming a virtuoso, dazzling audiences, and developing a refined appreciation of musical excellence. Yet the person hates the activity. He plays the piano only to make a living and he longs for the day when he can be done with it. Some think that such a person does not benefit from playing the piano. It is all wasted time (Dworkin, R. 2000: 267–274). Our question is not whether the person benefits here, but whether the piano playing enhances the quality of his life. Our answer to that question is hedged; for, on the one hand, his achievements and his appreciation of excellence are genuine goods, enriching the quality of his life; but, on the other hand, his hatred of this activity is inapt. Those who live well should value the goods in their lives, not despise them.

The piano player we are imagining certainly is an unusual case. Generally, people value what they are good at; and if they do not value an activity, it is very unlikely that they will be very good at it. Despite its artificiality, the case illustrates the key idea. The quality of a life is a function of both the goods it contains and the attitudes it manifests toward those goods. Our piano player would live better if he loved what he did.

Imagine next a person enmeshed in base pursuits. She spends much of her time playing card games, watching reality television, and smoking dope. Further, she is a hustler, taking pride in her skill at defrauding others. The lack of goods in her life and the viciousness of her character ensure that her life is one of low quality. Here, the pride she takes in her life, and the favoring attitudes she has toward the pursuits in it, do not enhance, but diminish, its quality. In general, fitting attitudes toward goods and bads in a person's life increase its quality, whereas wrongly oriented attitudes decrease its quality.[12]

Reflection on this general point provides support for one of the more controversial claims I advanced earlier about the ideal of self-mastery. I claimed that self-mastery has a point. We exercise our rational powers so as to believe truly and live well. Self-mastery, accordingly, is a success concept.[13] Its realization manifests effective rational self-control. This establishes a tight link between the realization of the ideal and the quality of a life. Since we have reason to care about the quality of our lives, we have reason to value self-mastery. But suppose all of this is denied. Suppose that one claims that self-mastery is a matter of leading one's life according to one's own conscious purposes and one's own perceptions of what one has reason to do, whether or not one's purposes are worthwhile or one's perceptions are accurate. This claim severs the link between the realization of the ideal and the quality of a life. For when a person's attitudes toward the goods and bads in his life are wrongly oriented, as they most certainly will be when the person has a false appreciation of what is true and good, then self-mastery may cease to be a good at all.

This austere verdict may be too austere, however. Closer attention needs to be paid to the notion of our attitudes being wrongly oriented. Several modes of wrongful orientation, in particular, are worth distinguishing. Loving what is bad or hating what is good can be the result of (1) willful rebellion, (2) culpable mistake, or (3) non-culpable error.[14] To illustrate these differences, consider a person, such as Manson, who values the domination of others. Suppose that he desires domination for its own sake, delighting in the degrading treatment of others. On this supposition, the person manifests rebellion against the good. But, alternatively, suppose he values domination only because he believes falsely that dominating others is a good, perhaps out of some distorted religious conviction. His belief, however, is defective. It originates from self-deception, or was adopted recklessly without serious consideration of the grounds for believing it. On this supposition, the person makes a culpable mistake. Finally, suppose that the person in question believes that dominating others is good, valuing it under that description, and that his belief is not defective. Given his upbringing and the evidence available to him, his false belief is

[12] For discussion and elaboration on this general idea see Nozick (1981: 429–433) and Hurka (1993), including Hurka's critical discussion of Nozick.

[13] Here there is a clear contrast with autonomy. There are multiple understandings of autonomy in the philosophical literature, but on all of them, one can be fully autonomous while failing to live well.

[14] Here I follow Hurka (1993: 178–180), although he does not use the terminology I employ.

not something for which he could be faulted. On this supposition, the person manifests a non-culpable error.

The third of these modes of wrongful orientation differs importantly from the other two. Here the person faultlessly stands for the good. He just mistakes where it lies. True, in the case of someone who values domination, this possibility is hard to credit. But, in other cases, where people have understandable, but false views about the good, their loving what they perceive to be good, but what is in fact not good, may not diminish, but enhance, the quality of their lives. (To be sure, if they realize bad or worthless things in their lives this will diminish the quality of their lives, but we are here focusing only on their attitudes toward these bad things.)

Does the possibility of non-culpable mistakes give us reason to revise the conception of self-mastery advanced earlier? I have argued that self-mastery should be understood in light of its contribution to the quality of a life and that this ideal can contribute to the quality of life only when a person's evaluative stance is responsive to genuine goods and not merely to perceived goods. Yet if it is allowed that when we make non-culpable errors about the goods (or lack of them) in our lives, the fit between our evaluative stance and the realization of these perceived goods in our lives can enhance the quality of our lives, then we have grounds for holding that self-mastery can contribute to the quality of our lives even when our evaluative stance is misguided.

This seems correct. However, and in tension with it, I have claimed that people have a background fundamental purpose to lead good lives, not merely lives that they perceive to be good. If this is right, then their mistakes about the good, non-culpable or not, will not mesh with this background purpose. This diminishes the degree to which they achieve self-mastery. Perhaps it will be objected that the background fundamental purpose is seldom conscious and that self-mastery is a matter of how effectively one's conscious purposes guide one's actions. However, one's evaluative stance includes beliefs and dispositions that are not immediately present to the mind. The fit between them and the way one leads one's life is surely relevant to one's self-mastery. A better objection insists that the background fundamental purpose is satisfied if one lives well, and living well requires only that one respond to the reasons that one non-culpably takes oneself to have. The excellence here is manifested in the skillful exercise of one's rational powers.

We can acknowledge that this kind of excellence contributes to the quality of a life. It is better to live well by skill than by luck. But this is not the issue in question. We now are seeking to understand the import of what I have been calling the background fundamental purpose of a rational agent. On reflection, we are not indifferent between a life in which we exercise our rational powers skillfully, but in which they misfire, and one in which we exercise them skillfully and they succeed in tracking the reasons that we actually have. Our preference for the latter reveals that it is our more fundamental purpose. That is why I have been saying that our rational powers have a point, and the point is to track the true and the good.

Some may deny that it matters to them whether they live well or poorly. When they deny this, they may make no mistake. Their error is not one of self-understanding but of not taking their lives seriously. They fail to respond to the reason to take their lives seriously, a reason which is not a reason in virtue of the fact that people happen to care about, or would endorse, living well rather than poorly. Some writers have referred to this reason as a reason of self-respect (Hurley 1989: 358–360; Dworkin, R. 2013: 205–209). Most of us have this kind of self-respect, even if many of us have never self-consciously considered the fact that we have it. For those who altogether lack it, might they nonetheless fully realize the ideal of self-mastery? Consider this case. Someone might not have the background fundamental purpose that I have been discussing, but she might succeed in responding to reason in all other respects. Her indifference to living well does not translate into her failure to live well. If she scored well on the other dimensions of self-mastery, could she not fully realize the ideal? I am inclined to say no. Self-mastery, on the view I have been advancing, is an ideal of rational self-control and this kind of control manifests itself in responsiveness to the reasons that we have, including the reason to care about living well rather than poorly.

Full self-mastery requires that one conduct one's life in accord with one's purposes, including most fundamentally one's purpose in living well. But if one lives merely under the semblance of rationality, then, while one may manifest attitudes toward objects that are perceived to be good (but in fact are not) that contribute to the quality of one's life, one's self-mastery nonetheless will be diminished insofar as one's perceptions are not accurate.

There is a further point to make. Authentic self-expression is an aspect of self-mastery, at least as this ideal is understood in a post-Romantic setting. But what is the value of authentic self-expression? How does it add to the quality of a life? The discussion in this section suggests an answer. The quality of a life, I have been stressing, is not simply a matter of the goods and bads realized in life. It also is a function of our attitudes toward those goods. Given our constitution and temperament, some of the goods available to us will "fit" us better than others. Our subjective valuations plausibly track this dimension of fitness (Railton 2003). Accordingly, when we pursue the goods that attract us and express our nature, we are much more likely to have fitting attitudes toward the goods in our lives. The piano player discussed earlier realizes an objective good, but its contribution to the quality of his life is not as great as it would have been had it been a good that resonated with him.

6.4 Liberty and Pluralism

In characterizing self-mastery, I have been urging us to keep an eye firmly on what makes it valuable. We should characterize it in terms that make its realization contribute to the quality of our lives. Yet, in proceeding in this way, it may seem that I have vindicated Berlin's main concern about the ideal. If self-mastery is the best articulation of positive liberty, and if self-mastery is understood in reason-responsive terms, then our freedom could be increased, or at least not diminished, by interventions that frustrate the desires and wills of our merely empirical selves. Worse yet, the appeal I have made to an alleged background fundamental purpose bears a suspicious resemblance to what Berlin termed "an occult entity" that expresses our rational will or "true purpose" (Berlin 1969b: 133).

How serious is this concern? A preliminary reply is that self-mastery is an axiological notion. Accepting it is fully compatible with accepting deontic principles that restrict how it can be promoted. One can accept that self-mastery is an important ideal of freedom and also hold that when we restrict the negative liberty of people, we disrespect them.[15] If not supplemented, the preliminary reply probably concedes too much to the critic, however. The reason why is well put by Taylor. Negative liberties come into conflict, and we need some way to distinguish the significant from the less significant liberties (Taylor 1985a: 217–220). Recognition of this point puts pressure on the theorist of liberty to identify criteria for ranking negative liberties in terms of their importance to the agent. If our concern is with liberty, then the criteria should be grounded in an ideal distinctively connected with liberty, such as the ideal of self-mastery (Kramer 2003: 428–441 – discussing autonomy).

[15] Doubtless, this claim needs qualification. We do not disrespect the murderer when we interfere with his negative liberty to commit his crime, for example.

Taylor asks the pertinent question. "Is not freedom at stake when we find ourselves carried away by a less significant goal to over-ride a highly significant one?" (Taylor 1985a: 220). Phrased differently, we can ask whether, from the standpoint of liberty, it is better to favor significant liberties over less significant liberties, when they conflict? Phrased in these latter terms, the answer seems clear. Indeed, Berlin himself recognized the need to gauge the significance of different liberties. To determine how free a person is, he claimed, we must attend to how important the liberties he has are to his life (Berlin 1969a: xxxix). This notion of importance was left unexplained by Berlin, but presumably, it is subjective in the sense that it refers to what the person himself takes to be important, or what he would take to be important if he understood his situation.[16] However, positive liberty understood as self-mastery must be more objective than this, for it must include within the notion of importance a reference to what we have reason to value.

Berlin's specter thus remains. On the view of positive liberty presented here, negative liberty can be sacrificed for the sake of values and concerns with which the empirical self does not identify. At this point, however, it is necessary to recall the independence dimension of the ideal. Those who achieve self-mastery must bring it about themselves. That is why implanted evaluative stances, while they might be effective devices for improving rational control, could not be effective means to realizing self-mastery. Implanted stances annihilate self-mastery by removing the self from self-mastery. Less extreme measures, such as paternalistic restrictions, need not have this annihilating effect, but they too would compromise independence to some degree. Nevertheless, it should be allowed that paternalistic measures could further self-mastery along the other dimensions to a sufficient degree to compensate for the deficit in independence. To this extent, Berlin's worry about self-mastery remains intact. Yet now it is much less clear that the worry speaks against liberty understood as self-mastery. Modest paternalism is a far cry from the "monstrous impersonation" of the real self for the empirical self that Berlin invoked.

The edge of Berlin's critique of self-mastery appears much sharper if one associates the ideal with the rejection of pluralism, as Berlin himself did.[17]

[16] The notion of importance referred to here is a revision to Berlin's earlier statement that importance refers not only to what the agent values, but also to what his society values. See Berlin (1969b, 130n1).

[17] In fairness to Berlin, the historical accounts of self-mastery that he criticized all assumed a monistic form.

> Pluralism, with the measure of "negative liberty" that it entails, seems to me a truer and more humane ideal than the goals of those who seek in the great, disciplined, authoritarian structures the ideal of "positive" self-mastery. (Berlin 1969b: 171)

But if self-mastery is placed in a post-Romantic setting, then this association is unwarranted. Berlin's pluralism is a pluralism of objective values and ends (Gray 1995: 38–75). This kind of pluralism fits well with an ideal of independent reason-responsiveness that allows scope for authentic self-expression.[18]

Berlin did not offer arguments in support of the kind of objective pluralism he asserted. If this pluralism were shown to be false or overstated, then we would need to rethink the ideal of self-mastery advanced here, placing it outside the post-Romantic setting. By the same token, any support for negative liberty provided by the truth of objective pluralism also would need to be reconsidered.

6.5 The Politics of Self-Mastery

Some will grant that self-mastery is an ethical ideal, but deny that it is a political ideal. They will say that it can guide us in our efforts to lead lives of high quality, but it should not inform political action. As I have explained, self-mastery has an intrapersonal, psychological component that encompasses a number of dimensions – integration, mesh, and reason-responsiveness. With respect to these dimensions, many will insist that the state should take a hands-off approach. It cannot promote this component of self-mastery effectively, and if it tries, it will likely do more harm than good (Pettit 2001: 127–128).

Suppose that we grant this line of thought. There remains the interpersonal component of self-mastery to consider. Few will deny that the state can be effective in securing the independence of those who are subject to its authority, and this independence is vital to self-mastery. Further, in identifying threats to independence, political officials may need to consider the ideal as a whole. For some threats to independence are more significant than others in virtue of their impact on self-mastery. Indeed, as just noted,

[18] Berlin's value pluralism is radical. On his view, incommensurability among values, ways of life, and options is pervasive, leaving little role for reason to guide practical decision-making. But one can accept value pluralism, while thinking that Berlin overstated the incommensurability of value and understated the power of reason to guide choice and decision (Nagel 2001).

modest instances of paternalism might advance self-mastery on balance, even as they diminish independence.

There is a further role for politics in creating and sustaining the kind of social environment that is conducive to the realization of self-mastery. Taylor raised the interesting possibility that positive liberty is fully realizable only in a certain form of society (Taylor 1985a: 229). This probably puts the point too strongly, but once the ideal is placed in a post-Romantic setting, it becomes important to attend to "the variety of situations" that form the backdrop of authentic self-expression. Perhaps an unregulated cultural marketplace will provide a wide range of valuable options for all, rendering otiose state efforts to secure the necessary variety. But perhaps not. Political support for high culture may be necessary to ensure that the opportunities provided by the culture, and the languages of qualitative contrast available to those within it, are sufficiently complex and rich. It is sometimes objected that support for high culture benefits only those who are well-off and takes resources away from more pressing problems. There is a kernel of truth to this objection, but it should not be overstated. High culture spills over and influences the wider social culture in complex and unpredictable ways, enriching it for all (Dworkin, R. 1985: 229–233).

Political support for high culture is, in this respect, a form of ethical education. When done well, it plays a part in shaping the culture of a society, and thereby the preferences and values of its members, in ways that can improve the quality of their lives. Reflection on this point should lead us to reconsider the supposition granted earlier that state action cannot effectively address the intrapersonal component of self-mastery.

The general outline of state-supported ethical education for self-mastery is clear enough, although it is unhelpfully abstract. The outline starts with a truism. The social environment in which we live and grow up profoundly conditions the formation of our evaluative commitments. With this in mind, the state can play an active role in helping to sustain and promote options in the social environment that instantiate genuine goods. By doing so, it can assist its members in their own efforts to lead lives that are reason-responsive and authentic, thereby helping them to achieve self-mastery.

Translating this general outline into practice presents several challenges. First, if state support for some options over others is too heavy-handed, then the independence that is necessary for self-mastery will be unduly compromised. Second, since not all worthy options can be supported, decisions will need to be made about what goods merit support. These decisions, if not made fairly, will be in tension with the pluralism that is recognized and presupposed by the (post-Romantic) ideal of self-mastery. Third, state efforts to favor some options over others run the risk of rigidifying current understandings of what is valuable. Finally, there is the familiar worry about the competence and motivation of state officials in modern societies to make the kinds of judgments and decisions necessary for any program of ethical education to be at all successful.

I will not try to respond to these formidable challenges here. Instead, I want to bring this chapter to a close by drawing a parallel between the politics of self-mastery and the articulation of the ideal of self-mastery. Self-mastery, as I have described it, is an ideal of independent, reason-responsiveness. Given value pluralism, it allows wide scope for authentic self-expression, but it does not give free rein to authentic self-expression. For any person who is serious about self-mastery, she must acknowledge that there are standards of reason to which she is answerable. The importance of discriminating higher from lower modes of living is thus built into the ideal. But an alternative understanding of self-mastery, one that is expressed well by a pure form of what I referred to earlier as the volitional conception, is also available. This alternative understanding of self-mastery severs the link between the ideal and the quality of a life, thereby calling into question its normative import. Yet there is no denying that this understanding of self-mastery resonates with many today. It finds expression in and is nourished by a model of politics that eschews all discussion of the content of a good life.

Ethical education for self-mastery does not make sense if there are no standards to inform it. However, once the standards are seen to be part and parcel of the ideal, ethical education becomes crucial to its realization. To be sure, much of this education must take place outside of the political domain in the wider society. For this education to do more good than harm, it also must respect the pluralism of value and be open to contestation and revision. Still, and notwithstanding the dangers it presents, a model of politics that invites citizens to reflect on, and take some responsibility for, the value of the options that their common environment provides to its members fits well with an ideal of positive liberty that requires individuals to reflect on, and respond appropriately to, the value of the options that this environment makes available to them in their own efforts to lead free lives.[19]

[19] Thanks to David Sobel for helpful discussion on some of the ideas in Section 6.3.

CHAPTER 7

Basic Freedom in the Real World

John Christman

In the various analyses of the concept of freedom in the political and philosophical literature, it is striking how distant these accounts often are from the language of freedom that seems most prominent in political discourse, namely in struggles for liberation and resistance to oppression. From abolitionist speeches and literature, to contemporary efforts to escape enslavement, tyranny, and economic deprivation, referring to the aims of such efforts as a freedom struggle is enormously common. Yet, most accounts of liberty or freedom – negative liberal views, neo-republican accounts, and many positive conceptions – fail to adequately account for the meaning of freedom in these contexts in crucial ways. This is either because they assume that the subject of freedom is a recognized member (citizen) of a functioning democracy and/or that the only institutional setting in which freedom can be enjoyed is a relatively idealized (just) polity.

However, refugees, migrants, the enslaved, and those suffering under oppressive regimes can be said to struggle for a kind of freedom that cannot presuppose such conditions. Either they search for a life in a host country in which they are not (and do not aspire to be) full citizens, or their only realistic objective in their journeys is to find protection in a political setting that is far from ideal. If we want to use the language of freedom to describe the aims of such struggles, then either we view such freedom struggles as entirely quixotic and utopian or we need to understand that concept in ways that are more nuanced than is typically found in the literature, or so I want to argue.

A motivating point for my discussion is to take seriously the abundant aspects of our current and historical condition that depart radically from

An earlier version of this chapter was presented at the American Political Science Association meetings, September 13, 2020. I am grateful to Maria Dimova-Cookson for the helpful comments on that version.

the simplified assumptions of (relatively) ideal social and political theory. For instance, it is instructive to note that arguably no current state conforms fully to the parameters of standard theories of justice and democracy, or at least a majority of people in the world do not live in such a state. Even many functioning democracies in the developed world are woefully short of these ideals, and those who live in conditions of tyranny, occupation, and repression seek escape from those conditions without an expectation that such an escape will find them in perfectly just political settings. Also, countless persons who have emigrated from their home countries fled persecution, disaster, and the like, reside in conditions that do not afford them citizenship status, and may not hold out much hope that they will be so afforded in their lifetimes. Indeed, many of those in such communities do not *aspire* to be given regular citizenship in their host countries, but rather seek different sorts of legal protections and community support. Must our conceptions of freedom be such that none of these types of individuals or groups can be labeled free? If their flight from earlier brutish conditions can be described as a search for freedom, will they never attain it?

In this chapter, I will use these observations as a springboard for an argument that we need an account of freedom that captures the aspirations and struggles of such persons and groups under a relatively realistic description of current conditions. Since many standard accounts of freedom tie that idea conceptually to membership in a stable, just (or nearly just) state, the discourse surrounding the plight of many people searching for "freedom" who are not and do not aim to be such members is not adequately captured.[1]

This is an especially poignant issue for many conceptions of liberty that lie in the "positive" terrain, since that conception often cashes out in terms of self-government and, by extension, to citizenship in self-governing polities. I will suggest, however, that the kind of self-government required by freedom (seen as the object of liberation struggles) need not entail full citizenship in a fully functioning democracy. This is in part because less formal, social practices rather than political participation form the contours of social life that constitute the self-government of many people. What is needed, I will claim is an account of *basic freedom* in a positive mode, an idea that lives up to the conceptual and normative requirements of such a concept and which can apply to those groups who do not enjoy (and may

[1] I will also argue that value-neutral negative accounts of liberty may escape this implication, but these views fail to capture the plight and aims of refugees (etc.) for other reasons.

not seek) citizenship in their resident country. I will attempt to sketch such an idea.

7.1 Nonideal Conditions and the Context of Freedom Discourse

Traditionally, political theorizing and the conceptual analysis of the key concepts central to it have proceeded as if such concepts apply to relatively settled, closed, and well-ordered societies. However, increasingly in recent decades, greater attention to the decidedly nonideal conditions of the social world has been in evidence. This is motivated by the observation that ignoring actual facts of victimization and the effects of injustice can serve to misdescribe the persons, interests, and social dynamics relevant to those concepts and the principles in which they function. Further, the dynamics of public discourse in the real world shape our intuitions about what such normative concepts must mean, so abstracting from the historical and ongoing conflicts in which such discourse operates can distort our modeling of those ideas and principles. And insofar as the rationale for developing such principles is to guide critique and reform (or resistance and rebellion perhaps), such idealized principles fail to appeal to members of actual societies who don't meet the criteria of persons described in abstract models.[2]

This is especially significant in the case of a concept like freedom, if only because that idea is so central to struggles against intolerable and oppressive conditions around the world and throughout history. The abolitionist movement in the antebellum United States, to cite only one obvious example, proceeded with ubiquitous reference to "freedom" as set against the condition of enslavement. Now granted, those ideas referred to codified legal distinctions that garnered their meaning from established laws and institutions where the "free" person was a category fully defined in law. Still, the idea of freedom should be explicated in ways that make sense of the language of those and related anti-oppression struggles, which of course continue on today, even if legalized chattel slavery has been abolished, and where the language of freedom is still ubiquitous.

This observation also highlights the ways that discussions of concepts like freedom assume that the backdrop against which that characteristic is enjoyed is a fully functioning state, presumably a constitutional democracy in which the subject of freedom is a citizen. However, one key aspect of the current condition that motivates rethinking of the idea of liberty here

[2] For discussion see Simmons (2010), Stemplowska (2008), and Mills (2005).

concerns the precarious status that countless persons have or hope to have regarding citizenship in fully functioning democracies. Large-scale and recurrent migration is now a permanent aspect of most societies, where it is reported that the number of international migrants reached 272 million people in 2019, up from 153 million in 1990.[3] An estimated 2.9 percent of the world's population live outside of the country of their birth, many without citizenship status in their host countries. Moreover, according to the United Nations, at the end of 2019, there were more than 79.5 million people forced from home by conflict and persecution. Among them are nearly 26 million refugees and millions more stateless people who have been denied a nationality and basic rights such as education, healthcare, employment, and freedom of movement.[4] Their initial escape from conditions of violence and oppression is certainly the first crucial step in gaining a significant degree of freedom for such persons. The United Nations also estimates that the average stay in refugee camps and "temporary" holding centers for displaced persons is seventeen years.[5] Clearly, such persons, who lack core resources but also live in a state of interminable statelessness, are not free, or not sufficiently free. But if so, what steps are needed to complete the process of freeing them from those earlier oppressive conditions, and what is the sense of "freedom" that is being invoked to answer that question?

A particularly unrealistic answer to this question is that they must establish full citizenship in a functioning and just (or nearly just) constitutional democracy. This is either because the nearest locations where those seeking "freedom" can plausibly hope to arrive are not fully functioning democracies, but closer to what John Rawls has called "decent hierarchical societies" (Rawls 1999: 64). Such social forms are nonaggressive, respect human rights, and have a generally legitimate and morally oriented legal system (for the most part) but do not afford full rights of democratic participation to all citizens. Often, those fleeing highly oppressive social conditions – that is, they seek *freedom* from such conditions – can only realistically aim to receive sanctuary in regimes of this sort.

Moreover, many members of migrant communities spend significant parts of their lives as noncitizens (guest workers, temporary residents, even illegal residents), and yet, as I will discuss later, they can in some cases

[3] UN Report on International Migration, www.un.org/en/development/desa/population/migration/publications/migrationreport/docs/InternationalMigration2019_Report.pdf.

[4] UN Report on Refugees, www.un.org/en/global-issues/refugees.

[5] UN High Commission on Refugees.

enjoy a relatively secure and meaningful social existence in their communities. This is not to say that such situations are by any means perfectly just, but the concept of freedom should not be tied to such a goal if it is to avoid the charge of over-idealization mentioned earlier.

Surely, there is a place for a language of "freedom" that is used to denote idealized conditions that require equal status in just or nearly just political settings. However, understanding the concept only in this way fails to capture the way this idea is used as a primary motivation for most actual people working to escape oppressive conditions, where the discourse of freedom is dominant in their rhetoric, manifestos, songs, and statements. What is needed is a conception of basic freedom that captures this use.

However, many standard models of freedom, from liberal negative accounts to neo-republican views, to Hegelian/Marxist recognition-based approaches, carry with them statist assumptions that tie the enjoyment of freedom to being a fully sanctioned citizen in stable functioning polities. As I said, this will pose a special challenge to positive accounts of freedom that tie that condition to political self-government. With this in mind, let us examine a selection of such frameworks.

7.2 Freedom for the Noncitizen: Received Views

It will not be necessary to survey all of the various models of freedom to make my point here, which is that many influential conceptions of that idea carry with them certain presuppositions regarding citizenship and highly functioning democracies, assumptions that I want, for various reasons, to question. I will briefly touch on negative conceptions and republican models before turning to classical positive ideas, showing that many such conceptions either carry the presupposition in question or, for other reasons, fail to express the idea of freedom at work in the various contexts in which we find it, such as struggles to escape oppressive conditions.

7.2.1 Normative Liberal Conceptions

Many thinkers in the liberal political tradition have followed John Locke in thinking that "liberty" is conceptually tied to the enjoyment of those rights and privileges that all human beings[6] enjoy by virtue of their natural

[6] Arguably, neither Locke nor many other thinkers in this tradition intended "all" here to really refer to all humans. For discussion, see Mills (1997).

rights.[7] Others may not make reference to natural rights in this way but still define liberty in ways that circumscribe that idea with reference to principles of justice, political morality, or other normative features of social and political life. One is free or deserves to be free, on these views, in the sense of being unhindered from pursuing *morally justifiable* actions. By extension, freedom in social settings means, on these views, being unobstructed from performing those actions allowed by just institutions.

For example, normative liberal views such as those held by Rawls and, in a different way, Ronald Dworkin claim that liberty refers to the array of rights and opportunities allowable under adequately justified principles of justice. Hence, one is free only in the sense that one enjoys rights under a just legal order. Of course, both Rawls and Dworkin acknowledge the idealized nature of their conceptions of justice, and they both make some mention of the application of their core concepts to nonideal conditions.[8] However, in both cases, the idea of liberty (or liberties) being used is conceptualized in a way that refers to the rights and opportunities that would be afforded to members of an established polity and ties the kind and level of freedom allowable in such settings to membership in these polities by principles of justice.

Now a fully normative conception of freedom is not necessarily alien to the discourse surrounding the enslaved, refugees, and stateless persons even if that idea is explicated in terms of established membership in a nation-state, although that context muddies the water quite a bit (as we will see later with the republican account). It is quite plausible to claim that freedom refers to those rights and prerogatives required by justice (or morality or natural rights) and claim that whatever those rights are, slaves (etc.) are made free only when they are granted them. But first, such views as they are found in the liberal framework typically refer to negative conceptions of liberty – i.e., rights and opportunities – rather than capabilities that enable persons the full exercise of freedom. I will argue later that these latter elements are needed for an adequate account. Also, the particular package of rights and liberties that any given regime will sanction will be highly variable and dependent on the historical and social context in which those liberties function. The conception we are seeking is meant to apply across cultural contexts, or at least to settings in which

[7] See John Locke (1967).

[8] In Dworkin's case, he specifically discusses the application of his idealized conception of liberty to the "real world" of imperfect justice (Dworkin, R. 2000: 172–180). Rawls's extension of his views to nonideal conditions can be found in Rawls (1999).

different political institutional structures are in play. Such context-dependent conceptions won't function adequately here.

For now, I merely want to point out that the normative accounts found in liberal philosophical theories of freedom refer to political settings with fixed boundaries and membership and with functioning institutions that conform to principles of justice. Extending these accounts to persons who cannot claim such membership will be tendentious at best.

Of course, other liberal theorists define negative liberty in ways that avoid normative implications altogether, defining freedom simply as the absence of constraints on action, neutrally described. The core idea in such a model is to see liberty as the absence of external constraints on one's actions, constraints that are intentionally put in place by others or at least are obstacles whose presence others can be held responsible for.[9]

On these views, degrees of freedom depend simply on the area of action a person is allowed (by others), making no reference to the nature of that area or its importance to the person. Now some defenders of negative liberty like Matthew Kramer insist that some reference to values must be made, such that the more a person values the opportunities afforded by the absence of constraint, the more free one is. Others have resisted this implication.[10]

However, even admitting that opportunity-freedom of this sort has general value for agents, it is not the kind of value that can explain the profound motivational force that calls for freedom have in the conflict situations I have been considering. Those who label their efforts "freedom struggles" do not simply want more open options of a generic sort, they engage in costly efforts to dismantle specific kinds of barriers to the leading of socially acceptable lives. These aims involve far more general and fundamental alterations in social conditions.

Now defenders of this negative notion could reply that such struggles are indeed aimed at greater opportunities and hence greater freedom, just of a (to them) very special sort. But the use of the language of freedom in these contexts indicates that the idea refers *specifically* to the overcoming of these particular obstacles, not merely as some among many that they face. That is, the discourses out of which we distill the conception of freedom here clearly do not view that condition as a simple scalar notion, where more freedom is better than less but no major thresholds need to be

9 This last point is emphasized by Miller (1983). Others who have developed a view of this sort include Carter (1999), Benn and Weinstein (1973), Kramer (2003), and Steiner (1983).

10 See Kramer (2003: 425–443) for discussion.

specified as being free, per se. Those fighting for freedom under oppressive circumstances and those fleeing conditions that turn them into refugees or permanent migrants, or those engaged in liberation movements, seek a kind of freedom that is in many ways a *condition* or *state*. The language of freedom and liberty across the ages is rife with references to being free, *simpliciter* – being a free person and being recognized, legally and otherwise, as such. Hence, even if we accept that freedom in one sense is a matter of degree, and indeed that opportunity spaces are one plausible measure of such a vector, another crucial idea that functions in liberation discourses in various social locations refers to an all or nothing condition, or indeed one below a significant *threshold* on a scale of degree, one denied to those living in oppressive circumstances.[11]

Of course, one must also be careful that the uses of the notion of liberty in some contexts is not simply synonyms for *justice*, and that the condition being sought is one of a just or normatively acceptable way of life. Again, if one can explicate the notion of freedom in a way that avoids this implication, one can skirt the objections often brought against such normative accounts, and this is what I attempt later. First, though, a look at other conceptualizations.

7.2.2 Republican Freedom

Another major development in thinking about the idea of freedom is found in attempts by Philip Pettit, Quentin Skinner, and others to reclaim the classical republican conception of liberty for use in contemporary settings. In Pettit's version of this view, freedom is defined as non-domination, which means being immune from interferences from other citizens or state institutions that are the product of arbitrary or unilateral decisions by those agents. Arbitrary interferences are those which emanate from a process that does not take adequate account of a person's interests. In contrast with freedom in the opportunity sense just discussed, non-

[11] As I mentioned, the history of the language of freedom admittedly arises out of times and places where legally designated conditions of being "free" or being a "slave" were part of the political and legal structure of the time. In classical settings such as ancient Greece and Rome, in various parts of Asia and Africa, and the western hemisphere prior to the late nineteenth century, the law reflected the status of being "free," "freeborn," manumitted (made free), and so on, to be contrasted with being a slave. Hence it could be argued that the categorical conceptualization of freedom inherits this codification, even if the subject is not slavery per se but victims of oppressive circumstances more generally (see Patterson [1982, 1991]). Still, finding a model that makes sense of this usage is an important philosophical aim.

domination means not only a lack of actual interference but also not being subject to possible interference due to the arbitrary whim of another. As Pettit puts it:

> The promotion of freedom as non-domination requires . . . that something be done to ensure that public decision-making tracks the interests and the ideas of those citizens whom it affects . . . It must be a form of decision-making which we can own and identify with; a form of decision-making in which we can see our interests furthered and our ideas respected. Whether the decisions are taken in the legislature, in the administration, or in the courts, they must bear the marks of our ways of caring and our ways of thinking. (Pettit 1997a: 184)

This implies that the republican state, for Pettit, will be a constitutional democracy guided by the rule of law, maintain separation of powers, and include strictures on majority rule. Additionally, all state decisions must be "effectively contestable" so that citizens' interests are appropriately tracked by government policy. Contestation will demand effective channels and forums for debate, and discussions will not mirror mere bargaining as citizens' desires will be shaped by the process itself and not merely exogenously given. Pettit argues that the conditions of non-arbitrariness require that methods of state decision-making be the subject of "common knowledge" and that citizens will see themselves as dominated when entire classes of individuals are afforded lower status than others.

Pettit sums up the core ideas of the republican conception this way:

> [E]qual freedom of its citizens, in particular their freedom as non-domination . . . is the primary concern of the state or republic. The second [idea] is that if the republic is to secure the freedom of its citizens then it must satisfy a range of constitutional constraints associated broadly with the mixed constitution. And the third idea is that if the citizens are to keep the republic to its proper business then they had better have the collective and individual virtue to track and contest public politics and initiatives. (Pettit 2014: 5)

Clearly, then, freedom in the republican model is tied to official membership in a particular form of state institutional structure. Pettit claims that his view is "non-normative" in that it will be a simple observable fact and not an evaluative judgment whether people's interests are being tracked in a way that renders whatever interferences they might subject to as non-arbitrary.[12] I am not at all sure he is correct in that assessment, as the

[12] For this reason, Pettit has, in more recent work, avoided the term "arbitrary" in favor of "uncontrolled." See Pettit (2012: 58).

question of arbitrariness will turn not merely on whether citizen interests are tracked but whether they are tracked *properly*. The latter determination is not merely a matter of observation.

Be that as it may, it is clear that being free in the republican sense will require legislative assemblies of a particular sort with deliberative mechanisms for the representation of commonly avowable interests, so that interferences with people's actions will not be arbitrary or uncontrolled. This is an ideal that is sometimes, but not often and never completely, realized in the world. In the many places and times when this ideal has not been realized, people lack republican freedom in Pettit's sense and the attainment of such a status will be nowhere on the horizon. But do we want to conclude, then, that freedom is impossible for such people in the foreseeable future and that their aspirations toward such a state are futile or meaningless? While a more detailed treatment of republican freedom on this issue is called for, if we can provide an account of basic freedom that answers this last question in the affirmative, then such a theory will have an advantage over the republican account in properly capturing both the aspirations and the attainment of large classes of persons.[13]

7.2.3 Traditional Positive Accounts

The approach to thinking about liberty that most directly ties it to already established membership in well-functioning states is the traditional notion of freedom as self-government, which is the central idea of positive accounts of freedom. I call these views "traditional" since they echo the ancient and enlightenment articulations of the idea that identifies liberty with the status and activities of citizens in self-governing polities. Classical republican accounts display this connection by identifying freedom with the *liber* of Roman law, a person (man) who is not a slave or otherwise dependent who actively participates in the governing processes of his political community. This status entailed virtues and obligations as well as privileges and immunities.[14]

[13] I should note that in the conception of basic freedom I outline later, albeit an avowedly positive notion, elements similar to what Pettit requires here will be included. A key difference, however, is that the locus of control or acceptance required for persons to have basic freedom in my sense will not refer narrowly to state institutions but social practices and cultural resources more generally.

[14] Pettit and Skinner argue that the Roman and neo-Roman theorists did not hold to this kind of positive conception, where participation is required (see, e.g., Pettit [2002] and Skinner [2012]). But (a) many did interpret them this way, and theorists like Rousseau and Arendt retrieved these ideas with the assumption of participation intact; yet (b) as I will argue in the next section, one can adopt a positive conception of freedom that does not require this sort of participatory citizenship.

This idea is reclaimed in the Renaissance with Niccolò Machiavelli in his Discourses, where freedom of the person is attached conceptually to the functioning of a free city (state). This notion is further developed in the Enlightenment period by thinkers such as Jean-Jacques Rousseau, who conceived of freedom as rule by the general will of which one was a part as a citizen – and not merely represented as such – in a democracy (republic) governed by the social contract. On this view, freedom is achieved by acquiring equal status with one's fellows in a political association that advances one's interests, considered in light of that association. One is free in that one obeys only oneself, albeit a "self" defined in relation to one's status as a co-member of a self-governing community.[15]

This connection between freedom and citizenship is best expressed by the oft-cited lines summing up the project of Rousseau's *Social Contract*:

> . . . to find a form of associations which will defend and protect with the whole common force the person and goods of each associate, and in which each, while uniting himself with all, may still obey only himself and remain as free as before. (Rousseau 1760/1987: 49)

In this way, Rousseau connects individual self-government with the collective (rational) self-government of an egalitarian democracy. He thereby epitomizes the thought that freedom requires membership and equal standing in a well-functioning democratic setting.

In his discussion of positive conceptions of liberty, Isaiah Berlin similarly traced how the idea of rational self-government (as a rendering of freedom) led ineluctably to the conception of a free person as a democratic citizen: "Those who believed in freedom as rational self-direction were bound, sooner or later, to consider how this was to be applied not merely to a man's inner life, but to his relations with other members of his society" (Berlin 1969b). These connections are developed further: "For if I am rational, I cannot deny that what is right for me must, for the same reasons, be right for others who are rational like me. A rational (or free) state would be a state governed by such laws as all rational men would freely accept" (Berlin 1969b). Hence, freedom in this positive sense cannot be understood apart from one's status as a citizen in a self-governing polity.

The motivation for seeing citizenship, indeed active participation in politics, as a requirement of (positive) freedom picks up on the note sounded by Rousseau and can be found in thinkers such as Hannah Arendt. For Arendt, the ideas "liberty" and "freedom" should not be seen as mere synonyms but

[15] For a reading of Rousseau that this gloss tracks, see Cohen (2010).

rather as distinguished by their different relations to citizenship status. On Arendt's view. liberty is akin to *liberation* and marks escape from oppression, but freedom requires political engagement in a constituted republic.[16] Only then can the self-government that defines true freedom be realized.

Arendt's (and Rousseau's) conception of self-government requires active control over the conditions of one's social environment enacted through the *political* institutions of one's place of residence. However, this requirement unrealistically assumes the possibility of active control, if not wholesale self-creation, of one's social existence by individuals by way of political structures. This assumes a level of control over one's embodied social condition that is unrealistic for all persons, but it also, over-narrowly, locates the prime mechanism of that control in formal political institutions. However, one's embodiment, sexuality, familial inheritance, ethnic background, and countless other factors shaping one's outlook and activities, cannot be said to be under our control. So why must we require this at the social level?[17] Secondly, various cultural, social, religious, and family practices will have much more impact on the way one is able to pursue valued ways of life than legal structures will, in many cases.

Rather than assuming liberty means capacity to create and control all aspects of one's social existence, I suggest that freedom requires the *acceptance* of one's condition, so that the projects and values one pursues can be considered as one's own, in a minimal sense (what I have referred to as "feeling at home").[18] As long as one's acceptance is not itself the result of manipulation and constrained circumstances alone, being able to embrace one's individual predicament and social surroundings and embark on valued projects is sufficient for the kind of basic freedom we want to capture here.[19]

As Amartya Sen puts it,

> As long as the levers of control are systematically exercised in line with *what I would choose* and *for that exact reason*, my "effective freedom" is uncompromised . . .. In modern society, given the complex nature of social organization, it is often hard, if not impossible, to have a system that gives each person all the levers of control over her own life. (Sen 1992: 64–65)

16 Arendt (1965: 22); cf. also Pitkin (1988).

17 An argument for a parallel point (concerning autonomy) is brought out in more detail in Christman (2009: chapter 7).

18 Cf. David Ingram's citation of Hegel's phrase "being at home with ourselves in an other" in his contribution to this volume (Chapter 5).

19 This is to make an oblique reference to the problem of adaptive preferences. For further discussion, see Christman (2014).

So, while more should be said on the matter, I am simply rejecting the semantic point Arendt makes that escape from oppression does not manifest freedom in a crucial sense, one which motivates persons in a fundamental manner and is central to freedom discourse at least since the abolitionist fights in the nineteenth century. The idea of basic freedom spelled out here is meant to express this very notion.

7.3 Basic Freedom

The outline of a conception of basic freedom to be presented shortly will, I hope, allow us to spell out a conception of liberty that accomplishes the twin goals of capturing the sense of freedom that forms the focal point for those struggling for liberation (better than other competitor notions) and avoids the commitment to citizenship status that most persons involved in such struggles cannot hope for and indeed often do not seek. We will be more precise later, but the general shape of this idea of freedom is this: To be free is to be allowed and enabled to pursue life activities with others that one can value, where, to speak more figuratively, one can feel in a minimal sense "at home." This doesn't mean one will be happy or successful or standing in ideally just relations with others – this is a concept of *basic* freedom, after all, and it applies to the imperfect world we live in. However, freedom here means being in a position to lead a life that has value for the person, given her sense of herself and her social identity.

As we mentioned, countless persons and groups are engaged in struggles to find or reclaim some semblance of a stable home environment after fleeing from, or overthrowing, oppressive conditions from which they are attempting to be freed. This means that millions of people live in conditions of seemingly permanent limbo, suspended between violent persecution, on the one hand, and stable and supportive social locations that they may call (a kind of) home, on the other. What is lacking is surely sufficient stocks of basic resources, including nutritional, educational, and housing resources, but also the ability to pursue projects and life plans in a setting that affords them social standing as independent and equal citizens.

One response to the precariousness of these conditions is to argue that securing citizenship status for persons fleeing persecution, whether in a host country or a reconstituted home state after sufficient reforms are instituted, is required for freedom. However, for several reasons I have alluded to and will elaborate upon, such measures are either not realistic in the foreseeable future or are not required for freedom in a sense of that term that captures the aims of those involved.

For example, as others have claimed concerning irregular migrants, social structures can be established within host countries that, while certainly far from ideal, provide a relatively stable setting within which migrant communities can establish a kind of home.[20] Nanda Oudejans puts it this way:

> [W]ithout denying the deplorable predicament of many unauthorized immigrants (particularly rejected asylum seekers or displaced persons in a refugee context), it should also be noted that irregular immigrants are not always struggling to survive and are not by definition excluded from a normal life. (2019: 448)

Indeed, securing full citizenship status can be counterproductive for some migrants. Oudejans continues:

> Indeed, unauthorized immigrants might have something to gain by remaining under the radar and keeping the arm of the (fiscal) state at length, not only because they fear detection, arrest, detention, and removal but also because a life in the periphery gives a certain sense of freedom, autonomy, and economic prosperity. (2019: 454)

Other analyses bear this out,[21] though we must be careful not to generalize; for people seeking freedom in their escape from oppressive and debilitating conditions are quite varied. I am certainly aware that countless people living under oppressive circumstances or seeking asylum are far from enjoying even basic freedom. And of course, gaining citizenship rights will in many cases be an important component of the struggle for that condition. But I want to at least claim that having such political rights bears only a contingent connection to the requirements for a free social existence, a condition that I claim is not always required.

In order to capture the aspirations of persons who lack a sense of home and stable social recognition (as well as resources and protections from persecution), one must, I will argue, see the freedom they aim for in a particular light, one captured by the idea of *socially effective agency*, a model that includes opportunities as well as enabling conditions and status recognition of a sort that need not presuppose well-established political standing in particular nation-states. Accordingly, such a view will have positive elements as well as negative ones – capabilities, authenticity, and

[20] See, e.g., Benhabib (2004: chapter 5). Also, following Bourdieu, we can say that different forms of social capital can be utilized by groups in securing capabilities and protections that allow them to pursue personal, cultural, and work lives that afford basic freedom. See Bourdieu (1986).

[21] See, e.g., Van Meeteren (2009).

social status conditions as well as opportunities to act. Let us, then, sketch the basic components of this notion.

7.3.1 *Basic Freedom as Effective Social Agency*

In general, the dimensions of freedom I want to sketch fall into the categories of *enabling* conditions, *authenticity* conditions, and *status* conditions, as I mentioned earlier. The first is meant to capture the idea that those who lack basic personal, social, and economic resources thereby lack an important dimension of freedom. The second refers to how one can lack freedom because of internal deprivations and pathologies such as addictions, psychological manipulation, and so on as well as being robbed of social, cultural, and political structures that allow one to live a life of value (where one is "at home"). Finally, freedom also requires that one's standing as a socially recognized candidate for agency be publicly respected.[22]

Now we should note that an emphasis on these positive features does not erase completely the relevance of noninterference to freedom.[23] A positive account of liberty will include requirements of noninterference or non-constraint as a requirement, but on the one hand, it will include a different account of what counts as a constraint and why their absence is important for freedom, and on the other, it will explain why this mere absence cannot capture all of what freedom is when seen as something of fundamental personal and social value.

7.3.1.1 *Enabling Conditions*

One of the longest-standing objections to traditional liberal accounts of freedom is motivated by the idea that noninterference fails to account for how social deprivation and lack of resources can systematically undercut liberty. The idea that freedom requires certain powers and abilities, as well as opportunities, picks up on Sen's requirements of agency freedom – namely, the enjoyment of basic capabilities for formulating and pursuing

[22] These elements mimic points made in other theorists' accounts of freedom, though not any one completely. See, e.g., Gould (1988, 2013), Honneth (2014), and Sen (1992).

[23] Indeed, one mistake that negative theorists make in criticizing positive notions is to assume that positive theorists, in Kukathas's words, are "not concerned fundamentally with the presence or absence of constraints upon individual action" (1994: 22). Depending on what is meant by "fundamentally," this is inaccurate. For a defender of positive freedom need not think negative notions are incoherent or wrong-headed, but merely that they are *incomplete.*

valued functionings.[24] These include, for example, both the absence of certain disabling conditions as well as access to various resources and social conditions that make decisions and choices feasible.[25]

For such an approach to be defensible, several challenges must be met. One is that the range of capabilities in question that define freedom must be described in ways that don't reduce to a narrow parochial understanding of human flourishing. Capabilities for the Buddhist monk are different from those of a striving business person.[26] Further, the view should not imply that disabled individuals who have acclimated to their condition and whose environments are such that they are not significantly hampered by them are described as failing to lead free, flourishing lives simply because of the fact of their "disability." Avoiding such implications is not an easy task and I merely flag them for now. My view is that the list of basic capabilities will be derivative from the condition of authenticity discussed later, specifically that the basic capabilities that comprise freedom for any individual will be those required for her to pursue paths of being and acting sanctioned by her (stable) practical identity.

The challenge, then, is to formulate an account of capabilities that is consistent with a relatively content-neutral (or broadly value-invariant) account of effective agency. These capacities will include both internal and external elements. Physical and psychological disabilities (properly understood), temporary or chronic inability to form stable intentions and act on them, as well as resources needed to engage in these intentional actions, will comprise capabilities in this sense. However, as Sen also argues, the capabilities in question will be specified without conditions of success: They are the requirements to *pursue* valued plans of action, not the successful pursuit of them. In this way, he argues, freedom is distinguished from well-being.[27]

[24] Sen gives an abstract rendering of the capabilities in question, namely whatever is required for the valued functionings that are constitutive of a person's being (Sen 1992: chapters 3–4). Martha Nussbaum, on the other hand, bases her conception of capabilities on an Aristotelean view of human flourishing (see Nussbaum 2001: 78–82). As will be clear from the text, I take a third route, namely a conception of capabilities tied to the person's authentic practical identity.

[25] For an earlier defense of a conception of freedom that ties it to access to resources, see Crocker (1980).

[26] This is to depart from the version of the capability view developed by Nussbaum, for example (Nussbaum 2001).

[27] Or as he puts it: agency freedom is distinguished from well-being freedom. See *Inequality Reexamined.* Also, some have objected that freedom-as-capability removes the unique character of freedom as a phenomenon and a value. This is because, allegedly, capability-freedom reduces the value of being free to the value of accomplishing goals. See, e.g., Carter (1999: 127, see also

Now it has often been claimed that adding positive requirements of freedom such as capabilities removes the distinction between freedom and, simply, *ability* or *power*. The sting of this charge can be removed, I think, if we understand the conditions of unfreedom to count as such only if they have a human source, that is, they are factors either put in place as a result of human activity or are ones that could be feasibly removed by it.[28] In this way, only when persons are disempowered by other agents, practices, social structures, and so on does she lose freedom by that token. Therefore, lack of freedom does not simply correspond to lack of power but only with lack of (a kind of) power whose absence can be traced to social sources.[29]

Further arguments can be offered for the inclusion of such a condition, though I will mention only two here. The first has been much discussed, and it is this: The notion of a constraint cannot plausibly be explicated without reference to the range of abilities that agents have that such constraints inhibit or undercut. A fence is a constraint on freedom of action only if it is high enough to block my path, which means I don't have the ability to easily scale it. If a reference to abilities is made there, how is it plausible to then claim that a *lack* of capability (properly defined) is not central to freedom?[30]

Second, imagine that the constraints a person suffers under are so severe that they, over time, debilitate her in pronounced ways; say the chains that bind one are on so long that one's muscles atrophy, so that when they are removed, one lacks the ability to move one's limbs effectively. Would not this disability be counted as a lack of freedom, even if it is in some way an inability *per se* at that point? If so, then the line between lacking a power/ability and lacking freedom (in the opportunity sense) is already blurry, so the claim that inclusion of capabilities in one's account is counterintuitive lacks force.

As I said, this discussion of capabilities is overly brief but it connects to the second dimension of positive freedom I want to defend, that of being enabled to pursue authentic projects as an effective agent in social space.

pp. 56–58). I attempt to respond to this problem in Christman (2012). For an overview see Robeyns (2011).

28 This bears some affinity to the "responsibility" view of constraints defended in different ways by Miller (1989) and Kristjansson (1996: chapter 6).

29 Cf. Pettit (2012), who claims that one lacks freedom when one's lack of resources (in my case capabilities) can be traced to the actions of other persons (Pettit 2012: 41–44).

30 As I said, this point has been much discussed, and I don't pretend to state this argument in a way that settles the issue. I merely want to gesture at the kinds of considerations that motivate this condition. See, e.g., Carter (2019: section 5).

7.3.1.2 *Authentic Agency*

Recall that we are asking what freedom might mean as an aspiration for those forced to flee their homes and in search of stable living situations, either back in one's homeland or in a new community. Before this is achieved, we can note that a key feature of life for such persons is deep and abiding alienation from their surroundings as potential long-term settings in which to pursue their lives. Of course, such alienation is hardly limited to refugees and migrants. The extremely poor, those forced into labor situations against their will, victims of discrimination and social marginalization, often cannot view their life options as minimally valued from their own settled perspective. The modes of life activities and plans that such a person has open to her are (we can imagine) of such paltry character that she lacks sustained motivation to engage in them, except perhaps as a matter of survival (or for the care of others).[31]

This last point is, I think, the fulcrum upon which to center the account of authenticity required for freedom, namely that the agent is able and allowed to pursue modes of being that she can see as minimally worth pursuing from her own reflective perspective. To use familiar terminology from another context, such modes of being will be sanctioned from the perspective of her practical identity.[32] That is, the self-understanding by which a person sees her life as worth living and which grounds her motivations and plans amounts to an evaluative perspective that organizes and guides her choices. The authenticity condition picked out here is merely that the options open to the person are ones that can be sanctioned from that perspective.[33]

We also need to point out the irreducibly social elements that structure this practical identity. One's value orientation makes essential reference to ways of life, not merely isolated choices, and such ways of life virtually always have interpersonal and social, as well as historical constituents, so that one's identity is shaped by social practices, traditions, religion, and

[31] Cf. Raz's claims regarding the requirement for autonomy, namely the adequacy of options faced by the agent (Raz 1986: 375). However, Raz gives little guidance to what such adequacy amounts to, except to say that such a range must enable the person to exercise "all the capacities human beings have an innate drive to exercise." He also claims that such a range must include choices with long-term consequences as well as short-term effects; and it must include enough variety to allow the person to exercise discernment in guiding her life by her own lights (Raz 1986: 375).

[32] See Korsgaard (1996).

[33] In other contexts, I have discussed authenticity in a similar vein as a condition of autonomy. The requirement is similar in this context, but freedom, even in its positive form, is not equivalent to full-scale self-government. Nor is the idea of authenticity here connected to identification with (or non-alienation from) first-order motives as part of a life narrative, as I have claimed autonomy demands. See Christman (2009: chapter 8).

cultural dynamics that cannot simply be constructed or recreated by one's own efforts. Social settings largely define what is minimally valuable for a person to pursue. In this way, freedom requires a basic sense of being "at home" in the world.[34]

This is the crucial point here. For the requirements of freedom laid out here include having opportunities and capabilities that allow one to live out a social existence that one can *accept* – seen as constitutive of a meaningful existence – not one that one necessarily fully *controls* or is the author of. I posit this in order to capture the ways that all our lives, the privileged and the deprived, are shaped by forces that did not originate with us and which we cannot, except at the margins, control. Yet for the fortunate among us, we can embrace these conditions as an acceptable structure within which a meaningful existence, including choices such a structure allows, can be pursued.[35]

Again, one's *political* status as a citizen or permanent resident or guest worker (and so on) will be contingently related to this ability to accept one's social condition, to "be at home" in the world. This involves functioning in a congenial linguistic community, finding meaningful work and life activities, engaging in caring relations, and so on. Whether one's ability to find such a social location and live within it may depend on having a political voice in the centralized state institutions that govern one's living area; but (importantly) it may not. There is no conceptual necessity that one stand as a *political* member of the broader community that shapes that existence. For the reasons I have been laying out, I take this as a particular advantage of this account.

This discussion of authentic value orientations will help further show why limitations on freedom should not be confined simply to constraints on *action* as such. For when one is not recognized as an agent with an authentic value orientation at all, or as a deficient or degraded version of an agent, one lacks freedom independently of what actions one is allowed to undertake viewed narrowly.

7.3.1.3 Status and Recognition

Many writers developing positive conceptions of liberty have stressed that interactions with others can support or undercut freedom in

[34] See Gould (2013: esp. p. 109), who makes very similar points.

[35] Moreover, tying freedom to one's practical identity in this way will allow us to give a better account of what constraints should be counted as limitations on freedom. For unlike the neutral counting of standard negative models, a constraint only counts as such for us if it frustrates the successful performance of a course of action deemed worth pursuing from one's (stable) practical perspective.

direct ways, specifically, that one can be rendered unfree due to lack of proper recognition by significant others in a way that both engages the intersubjective structure of thought and intention as well as affords the person with the standing as an agent encountering other agents on those terms.[36]

I agree that the kind of freedom fought for in abolitionist struggles and migratory quests for home and the like (which I am using as the touchstone for this analysis) requires that one has a kind of standing in a community as a person worthy of freedom. Relegating persons as dispensable or as subhuman or as enslavable implies that freedom does not apply to them, their effective social agency is not a pressing concern.[37]

Consider conditions where groups are subject to pervasive derogatory attitudes that essentially prevent them from living in public as themselves (without facing such degradation). Persons facing such discrimination are thereby regarded as unworthy of full participation in the social and political world in which they reside.[38] Racist attitudes can prevail to an extent that undercuts effective agency long after nominal legal protections are put in place to prevent overt interference and constraint. When this is the case, people are prevented from engaging in socially effective agency, simply because they are denied the social resources required to *be* the kind of person they identify as, in public and without shame.[39] For these reasons, I suggest that a condition of social status whereby a person is publicly treated as a *candidate* for free agency is required for freedom itself. This follows from the view developed so far of effective agency, without relying on a full commitment either to Hegelian conceptions of agency, object relations theory in psychology, or other such theoretical foundations adopted by others to require recognition for freedom.[40]

36 See, e.g., Honneth (2014).

37 I have argued elsewhere, however, that the *terms* under which persons are described that ground this recognition must be determined by the persons themselves, and not imposed by the dominant groups in a society (Christman 2020).

38 Pettit argues that (neo-) republican freedom reconnects that notion to a guarantee of *honor* and hence restores the status requirement to the idea of liberty. He argues that where it is public knowledge that persons are immune from uncontrolled interference – are not dominated – such honor will be afforded to them (Pettit 1997b: 64). However, this describes a merely *contingent* connection between freedom (as not being subject to arbitrary interference) and one's status as a person able to conduct her own affairs with the abiding acknowledgment by others of her capacity to do so. It also, I think, gets things the wrong way round: to be free requires that one is recognized as a candidate for freedom, not that being such a candidate will (likely) afford you such recognition.

39 Cf. Amartya Sen's defense of a similar consideration (Sen 1992).

40 That is, this view departs in this narrow way from similar claims made by Honneth (2014), views with which I am largely sympathetic.

Also, and more to the present point, enjoying the socially recognized status of being a free person is defended because of its ties to one's ability to engage in minimally valued pursuits. This may not require being a *citizen* or an active participant in institutionalized politics. That depends on the contingencies of one's circumstance: when lack of political status and the related control undercuts one's ability to pursue valued aims, then citizenship is required for freedom. However, when one can stand in a social space with dignity and accept one's opportunities for pursuing a valued life without the status of citizen (as is sometimes the case), then citizenship is not required for basic freedom.

7.4 Conclusion

In this chapter, I have attempted two related things. The first was to challenge the idea that freedom and citizenship should be conceptually intertwined. I had two sets of reasons for doing this: First, freedom in the sense of being able to live a life of one's own does not require in all cases the kind of direct political control that citizenship and advanced democratic practices enable, valuable though those things are. Second, assuming citizenship in one's idea of freedom fails to capture the discursive logic of countless people whose life situation and long-term prospects do not include citizenship in fully or nearly just democracies.

My second objective here was to sketch the major elements of a positive conception of liberty that avoids such presuppositions but nevertheless captures the state that is so valued both inside and outside of well-established democracies. Of course, this is merely a sketch. For now, however, I merely want to paint the general picture of what freedom in a positive sense might look like in order to capture the value in question as it motivates those struggling so desperately to achieve it.

CHAPTER 8

Reframing Democracy with Positive Freedom
The Power of Liberty Reconsidered

Carol C. Gould

8.1 Introduction

Contemporary democracies are facing ever-increasing threats of an authoritarian rule on the part of their own leaders, along with the emergence of powerful white nationalist social movements. In the United States, democracy continues to be undermined by powerful monied interests, whose influence over voting, and over politics more generally, has intensified following the Supreme Court's Citizens United decision. At the same time, the core right to vote is being curtailed by many US state legislatures, with endorsement from the courts. In this difficult political context, those committed to reform have called for a recommitment to democracy, including restoring and expanding voting rights, and limiting the power of money. Yet, several theorists (myself among them) have argued that we need to go beyond this, not only by deepening democracy but also by expanding its domain, extending it to corporations and firms and to social institutions (Gould 1988, 2014, 2019; Schweickart 2002; Landemore and Ferreras 2016), a view that has also been proposed in feminist ethics, e.g., as caring democracy (Tronto 2013).

In this chapter, I want to argue that a key element is missing in the standard analyses of democracy's difficulties, one that is at least partly theoretical and normative in nature. Although some have acknowledged that democracy cannot be limited to the bare formal requirements for periodic elections and majority rule (themselves often honored in the breach), what is even more problematic is that the notion of liberty which grounds much democracy theory is itself deeply flawed. I will argue that the deeper meaning of freedom has been obscured within the dominant liberal democratic tradition, taking this to include both liberal and libertarian approaches. Although authoritarianism falls outside both of these more mainstream approaches, it benefits from the fecklessness of the traditional understanding of liberty, which also, I believe, enables it to propagate itself in perniciously inegalitarian as well as antidemocratic ways. Of course, the current (re)emergence and growth of authoritarianism is mainly due to empirical determinants rather than to these defects in political theory, but I believe the latter contribute to the plausibility of these antidemocratic movements. In fact, sometimes the policies promulgated by authoritarian leaders or movements that support them appeal directly to these liberal or libertarian conceptions of liberty which provide them with a degree of cover and help them to gain a foothold through democratic procedures. It behooves us in this dangerous context, then, to return to the old question of the meaning of liberty or freedom which undergirds our democratic commitments, and to inquire into the adequacy of prevailing understandings. We also need to consider what conception of freedom could better accord with, and lend support to, the deeper and more expansive democracy that is urgently needed in the present.

8.2 Liberty as Absence of Interference

It is interesting to observe that the current – and still dominant – conception of liberty was foregrounded by Isaiah Berlin specifically to counteract one specific type of authoritarianism (or, perhaps, totalitarianism), namely, the one that is thought to have characterized the former Soviet Union in the Cold War period. Writing in the late 1950s, Berlin defended a negative notion of liberty as freedom from interference, or freedom from external impediments to an individual's free choices. At the same time, he railed against the understanding of freedom as involving positive aspects, which he understood in terms of a Kantian notion of self-determination. He claimed that positive liberty in this sense would transform itself into self-mastery and ultimately (through Marxism apparently) to endorsing the dominion of the state over the individual, by virtue of its putative claims to know what is good for the individual. C. B. Macpherson and several other writers have challenged the non sequiturs in Berlin's argument, I believe generally successfully (Macpherson 1973: 95–119; Gould 1988, 36–38; 2013; Edge 2013; Tutor 2018). Clearly, Berlin's approach was based on a range of philosophical commitments beyond his notion of liberty, including pluralism in values (Crowder 2004). Yet, the core problem from my standpoint lies in his narrowing down of freedom to the very limited aspect of freedom from external interference, especially on the part of the state, while also radically individualizing liberty, separating it from its conditions, and ultimately leading to counterintuitive conclusions. One of these was developed in a critique by Gerald A. Cohen, in particular, the implausible implication that poverty does not limit a person's freedom (Cohen 1979).

Any notion of the freedom *to* do something, as positive freedom, is banned in Berlin's view, as is the related notion of effective freedom. In the face of these restrictions, and after many years of discussion and back and forth about Berlin's two concepts, a recent tendency has been to propose that we dispense altogether with the notion of positive freedom, because it is said to lack any point or because it is too controversial. Others argue that Gerald MacCallum (1967) long ago convincingly showed that there cannot be two types of freedom, since all understandings of freedom can be formulated as the freedom from X to do Y. However, I think that MacCallum's observation can instead be mobilized to defend the idea that a merely negative notion of freedom is inadequate and that it must be supplemented by a positive one. I want to argue along those lines, but not merely insofar as the "from X to do Y" formulation is required as a formal property of freedom statements. Rather, I suggest, the positive moment follows from a reflection on who the agents are who are said to be free and what the value of freedom is for them. In the view I propose, when positive freedom is correctly interpreted, it does not limit negative freedom in the main, or undercut it, but rather can be seen to supplement it in essential ways. A similar reflection on negative freedom also leads us to reinterpret it in some important ways. In the course of this analysis, I will suggest that other "positive freedom" views like those of Amartya Sen (1985, 1999) and Cohen (2011b), and more recently that of John Christman (2015), are not fully adequate, although they point us in helpful directions. Finally, we will be in a position to draw some implications from the robust account of positive freedom sketched here for deepening and extending democracy in ways that could help to prevent the authoritarianism that threatens to undermine it in the present.

8.3 The Positive Freedom Account

Given the common-sense observation that someone who is impoverished or otherwise lacks the means to do something they would otherwise choose to do is not, in fact, free to do those things, we can wonder what that implies for an adequate account of freedom. Many strategies have been implemented against Berlin. Among them have been rather contorted (in my view) attempts to build a range of conditions for free action into the notion of negative liberty itself, to show that even accepting Berlin's narrow view, the absence of the provision of required means constrains liberty. This move can be found in Macpherson's early rejoinder to Berlin's critique and in Cohen's account of freedom and money (Macpherson 1973; Cohen 2011b). However, to my mind, such views that try to shoehorn the multifarious conditions of liberty, including the positive availability of means like money or access to property, into negative liberty, end up with convoluted and implausible accounts that disregard MacCallum's helpful observation that all liberty is both from and to.

Some other approaches explicitly adopt a positive freedom conception, including Sen's well-known account of capabilities. However, as Cohen observes in his critique of Sen, the notion of capabilities does not work well for some key liberty-enhancing states, such as freedom from malaria, although it may work well for freedom from poverty and the associated capability. Cohen notes that in Sen's eagerness to put the focus on activity (a focus that my view shares with his), he is forced to stretch the notion of capability to the point where it does not actually refer to an action or an ability to function but also includes states of affairs (like freedom from malaria or freedom from poverty) that may not require activity on an agent's part. The notion of functioning can also be overly narrow: While it certainly applies to human needs, it is not clear how it relates to more developed capacities that go beyond these basic needs, or how it applies to states of affairs that advantage people without requiring an activity on their parts or that do not pertain to their functioning taken as an activity (Cohen 2011b: 44–60).

I want to suggest how the view of positive freedom that I have previously developed avoids many of these weaknesses in existing views. It offers a more capacious account that incorporates a more adequate conception of both basic and developed freedom, and sees freedom as integrally related to its various conditions. The approach is at the same time more fully relational than existing ones. Yet, I believe it does these things without becoming a perfectionist approach and while retaining a core notion of free choice. I believe this view also has advantages over the many notions of freedom that focus on autonomy, whether individual or relational, even if they add in a notion of authenticity, as Christman does (2015), an emphasis we can also find in Charles Taylor's early critique of negative liberty (1979). In some contrast with these various interpretations, I focus on a more dynamic notion of human agency as developing over time and as proceeding not merely as a relation to oneself or one's authentic desires or as exclusively as an action of the self, but as necessarily proceeding through relations with others and with the natural world. It is thus based on a distinctive social ontology of what I call *individuals-in-relations*, in a way that contrasts with the still prevailing individualist ones characteristic of liberalism or libertarianism.

The perspective proposed here does not deny the importance of freedom from external constraint, but sees this as insufficient, even as an account of negative liberty. Rather, we need to add in not only the freedom from internal constraints which may hinder or interfere with an agent's choices (Taylor 1979) but also the freedom *from* domination, exploitation, and oppression. This approach retains the idea that freedom is both *from* and *to*, and accordingly, it does not replace negative freedom with positive freedom. However, a crucial question is what the "to" signifies. Freedom to do what? Here, I advance a broader account than other positive freedom views, including the capabilities approach. It is a freedom to develop oneself both individually and jointly with others, understood as the *development of capacities* (which can go beyond capabilities for basic functioning, though it includes those). It also can extend to the traditional liberal notion of *realizing projects* or aims of one's choosing. Also, a final parameter for the "to" element is the *cultivation of relationships*, in accordance with the centrality this account would give to our sociality.

However, if we look at this array of "freedom to's," we find a somewhat different notion of agency itself. The conception here is distinctive in that it sees agency as extending beyond free choice at a given moment (although it presupposes that), in developing overtime in and through social relations and as operating in a socially transformed natural environment; that is, as embodied and embedded in these relations. These relations include those of a person to themselves over time as well, as proposed in authenticity accounts. Beyond this, it emphasizes biographical or narrative dimensions which are essential to understanding an agent's self-development. These dimensions also have an analog in collective contexts, where groups have historical and developmental dimensions that characterize their free activity over time and where freedom can analogously be taken in this self-transformative sense. (However, the attribution of such freedom to collectivities obviously would require both elaboration and qualification in various ways, to avoid the idea of entirely unitary processes of choice and decision-making by such groups.)

The conception of freedom as developmental thus can be seen to preserve the importance of free choice but it recognizes that for such choices to be real or effective over time, what is centrally required is the agent's relation to a set of conditions that enable the activity as free activity. In the account I propose, the conditions include the absence of constraint that is recognized in negative liberty accounts along with the new requirement of freedom from domination and exploitation. Crucially, however, the self-transformative activity that constitutes our free action also involves access to a set of positive or enabling conditions of action. These positive conditions, moreover, are not merely external ones instrumentally required for an action's efficacy, as Berlin apparently thought of them, but are partly constitutive of the action itself.

From this perspective, Berlin was wrong to sharply separate freedom from its conditions. His view was possible only for one operating with a radically individualistic account of the person, which fails to see how our free action always operates in and through social and material conditions that facilitate it. These conditions are integral to the activity itself and not separate from it. We can see, therefore, that Berlin was correct to associate positive liberty with the tradition of Hegel and Marx, but not in the sense he thought. It is not because positive liberty would lead to a holistic or dominating state, which in fact does not follow, as Macpherson ably demonstrates (1973). Rather the positive liberty account has roots in the Hegelian notion of objectification, which conceives action as a relation to others and to nature (the latter being especially prominent in Marx's version of objectification), and understands freely chosen activity along similar lines as a process that necessarily engages with others or with the natural world (Gould 1978, 1988). Accordingly, agency should not be understood as the simple repetition of bare free choices, or as the expression of preferences, even if these are autonomously chosen, but rather as a process of growth and development over time. Clearly, such a process does presuppose the capacity to make free choices or to act on conscious purposes. I identify this with the intentionality characteristic of human activity. However, when such choices are taken as those of embodied social individuals, the relation to others and to nature is not merely an add-on or a contingent feature of free activity, but part of it. Moreover, in this vein, the processiveness over time is best conceived not only as the realization of individual goals or projects, but as involving the development of capacities and the cultivation of relations. It is in this sense at least potentially also a process of the flourishing of individuality in freely chosen ways.

Some might object that this view fails to capture the fact that free choice, even if constrained, can presumably shine forth even in miserable conditions, e.g., when a person is imprisoned or even enslaved. This might be conceived as a sort of ontological or metaphysical freedom. However, I think it is more than that and has phenomenological dimensions as well.

My view sees the capacity for this sort of free choice as an experiential feature of basic human activity understood as intentional activity. Yet, the view I propose also recognizes that for these choices to be effective, they necessarily require access to various means, including not only freedom from constraining conditions, but also a set of enabling conditions of action.

Interestingly, the set of human rights that were promulgated by Eleanor Roosevelt and the other drafters of the Universal Declaration of Human Rights (UDHR) and that have been elaborated in the human rights covenants and treaties up to the present do a reasonably good job of laying out these fundamental conditions of action. I have elsewhere argued that these rights should be understood in the first instance as social claims on others for their fulfillment, which are subsequently worked up as legal rights (Gould 2014). I believe that they can give us useful guidance regarding the range of conditions needed for freedom in both its negative and positive senses, provided that they are taken to include social and economic rights, and not only the first generation civil and political rights. Moreover, I have suggested that we can distinguish between a set of basic or primary human rights, namely, those necessary for any human activity whatever, and other, secondary, human rights, which encompass those needed for the further development or flourishing of human capacities, the fulfillment of long-term projects, and the cultivation of relationships throughout a person's life.

Note then that there are not two different and conflicting conceptions of liberty. Rather, we have free choice, evident in basic human intentionality, and also its development in relations with others and over time in capacities and projects. I suggest too that a similar transformative process can analogously be found in joint or common forms of activity, oriented to shared ends.

The deeply egalitarian feature of this account can be seen by reflecting on the basic capacity for freedom that is found in human activity itself as an intentional process. As a fundamental feature that we recognize in each other, this capacity for free choice supports claims to human rights by each individual, and is one of the components of human dignity which lies at the core of human rights norms. By reflecting on basic human activity as free activity, yet as an activity that involves development and that essentially requires conditions, we can further see that in virtue of people's equal agency (as a capacity for such freedom), no one has more of a right of access to the conditions that enable flourishing or self-development than does anyone else. This amounts then to a principle that I have called *equal positive freedom*, as a principle of justice. That is, each has an equal right of access to the conditions of self-transformative or self-developing activity.

8.4 Replies to Some Objections and a Demonstration of the Power of Positive Freedom

It may be objected that this conception of freedom, which sees real freedom in the ability to act beyond the bare capacity for free choice, confuses freedom with power. However, this elision is ultimately accepted in my account. Given the extended sense of freedom as development based on the capacity for free choice but not reducible to it, real freedom can be said to coincide with the power to act. Such a merging of freedom and power is not unheard of in the history of philosophy, even if it is not standard. Yet, given that freedom in my view requires the absence of domination and not only the absence of external interference, it would not condone *power over* in the sense of such domination or as exploitation or oppression. Moreover, inasmuch as the individuals who act are conceived as social individuals or individuals-in-relations, very often their freedom will take the form of what has been called *power with*, or the sort of power which can only be exercised in common with others (Arendt 1963, 1969; Allen 1998; Gould 2014). This will have import for the understanding of democracy to be considered in the next part of the chapter.

Another objection to the view put forward here concerns its claim that negative liberty as the freedom from interference that would protect free choice can in fact conflict with positive liberty as a process of self-transformative activity requiring the provision of enabling conditions, where the latter would require economic redistribution and thus would potentially interfere with liberty in the first sense. There is also the even more straightforward traditional objection that the equality posited in the notion of equal positive freedom would necessarily lead to interference with people's liberties. These familiar right-wing arguments would require fuller rebuttals than I can give here. But for our purposes, we can note with respect to the first objection that the claim here is that there is a harmony in principle between free choice and its realization in concrete forms of activity (through an agent's operating on the conditions of action). In fact, the free choice of activity taken alone is something of an abstraction from such processes of self-transformative activity, in the sense that they are only effective insofar as conditions are available, and are most often only moments in what are actually extended processes over time. While it is evidently the case that some redistributions would involve interference with unlimited free choice (assuming this is possible) or constraints on it, these redistributions may well be necessary for "real" freedom as the freedom to develop capacities, realize long-term projects, and cultivate relationships. At the same time, the view proposed here suggests that there are good freedom-based reasons for protecting the civil and political human rights usually encompassed under negative liberty, while at the same time moving to realize social and economic rights. That these rights are compossible is posited in the various declarations and covenants that frame the human rights movements and institutions since 1948, but the actual balance among the rights has to be determined in well-conceived public policies. Another factor that mitigates possible conflicts between negative and positive liberty derives from the fact that both pertain to equal individuals. Thus, negative liberty is not unlimited, but qualified by the equal liberty of others, and the same holds for equal positive freedom, which presupposes negative liberty but goes beyond it. I suggest then that all forms of liberty can therefore be understood as constrained by the demands of justice.

Before proceeding to the implications of positive freedom for strengthening democracy, it will be useful to briefly explore the power of this positive freedom notion for illuminating a particular case. We can consider its importance for understanding one of the central normative disputes that have arisen in dealing with the devastating COVID-19 pandemic that has afflicted most countries around the world.

Opponents of governmental "stay-at-home orders" and the promulgation of requirements for social distancing have demanded that these constraints be ended on grounds of "liberty." Clearly, those opponents' reference to liberty is to negative liberty, as the individualistic freedom from external interference (by the state). We can easily recognize that these demands are dangerous and misplaced but it is not easy to say why they are if one remains simply within a negative freedom perspective. The argument against prematurely removing these public health orders or requirements is often framed in terms of the greater good, or some notion of that sort, where the greater good remains vague and undefined. Alternatively, some argue that carriers of the virus have no right to infect others. While these are indeed plausible ripostes, the protesters can also be criticized for not properly appreciating the real meaning of liberty or freedom. If freedom is that of social individuals and integrally requires access to conditions, a person's freedom would directly be impacted not only by the virus, were they to catch it, but by their inability to get adequate care from an overextended health care system. It would also be to disregard the degree to which the self-development of any person is dependent on the cooperation of many, if not all, others, in not furthering the spread of the virus and increasing the danger it poses for all. We can see too that cooperation here is not merely instrumentally useful for the realization of the capabilities or capacities of others. In the case at hand, the ability of each to avoid getting sick or even dying, as a condition of their own freedom, depends on the forbearance of others in not exercising their "liberty" to jeopardize the lives of the first. Indeed, it is likely that one can develop the sort of argument required here even from Mill's traditional harm principle or simply from an equal liberty interpretation of negative liberty. However, the argument is clearly strengthened when the relational aspects of positive freedom are taken into account, and in which a range of conditions – including a human right to health or healthcare – are seen as essential to it.

8.5 The Implications for Democracy

I suggested at the outset that the current problems with democracy and the concomitant growth of authoritarianism are not only empirical phenomena but reflect weaknesses in the relevant political theory, and in particular the conception of liberty on which contemporary democracy is based. We have seen that this conception is currently one of negative liberty, or freedom from state interference with individual choices, which calls for their protection by various civil and political rights. Within liberal theories, these rights are sharply differentiated from economic and social rights (which tend to be denigrated) in large part because of negative liberty's exclusive focus on such freedom from state interference. Even though civil and political rights in fact must be guaranteed by means of positive state provision (e.g., the provision and maintenance of a police system, courts, etc.) in the same way as economic and social rights, like those calling for education, welfare, and health (Shue 1980), this sort of positive provision is disregarded in these liberty accounts.

It is undoubtedly the case that ideological factors often play a role in the appeal to liberty and the concomitant denial of social and economic rights. Thus, the critique of state interference is often advanced by corporate lobbyists or wealthy donors who are interested not in equal liberty per se but profits and the preservation of their wealth and the diminution of taxation, all of which motivate their concern with state interference. This preoccupation reflects the historical connection of liberty with private property and the capitalist system. The donors and corporate agents may in turn seek to encourage social movements in defense of their favored conception of negative liberty. However, we have already seen that the norm of equal liberty itself, even when understood in negative terms, has some significant critical potential, and can perhaps be interpreted in a way that grounds a critique of such self-serving interests and actions based on them.

Moreover, negative liberty can itself be interpreted as rightly including freedom from domination and capitalist exploitation, as we have seen. A positive freedom account goes further, however, and fully justifies economic and social rights by adding to the requirement of freedom from deleterious constraining conditions the importance of the availability of a range of enabling conditions for free activity. In this perspective, social and economic human rights are essential for self-transformative or self-developing activity, which also lends further support to appending to absence of interference the further negative requirement of freedom from domination or exploitation. Beyond this, to the degree that social and economic rights are in fact equal rights and call for responsiveness to basic human needs, the positive freedom account would insist on a far more egalitarian distribution of income and wealth than presently exists, and additionally would oppose the intrusion into politics by powerful monied interests, which subverts the political right to democracy itself. Moreover, to the degree that basic conditions for people's free life activity go unrecognized, including their required access to food, health, and education, they are unable to effectively exercise their democratic rights even in the traditional and limited sense of voting that is at the heart of the liberal democratic ideal. Crucially for our purposes, a principle of equal positive freedom provides a ground for implementing much more robust, and also more extensive, democratic participation than on the negative liberty account. This can be seen by reflecting on its implications in contexts of what I have called common activities, where groups or institutions are organized around meeting shared ends.

I have proposed the notion of common activities to characterize the set of interlocking institutions and social and political practices which tie people together in public (taking the latter in an expansive sense to include most of economic life). The commonality or collectivity involved in their activities is not necessarily a unitary one such as is found in corporate agency accounts (e.g., List and Pettit 2011), although it does involve institutional contexts that are organized to meet a set of shared goals or aims. The aims may not be fully explicit or determined by collective decisions but are incorporated into the institutional design which is functionally oriented around such aims or ends. The institutions in question need not only be political in nature, but also include economic organizations like corporations and other business firms, as well as social organizations like voluntary associations.

A crucial presupposition of the positive freedom account comes into play here. Inasmuch as individuals are social beings, the ability to take part in such common activities is itself a necessary condition of their self-developing activity. And as we have seen, equal positive freedom requires prima facie equal access to the conditions of self-development. What this entails in the case of common activities are individuals' rights to take part in these activities as members. However, inasmuch as the individuals are agents characterized by a capacity for free choice, no one has more of a right to exercise their agency in these common activities or to determine its course than does any other. They must have equal rights to do so. An opportunity to take part in decisions about the course of these common activities thus preserves the right to self-determination that each of them has as an individual and would be required if none are to be dominated by the others in such activities. Yet, since this is a joint or common activity, they must necessarily co-determine the activity. No one of them can decide for all the others how it is to proceed. But such codetermination, in which each joins in the decision making as an equal with the others in fact amounts to a right to democratic participation in decision-making about these collective activities. It generates a right to democracy which, as one of the necessary conditions for free self-developing activity, can be seen as itself one of the human rights.

In this approach, democracy is evidently both deeper and more extensive than it is on the negative liberty view. It requires actual opportunities for participation and for deliberating with others about the direction of joint activities. Such opportunities and the correlative equal right to participate in decisions and planning extend broadly to all institutional contexts, where we can find common activities defined by shared aims. Thus it pertains not only to political institutions, including governments at all levels (including local and national, as well as transnational ones, Gould 2009). However, democracy would also be important within economic firms, where it takes the form of what has been called workplace democracy or, perhaps more appropriately for contemporary extended workplaces, democratic management (Gould 1988, 2014). Such democratic rights of participation would seem applicable to many social institutions as well.

At its limit, a positive freedom approach would also support the relevance of the norm of reciprocity, if not full democracy, to interpersonal contexts of action that are not institutionalized (Gould 1983, 1988). At the very least, we can observe that democratic decision-making in institutional contexts would be supported by the quasi-democratic practices of reciprocity and solidarity in interpersonal contexts. Empathy with the situation of others, standing with them, and listening to their voices applies in both domains and would improve communication and deliberation in both formal and informal contexts (Gould 2007, 2014, 2020). In broadening the scope of democracy in these ways, such a positive freedom framing of it comes close to John Dewey's call for seeing democracy as "a way of life" (Dewey 1927a [1916]). Along somewhat similar lines, Macpherson writes of democracy "as a kind of society – a whole complex of relations between individuals – rather than simply a system of government" (Macpherson 1973: 51).

Just to elaborate a bit on the still relatively unexplored notion of democratic management at work and in social organizations, we can note that this is not to be taken simply as a matter of voting, or as a requirement to decide everything directly by democratic means. It would not be possible to subject all policies to meetings and votes, but it does require real accountability of managers to all who work in a given organization (or are members of it) and extensive opportunities for all who work there to participate in framing policies and having ongoing input into their formulation and execution. The positive freedom notion, which emphasizes the expression and development of agency over time, where this is understood as the equal agency of all members, requires the cultivation of such opportunities for codetermination. I have discussed possible models for such democratic management elsewhere (Gould 1988, 2014), but clearly much more theoretical attention is needed to work out constructive and viable ways of enhancing work and a social life that implement such a democratic approach.

We can finally observe that aside from the intrinsic requirements for more extensive forms of democratic decision making in societies, instrumental considerations support the idea that such pervasive democratic practices would go a long way to address contemporary feelings of powerlessness, which provide a fertile ground for authoritarian ideas, and would also contribute to establishing some measure of equality among participants in these self-managing and self-governing contexts of life (Pateman 1970; Gould 2019). Although it must be acknowledged that contemporary politics is currently heading in a different and undemocratic direction, the only real remedy for democratic deficits is such an efflorescence of democracy, not only deepening our politics but addressing some of the exploitation, domination, and profound mal-distribution in the economic realm.

In conclusion, one can propose that only a positive and egalitarian conception of freedom such as the one elaborated here is able to rescue liberty itself from its current peril. From this perspective, making freedom effective by seeing it in relation to its conditions may well be a necessary prerequisite for the continued existence of any form of liberalism itself (including those features important for more cooperative politics in the future). Moreover, I would hope that this alternative reading can be of some help to contemporary social movements in their crucial efforts to supplant the forces that presently threaten to undermine existing democracies. However, the practicalities of how to accomplish that would need to be addressed in subsequent research.

CHAPTER 9

Disability and Positive Liberty

Nancy J. Hirschmann

Positive liberty is not a simple concept, and certainly not as simple and straightforward as negative liberty; it is defined differently by different scholars, as illustrated in this volume. From Isaiah Berlin's (1969b) original formulation of state-engineered totalitarian mind control to Taylor's (1979) individualist second-guessing and self-realization view, to other more complex and socially located incarnations (Hirschmann 1996), positive liberty's meaning has had considerably more variability than the straightforward "tough-minded" negative liberty concept, with its noninterference and "open doors" imagery that Berlin (1979) theorized. The relationship of disability to positive liberty thus will depend on how positive liberty is defined. In the process of considering positive liberty from a disability perspective, however, disability also shows that some variants of positive liberty as the positive provision of resources could actually be construed as variations on negative liberty, which starts to look more complicated and perhaps a little less "tough." This is an important aspect of positive liberty.

In my previous work on feminist conceptualizations of freedom (Hirschmann 2003, 2008), however, I have argued for a more complex understanding of positive liberty as entailing the social construction of the choosing and desiring subject. I have explored the ways in which the social construction of women and men, femininity, and masculinity, have produced and shaped desires and choices throughout the modern history of liberty theory, leading us to question who the "subject" of liberty is. I have argued that dominant understandings of freedom – most particularly negative liberty, but also certain variants of positive liberty that depend on the notion of a "true" self and the dominance of the "will," or rational deliberative choice, over the "want," or desire – operate from a conception of the subject as white, male, heterosexual, and for the most part propertied. However, "he" is also decidedly not disabled.

Perhaps ironically for my argument, this would seem particularly true for many variations of positive liberty. Its focus on the "true" will and the critical evaluation of desires echoes familiarly with ableist claims about disability as a tragedy, loss, or lack. The common view of the disabled subject as an object of pity, disgust, and aversion makes it difficult to imagine any "true desire" in a disabled person other than not to be disabled; disability is something that nobody could possibly be content with, much less actively desire, the thinking goes. The link between freedom and the will, moreover, with its stress on rationality and autonomous self-reflection as we weigh conflicting desires to try to determine the "truth" might seem to eliminate cognitively impaired persons from the start; such elimination would seem to be built into the very conception of positive liberty (Francis 2009; Davey 2015: 133). That may not bode well for an argument seeking to recuperate positive liberty for disability.

9.1 The Negative Roots of Positive Liberty

Thus, it is not surprising that the vast majority of those who work and write on disability issues, particularly those who themselves have impairments, tend to take a negative liberty approach, portraying themselves as fully aware of the limits that society places on them, the barriers and obstacles that have been put in the way to impede them in their straightforward desires. In fact, the very core of the "social model" that disability scholars have theorized and developed in response to such obstacles defines "disability" entirely as a product of barriers and restraints. That is, on this model, my vision or mobility or cognitive function may be "impaired," but what turns such impairment into a "disability" is the creation and persistence of such socially produced barriers. "Disability" is, by definition, a condition of unjust restriction of persons with particular impairments. These limits and barriers often pertain to issues of design, ranging from curbs, stairs, and the lack of elevators to door width and countertop height (Keates and Clarkson 2003; Pullen 2011). Even smaller, apparently innocuous things like drinking straws, eating utensils, sidewalk surfaces, fragrances, flashing lights, or a single, apparently small step up into a building or room can pose obstacles to persons with mobility impairments.

However, at least as important to consider within this social model framework are prejudicial social attitudes that assume that all disabilities equate to complete incapacitation, as if physical disability produces intellectual disability, and as if intellectual disability entails complete incompetence and lack of understanding, desire, preference, and subjectivity.

Disabled persons have been and still are presented with many attitudinally based barriers to achieving what they want, even basic wants such as meaningful work, or even sometimes any kind of work, often further condemning them to poverty. A clear example is the experience of April Dunn, who despite being an honor roll student and never missing a day of classes was prevented from graduating from high school because she could not pass a standardized test required by the state for graduation because no accommodation was made for her cerebral palsy. She was thereafter prevented from obtaining employment for positions for which she was otherwise qualified (Hawkins 2020). Someone who uses a wheelchair is deemed less desirable as a professor and teacher; a deaf person is assumed to be unable to use a telephone; a young adult with Down syndrome is viewed as incapable of bagging groceries. The fact that many such persons in fact can and do perform these jobs is frequently outweighed by the assumption that the accommodation required to make that possible is excessive.[1] As Dan Goodley puts it, "compulsory able-bodiedness functions by covering over, with the appearance of choice, a system in which there is actually no choice" (Goodley 2011: 41). Even the group "Disability Justice," which is considered a "second wave" of the disability movement that focuses on fighting the negative impact of ableism that falls disproportionately on persons of color, queer, and trans persons who have impairments – including being viewed as disabled by virtue of differing from the white heterosexual norm – focuses on external barriers to access, rather than exploring the ways that disability may be conceptualized and lived differently to create different desires among differently situated disabled persons.

In this model, disabled persons claim they are unfree to pursue their desires, a clear violation of negative liberty. However, a positive liberty approach, with its extension to internal barriers, prompts us to ask: what are their desires?[2] This is a fraught question because it is often assumed by others that disabled people desire unrealistic goals – generally predicated on an underlying desire not to be disabled. Should we devote billions of dollars to an elusive cure for spinal cord injury, which affects relatively few people, if that means less money for education, or general health care, or even curing diseases that affect much larger numbers of people such as

[1] The disability literature views these claims as so common as not to merit specific references for each of them, but a sampling of disability literature in which such claims can be found include the articles in Davis (2017).

[2] I use "their" rather than "we" despite having several disabilities following common editorial usage, just as I use "their" to refer to women as well, although I identify as a woman.

cancer or heart disease?[3] Technologically advanced prosthetic limbs, seen by some as superior to "natural" limbs, are very expensive; should society have to pay for them or should it only pay for less expensive, more basic prosthetics, and disabled people who cannot afford them need to accept their bad luck?[4] Such objections build on beliefs that disabled persons are selfish, greedy, and unreasonably demanding in an unceasing effort to be compensated for their bodily misfortune, a notion that is also seen by disability scholars as itself a significant obstacle to disabled persons' freedom. Because as long as their desires are deemed unreasonable, they can be denied or ignored while the nondisabled comfort themselves through justified pity, ignoring the multiple ways in which society expends significant resources to support their own preferences.

Such attitudes clearly demonstrate an ableist bias. Jacobus tenBroek's groundbreaking argument about the "right to live in the world" articulated a vision of disabled persons as no different from nondisabled, with the same basic desires, wants, and needs, such as using buses and trains, moving along sidewalks, being hired for and holding a job for which they are qualified, and having a family. Arguably mapping the social model, he maintained that it was not the intrinsic condition of disability that prevented people from doing these things – in his specific focus, persons with vision impairment – but rather a thoughtlessness about disability that decreed the world too unsafe and difficult for them to navigate, which led to the conclusion that they should stay in their homes or institutions and that they were unreasonable to desire to go out in public. tenBroek, by contrast, held that the exaggerated risk of harm was an unreasonable justification for the denial of basic civil rights of disabled persons to pursue desires that are common to most people. He argued for using the law of torts to hold municipalities responsible for *creating* unsafe conditions in the built environment, for *preventing* access to common carriers, and for *failing to protect* disabled citizens from employment-based and other forms of discrimination. From placing barriers around open manhole covers to wheelchair ramps into buildings and Braille signage in elevators, to nondiscrimination legislation such as the Americans with Disabilities Act (ADA) requiring employers to accommodate bodily difference, disability scholars, lawyers, and activists have sought the removal of barriers to the

[3] The actor and quadriplegic Christopher Reeve was a strong advocate for a "cure" for spinal cord injury. The common utilitarian objection is a more generalized variant on Peter Singer's argument (1993, 2009).

[4] See Hirschman (n.d.) on the problems with so-called "luck egalitarian" approaches to disability.

full participation of disabled persons in civic life, generally through the provision of things that were previously missing (tenBroek 1966).

One can easily see that such efforts have entailed the first and most obvious sense of positive liberty, namely the positive provision of resources to enable people to take advantage of negative liberties. For instance, young people who cannot afford tuition need to be provided with free access to public education or scholarships and other resources such as books and computers. People who lack adequate nutrition, health care, or shelter need to be provided with such goods either through monetary payments enabling them to purchase them (cash), through direct provision of the goods (e.g., food banks), or some combination of the two (e.g., food stamps), depending on which method is the most effective in achieving the goal of maximizing the negative liberty to pursue health, comfort, and security. For instance, a large camp of tents is not a level of sufficiency for the attainment of freedom; nor are soup kitchens. Positive liberty would, like the capabilities approach, require a sufficiently robust provision of such resources to rise above a minimum threshold (Terzi 2015). Old fashioned affirmative action might fall under this category as well, in providing a way to overcome less tangible but no less serious barriers to achievement such as racist and sexist attitudes in hiring.

Disability offers many examples of this type of positive liberty. Accessible space for those with mobility impairments, such as wheelchair ramps and elevators, can (and in many countries, now must) be included in new construction, and are in many instances added on to existing structures. "Curb cuts," or depressions in the curbs at intersections, have been made in many cities enabling wheelchair users to move on sidewalks. When such mobility resources for one disability are obstacles for others – for instance, those with vision impairment for whom curbs provide valuable signals – this has been addressed in many (but not all) curb cuts through the addition of specially textured surfaces in the pavement, providing a different signal to such pedestrians and restoring their freedom of movement. "Talking" crosswalk signs similarly provide a positive addition to the streetscape that enhances the freedom of movement for persons with vision impairments. Straws, the new demon of the environmental movement, can be made sustainably for persons with upper body disabilities who use them to drink fluids. On a more complex level, one could also readily argue that employment programs to hire intellectually disabled persons for lower-skilled jobs help provide them with income and independence as well as a feeling of social inclusion and usefulness; that physical and occupational therapists help people with a variety of disabilities figure out how to navigate social and physical barriers in the built environment; and even that sexual surrogates can help provide people with some disabilities, such as paralysis, achieve sexual pleasure (Mintz 2014). All of these achievements could easily fall within a capabilities framework or a human development framework, consistent with the ideals of positive liberty (Sen 1999).

They could also fall within a negative liberty framework, however, which raises some questions. As Thomas Hobbes argued, "A FREE-MAN is he, that in those things, which by his strength and wit he is able to do, is not hindered to do what he has a will to" (Hobbes 1985: 21, 262). This very strong account of negative liberty seems to take ability as given: if I cannot walk and must use a wheelchair for mobility, stairs do not constitute a "barrier" to my liberty, but only present a condition that I am "unable" to surmount. The vast amount of attention paid to Hobbes's conception of liberty generally fails to question this "ability" requirement, and indeed it is fair to say that it is taken as a truism in contemporary freedom theory that freedom presupposes ability (Flathman 1984; Raz 1986; Benn 1988; Swanton 1992). The influence of this apparently small part of Hobbes's argument – one that is generally ignored in favor of the notion of interference, obstacle, and barrier – is actually quite significant. As Berlin argued, "If I say that I am unable to jump more than ten feet in the air, or cannot read because I am blind, or cannot understand the darker pages of Hegel, it would be eccentric to say that I am to that degree enslaved or coerced" (Berlin 1969b: 122). Freedom presupposes ability, as Hobbes maintained.

A disability perspective seeks to interrogate what is meant by "ability": am I "unable" to enter a building that requires one to climb stairs because my legs do not work, or because the building was designed without my wheelchair in mind? Who gets to decide how this situation is framed? Why can I not consider the stairs a barrier to my body, rather than my body as unable? Moreover, from a disability perspective, Berlin's equation of blindness to being unable to jump ten feet in the air – a common trope in the negative liberty defense (see Flathman 1984, for instance) – seems crudely ableist, since nobody can jump that high, as if the goal is to point out how ludicrous such claims would be. Yet it was not difficult in Berlin's day to provide a blind person with a book in Braille (today, computer technology makes many books even more accessible). Thus, it is worrying that the apparent compatibility of the "positive provision of resources" version of positive liberty with an expanded view of "barriers" within negative liberty might require us to retain some of these other underlying foundations of negative liberty that are quite ableist. Feminists have argued that the subject of liberty is a white propertied male, and this has raised our suspicions about whether the concept of liberty is itself masculinist (Hirschmann 2003; Jamieson 2003; Chambers 2008). I suggest that the subject of liberty is also decidedly nondisabled, and that theorists should be equally suspicious of simple conceptualizations of positive liberty as potentially deeply ableist.

9.2 Internal Barriers and Social Construction

In addition to this resonance with the worst aspects of negative liberty, there are other reasons that I find this version of positive liberty inadequate for disability. First, it depends on an extremely strong version of the social model: disability has virtually nothing to do with the body, but everything to do with social attitudes and the built environment (Retief and Letšosa 2018).[5] Yet increasingly, disability scholars are recognizing that some aspects of disability pertain to the physical body, such as pain. The distinction between "impairments," which all bodies have, and "disability" as a condition produced solely by the social (both attitudinal and physical) response to different impairments, ironically erases the body (Wendell 1996: 181; Siebers 2010). Tom Shakespeare, an early articulator of the social model, has argued that environmentalism reveals the limits of that model, as "it is hard to blame the natural environment on social arrangements." "Natural" barriers such as cliffs or steep forested slopes or loose sandy beaches, in his view, prove that "people with impairments will always be disadvantaged by their bodies."[6] On another level, Margaret Price (2015) has argued that bodily impairments have materiality to their disabling properties; that bodies in a sense have a "will" that escapes the bounds of the social model, and indeed of the social altogether. The body, such theorists contend, sets conditions on – and even limits to – the ways a person interacts with the world around them, including other people. While such scholars agree that the things that social model partisans advocate are vital and necessary, they are not sufficient for a full understanding of the experience of disability (see also Siebers 2010). Yet the body itself interacts with and is influenced, even produced, by the environment; new work in

[5] Though they say the social model entails viewing disability as a "social construction," they actually describe it simply as a one-dimensional category of oppression and ignore the more complex notion of social construction I develop here (Retief and Letšosa 2018: 3–5).

[6] Shakespeare (2006: 45–46). See also Kafer (2017: 202).

epigenetics and neuroscience shows that even the way our genes work responds to environmental factors like stress and pollution in significant ways (Amundson 2000; Roberts 2016; Tremain 2018).

Second, and perhaps in a contrary direction, this conception of positive liberty fails to capture the depth of social construction in discourse and language, leaving it only at a superficial level of "socialization" or "discrimination." Consider, for instance, the linguistic separation between disability and impairment offered by the social model; the latter can be as value-laden and pejorative a term as the former. Impairment refers not simply to bodily "difference," but to a lack of function measured against a standard of supposedly proper or normal functioning – standards in themselves that are socially constructed through systems of power and which in turn produce the meaning of impaired and disabled bodies. Shelley Tremain has argued that "the strict division between the categories of impairment and disability that [the social model] is claimed to institute is in fact a chimera" (Tremain 2001) because "impairment" is treated by the social model as "a naturalized construct of the relations of power that the model was designed to rebut" (Tremain 2001: 634). That is, if the social model is supposed to assert the social location of bodies, and the meaning of bodies is located in the ways that they are read and responded to, then impairments themselves seem to contradict and undermine this, because they are "theorized as essential, biological characteristics (attributes) of a 'real' body upon which recognizably disabling conditions are imposed." Instead, Tremain insists, "impairment" is a term that, just like "disability," must be instead theorized "as constructs of disciplinary knowledge/power that are incorporated into the self-understandings of some subjects" (Tremain 2001: 632).

Though these two objections seem contradictory, I believe they are complementary. Insofar as what we call "disabilities" are as socially produced as lack of education, which is generally a function of economic inequality as well as racial and gender discrimination, it adopts only the first layer of social construction that I articulated in *The Subject of Liberty,* namely ideology: The perpetuation of false beliefs about members of a subordinate group that feed into the power of a dominant group. At this level of social construction, certain targeted subordinate groups are oppressed by social relations that are changeable, sometimes more easily so than we wish to admit.[7] If those oppressive social relations would end, the members of the subordinated group would return to a basic "default"

[7] For instance, the lack of education has been identified as the single most important factor influencing wealth and poverty, not to mention (women's control over) fertility (Sen 1999).

of their "true natures." This is the fundamental idea underlying positive liberty as a positive provision. However, the model of the subject that this view implicitly relies on is the same liberal individualist model that feminists and others have long critiqued: I want what I want and you're standing in the way. You may be standing in the way of my even knowing that I want it, as well as in my way of pursuing it, but you need to stop oppressing me. For a disabled person is just a "regular" person, no different from anyone else, who happens to use a wheelchair or a seeing-eye dog or talks with her hands.

Certainly, this is not how many would characterize their own arguments, but it is what I am suggesting is the philosophical edifice that makes possible these sorts of arguments (see also Tremain 2001). My critique centers on the possibility that such assumptions underlie, and therefore threaten to undermine or at least seriously weaken, uses of positive liberty to characterize the positive provision of resources. To this end, other aspects of positive liberty need to be included in this kind of framing of positive liberty. For purposes of my argument, what is important is the fact that what is missing from the version of positive liberty as the positive provision of resources is an allowance that these conditions, both social and physical, are mutually constitutive and deeply intertwined, and inevitably help produce subjectivity. This occurs at the second and third layers of social construction. The second layer I have called materialization, and is where the ideology produces material social relations and institutions that produce the very facts that the ideology asserts. For instance, if it is declared that the world is too dangerous a place for disabled persons and they should stay in their homes, then no effort is made to provide basic adaptations such as wheelchair lifts on buses, making it more difficult for such persons to move around a city. If deaf persons are perceived as mentally deficient, they will be institutionalized and denied education and communication skills, thus ensuring intellectual damage (Burch and Joyner 2007).[8]

This brings us to the third layer of social construction, namely discourse. What I particularly wish to explore is what I consider my primary contribution to the idea of positive liberty, namely the social construction of subjectivity and desire. In *The Subject of Liberty* and *Gender, Class, and Freedom in Modern Political Theory* (Hirschmann 2003, 2008), I was able to draw on a long history of feminist critique of desire, and the ways that femininity is defined to be in line with certain desires, such as marriage,

[8] See Hirschmann (2003: 79–80), for parallel examples pertaining to gender.

maternity, and nurturance. It seemed obvious to me that we could plug women's experience into a more complex, nuanced, and sophisticated notion of "social construction" where women's desires could be understood not simply as "false consciousness," but as a complex negotiation between external factors such as the family, sexual relations, workplace discrimination, religion, and cultural practices, and internal factors of desire to suggest that what is internal is to a significant degree externally shaped and influenced, if not outright generated or caused, and that these all needed to be understood within a discursive framework of a gendered language and set of discourses that defined what it means to be a gendered person.

Should not this be applicable to disability? This is trickier. On the one hand, as I have shown already, we can see disability as a socially constructed category as much as gender and race are: what defines someone as disabled is the way that a particular body and its capacities and interactions with the physical environment are read and interpreted. This changes over time and culture: 300 years ago, in the West at least, a woman aspiring to be a university professor would have been viewed with astonishment and deemed "unwomanly:" today we accept it as normal (as we do paying them less than their male colleagues). Similarly, 300 years ago my vision impairment would have categorized me as a blind person; today, eyeglasses and contact lenses are prostheses so commonplace that we do not even think of them as prostheses. Much of this is due to technological change: advances in technology for the mass production of corrective lenses which spawned a fashion industry in frames, just as medical advances in birth control freed women to enter into the public sphere of work in sufficient numbers to pressure social acceptance of women in positions of professional prominence. Simultaneously, social movements emerged in the struggle to normalize heretofore radical and marginal viewpoints, whether the feminist movement or the disability rights movement.

On the other hand, the long history of abuse of disabled persons requires caution in asserting that their desires are as constructed as anyone else's, even though that must be true (Baynton 1996, 2016; Burch and Joyner 2007; Schweik 2010). I hesitate to make a critique that may look to many disabled scholars like appropriation by an apparently nondisabled (because all of my disabilities are invisible [Hirschmann 2015]) straight white woman who is seeking merely to destabilize the gains achieved over the past several decades. That is, of course, not my intention. But even so, as someone with invisible disabilities who will "pass" as nondisabled unless I make the effort to make my disabilities visible, I recognize that I occupy a relative position of privilege within the hierarchy of disability that an ableist society produces, not to mention the disability community itself, parallel to "colorism" within the black community (Gonzalez-Sobrino and Hughey 2016). Yet I believe these arguments are essential to understanding the critical role of positive liberty to disability.

At the very least, disabled persons' desires operate in the same socially constructed contexts as gender, race, class, religion, and so forth, because disability cuts across all other identity categories. Yet it can readily manifest itself differently. For instance, disabled women may be desexualized, seen as incapable of fulfilling the roles that define gender, such as motherhood; disabled men may be demasculinized, seen as impotent, deprived of the phallus, symbolically if not literally. Yet the framework of gender nevertheless operates as a defining framework for experience to shape and construct desire.

For instance, Amber Knight takes up disabled women's reproductive freedom. Knight defines "positive liberty theory" in terms of "the public provision of the conditions necessary to take advantage of negative liberties, and also concerns itself with actively dismantling internal barriers to freedom" (Knight 2017: 79). Eugenics has played a powerful role in seeking to control the sexual reproduction of women with disabilities. Knight shows that women with disabilities are often denied access to reproductive technologies, and in many cases even to sexual partners, because of the ways that institutional settings are arranged. They also experience "the training against motherhood" (Knight 2017: 82) that is particularly directed at disabled females, who are assumed to be incapable of raising children and/or likely to pass disability on to their offspring (Knight 2017: 75). Knight thus notes that "women with disabilities may choose to forgo motherhood because they have been bombarded with the social message that they are not 'mother material'" (Knight 2017: 78).

This "bombardment" certainly deploys an imagery that suggests such women's supposed preferences are externally generated by hostile sources that seek to colonize disabled women's desires. It is social construction at the crudest and most obvious level of "ideology," or the false representation of a class of human beings along lines that serve the power of a dominant group (Hirschmann 2003). Hence, "If we take the internal barriers to free choice seriously, it follows that the community is obligated to actively combat degrading stereotypes that portray women with disabilities as asexual, incapable of parenting, and breeders of defective offspring" (Knight 2017: 78).

Within this account, the lines between positive and negative liberty start to blur – as I believe they should in most cases, because all internal barriers are situated within social contexts that have produced, shaped, and defined them ideologically, materially, and discursively.[9] However, I think that a positive liberty approach also requires us to dig deeper. For even prior to such constructions of disabled persons as unworthy of becoming potential reproducers, Knight notes that disabled persons are often denied sexuality, both in how they are conceptualized and treated by their families and caretakers, and subsequently in their opportunities to develop sexual relationships (Knight 2017: 75–76). So, the historical sway of the social construction of persons with disabilities may seem to run counter to the social construction of nondisabled persons, and particularly girls and women.

But does it really? The reason that reproduction is seen as such a fraught ethical, social, and political issue for disabled women in the first place is the same as it is for "all women," even regardless of whether they can or want to become pregnant. It centers on the ways in which femininity is constructed as a larger framework into which disability is fitted, particularly a framework of reproductive fertility and the function of motherhood. If patriarchal ideology dictates that women's function is to serve men's sexual needs, including their needs for heirs to continue lineage and property, to control women through the patriarchal nuclear family, and through the uneven sexual division of labor, then part of the construction of disabled femininity is its elimination from those very criteria. In this sense, one could just as readily argue that the denial of reproduction to disabled women could be seen as "liberating" women from sexist norms that women's "function" is to reproduce, that women's identity is tied up with their reproductive capacity, and that all their other options in life need to be filtered through the overwhelming priority of their reproductive capacity and role (Asch and Fine 1988). Similarly, Knight's call for "supported decision making," particularly for women with cognitive disabilities, can on the one hand help reconstruct our understanding of freedom, for as she argues, "choice does not have to be radically individuated, but can be undertaken in a collaborative manner" (Knight 2017: 78), in this case involving support networks that can assist disabled women with reproduction and care for infants and children. However, on the other hand, these networks and the persons who form them are always

[9] See Hirschmann (2003: chapter 3), for my account of three layers of social construction: ideology, materialization, and discourse.

already involved in the networks of patriarchy and the social construction of femininity as locked into reproductive capacity and performance. No matter how much they might engage a pro-woman "maternal thinking" (Ruddick 1989), or seek to resist patriarchal appropriations of women's bodies and the reproductive process (O'Brien 1981), they nevertheless replicate and reinforce the idea that pregnancy and parturition are essential to femininity: to realize one's status as a woman, one must reproduce. So how reliable can they be in terms of producing "free" choices?

Similarly, Mark O'Brien's quest to employ a sex therapist (an account that became the basis for the movie *The Sessions*) demonstrates a certain facet of what I am talking about.[10] He says that "what separated me from [pursuing people to whom he was attracted] was fear – fear of others, fear of making decisions, fear of my own sexuality, and a surpassing dread of my parents." Though at the time of writing this article, and presumably sometime before, he identified this fear as a barrier – an internal barrier, in true positive liberty fashion – to doing something he wanted to do, up until the point of seeing his emotion *as* fear and *as* a barrier, what role did this emotion play in forming his subjectivity as a person who was not sexually active? He particularly notes the presence of his parents, "who seemed to have an uncanny ability to know what I was thinking" in his self-imagining, and this shaped the way that he thought of himself as a (non)sexual being. For it was not that his parents didn't talk about sex; in his mind, they fostered the notion that "no one did." This "self-hatred and fear," he posits, emerged from this sexually repressive environment. Yet his body would assert its needs when he could not control having erections and orgasms when being given baths by attendants, who also never spoke with him about it.

All of these things, in generating his "self-hatred and pessimism," entail a positive liberty concept of "internal barriers." However, they also demonstrate that such internal barriers are externally generated by his interaction with and treatment by others. Indeed, O'Brien questions whether he would have needed a sex therapist if he had had "intensive psychotherapy," beginning from when he got polio as a child, speculating that it would have allowed him to reject "the cultural standards of beauty and physical perfection" that he felt led to his self-devaluing. This can lead to the conclusion that positive liberty requires the provision of enabling

[10] Mark O'Brien, "On Seeing a Sex Surrogate," *The Sun Magazine*, May 1990, accessed online March 1, 2020, at https://thesunmagazine.org/issues/174/on-seeing-a-sex-surrogate. Since there are no page numbers in this online article, all quotes from this discussion will not be further footnoted.

resources; Kevin Mintz argues that sex therapy is one such resource that society should provide to help disabled persons fulfill their desires (Mintz 2014).

We must, of course, accept O'Brien's account of his experience of these feelings, for we have no external referent to serve as a basis for "second guessing" him; yet Taylor indicates that this is a vital part of positive liberty (Taylor 1979). For instance, one might ask whether the internal barriers were simply internal, in that O'Brien never liked his body – something that is true for many people, male and female alike of different ages, whether or not they have a disability – and so he interpreted what were, in fact, neutral interactions with his parents or others in a negative or oppressive way. Similarly, it is possible that his perception of emotions like disgust in his caretakers is a projection; perhaps they in fact cared for him with respect and, for instance, did not object to his erections or ejaculations while bathing but did not speak to him out of sympathy for his evident embarrassment and respect for his privacy. Perhaps he was seeking to rationalize his own fears and anxieties about rejection and attractiveness, which most humans share. Perhaps this really was just all "him."

As I argued in *Subject of Liberty*, however, internal barriers are rarely simply or exclusively internal, because as human beings we live in relationships with others that always frame, shape, and make possible our experience of ourselves. So this hatred of his own body might come from observing the motor skills that others have and feeling angry that he lacked such power; or from feeling resentful of his profound dependency on others who he might not even like, but who must help him perform the most mundane actions that others take for granted. Even if his anger and resentment might come from some genetic makeup of his personality that seeks total independence – perhaps he produces too much testosterone, and his impulses are thwarted by a body that seeks to act aggressively – such genetic tendencies would unavoidably be triggered, shaped, and fed by his experiences with others.

All such speculation, no matter how remotely possible – or even viewed as offensive from a disability rights perspective – should be considered if we are to engage a full understanding of freedom, for as Taylor notes, "second-guessing" persons' motivations is central to positive liberty, no matter how troubling it seems (see Hirschmann 2020). However, we need not grant it dispositive force: the account of his narrative, and how he perceives his own feelings, must also be given appreciable consideration. O'Brien exhibits, after all, the central philosophical requirement of self-reflection, and that, in the standard discourse of positive liberty, carries weight. Assessing his freedom through this individualist focus becomes a complicated task with little hope for a satisfying conclusion.

9.3 Positive Liberty and the Social Construction of Desire

A social constructivist framework can save us from this sort of individualistic psychologizing to engage a more political approach to the idea of internal barriers as socially produced. Along with saying that internal barriers are not just internal, however, it also forces us to confront that they are not just "barriers," they are also importantly constitutive of who we are. As Tremain observes about Michel Foucault's theory, "social power is productive of the objects on which it acts and is diffused throughout society and culture rather than first and foremost repressive and centralized" (Tremain 2001: 21). She argues that the very category of "impairment" and "disability" are themselves functions of this kind of productive power even as that power is simultaneously repressive. This theme, which I developed in *The Subject of Liberty* (Hirschmann 2003), is important to understanding the gendered character of our understanding of freedom; here I am suggesting that it is also important to understanding the "enabled" character of freedom, the ways that supposedly "able-bodied" persons are made so in part by the way society is structured, including the way that we perceive the body and its relationship to the physical environment, whether natural or built.

Returning to Knight's example, for instance, we cannot conclude that a desire for a child is uncomplicated by sexist ideals of femininity; indeed, ways of thinking about reproduction are part of the apparatus of gender. Yet rather than that being a reason to simply reject them, those ideals help constitute us as human beings and play an important part in shaping desire. Sexist ideals of femininity and masculinity are part of every person's experience and identity in any society where "gender" exists as a binary concept; whether they embrace those ideals or reject and react against them, they constitute the possibilities of meaning for all persons as long as gender exists as a conceptual category of social organization and personal identity.[11] Similarly, ability is a conceptual framework for organizing bodies and persons. As Rosemary Garland-Thomson's notion of the

[11] My qualified language is meant to acknowledge that there are some minority cultures, particularly aboriginal, where gender does not appear to be a binary in the dominant framework; but even in such cultures, gender is a significant demarcation of difference. See for instance Towle and Morgan (2002).

"normate" posits, many cultures deploy an idealized vision of the "able--bodied" person who is in perfect health and physical strength – always white, and almost always male – an ideal that hardly anyone can ever achieve, since even remarkably fit athletes can get sick (Thomson 1997: 8; Keh 2020). Yet it serves as a demarcating fantasy to separate "able bodied" from "disabled." Accordingly, "disability . . . is the attribution of corporeal deviance – not so much a property of bodies as a product of cultural rules about what bodies should be or do" (Thomson 1997: 6). Such attribution does not merely describe what already is, but creates or produces it: not to say that the term "paraplegic" itself causes someone's legs not to function in the way that the majority of human legs function, but rather that it creates a particular way of seeing that function as it relates to that body.

Similarly, unable to move his arms or legs, O'Brien is clearly in need of the help of others to experience sexual pleasure, as he cannot masturbate; in conducting the therapy, the sex therapist seeks to individualize sexuality so that it is an expression of pleasure for O'Brien, and that is determined to a significant degree by the possibilities of his body. S. Graby and A. Greenstein claim that "the 'polymorphous' sexuality of disabled people, in which – even in heterosexual relationships – heteronormative sex acts such as penis-vagina penetration are deprivileged, can expand the boundaries of the erotic in positive and productive ways . . . bodily difference can productively open up routes to challenging and subverting restrictive sexual norms and inventing new forms of pleasure" (Graby and Greenstein 2016: 242). In the film version of his story, the therapist helps him, to a limited extent, explore what areas of his body are available for erogenous pleasure and different techniques and methods that he can deploy. However, in O'Brien's own essay, the sessions focus primarily on standard ideals of heterosexual intercourse. In both cases, the therapy, including both O'Brien's expectations and the therapist's approach, is also shaped by both his and her conceptions of masculinity and heterosexuality, which are constructed by a wider culture as well as O'Brien's relation to that culture as a disabled man. For instance, the assumed starting point of his story is the desire to have sex with a woman, but he does not apparently consider his choice of a female therapist rather than a male, as if sexuality were naturally predetermined rather than socially produced. Moreover, the larger question of how he, as a disabled person, comes to the experience in the first place, is never addressed; we are expected to accept the notion that heterosexual desire is natural. We want to acknowledge physiological response; but as Judith Butler has forced us to ask, are physiological responses and the experience of sexual pleasure not themselves culturally mediated? So, we would need to consider how clients got the sense of self and desire that they brought to the sexual surrogacy therapy sessions in the first place, and how they change the ways that they think about themselves and their desires – which O'Brien apparently does not. In the film, O'Brien is portrayed as having overcome all obstacles, and concludes with a screenshot telling us that he married a woman, but he concludes his essay with a rather unsatisfying resolution, that although he had achieved his goals, obstacles remain. One might think that this would cause him to pursue the therapy further, but he ceases, not merely because he is worried about cost, but because he feels awkward with the therapist after failing to maintain an erection for more than a minute after penetration, again invoking a standard ideal of masculine sexuality.

Finally, we need to ask what is particular to disability about this, given that all women and men are told by popular media what "good sex" and "femininity" and "masculinity" mean: a disabled woman or man who has gained their primary understanding of sexuality from the movies may well think that twenty seconds of vigorous sexual intercourse is all that they need and want, and indeed define that as an ideal of feminine or masculine sexuality. Is fulfilling such a desire a genuine expression of freedom, since the way sex is portrayed in the movies is so phallocentric and misleading? When they fail to achieve it, will they reassess it or will they simply internalize that as a failure? Does disability simply constitute a series of barriers to achieving sexual satisfaction, or is it just as socially constructed as nondisabled experience, even if in a different way? Relatedly, if a disabled person has been told all their lives that they are not sexual beings, or even further, if they have been surgically altered to forestall their becoming sexual beings in the first place, as in the case of Ashley X (Kittay 2011) or, in past eras, the castration of intellectually disabled men, then the nature of desire itself and how sexuality is imagined and produced through disability experience are open to question and require a deeper understanding of positive liberty than the simple provision of resources.

Eli Clare illustrates this deeper understanding which I believe is helpful to freedom. A hiker and climber, he embodies the idea of the "supercrip," the term for a disabled person who strives to achieve beyond what is perceived as the "limits" of their disability. Supercripdom entails the disabled person who does what others assume, or have told him, he cannot do, whether that is climbing a mountain, competing in the Olympics, or even finding a lover (Clare 2009: 3). Most nondisabled persons would not see the supercrip as having an internal barrier, but rather as an internalized empowerment (see Kafer 2013). However, Clare offers a different perspective and writes about "internalizing supercripdom" as a potential blockage to his own self-acceptance.

In a climb up Mount Adams, in New Hampshire's White Mountains, Clare finds the going more challenging than expected, despite his considerable experience climbing and hiking, due to wet conditions. The limitation he experiences, he recognizes, is located in the physical rather than social – what prevents him from achieving his goal is not about curb cuts or signage but his body's particularity, the extra energy it takes to calculate where and how to take each step, and the realistic fear of the consequences of injury, as opposed to his nondisabled hiking companion who can climb much more quickly and has more room for error. His experience of his body is part of what shapes his intellectual and emotional experience of this event: not only his determination to climb, but his frustration at being unable to complete it. The body is located within normatively social frameworks, however, and "the mountain as metaphor looms large in the lives of marginalized people" (Clare 2009: 2) where being on top of the mountain is socially valued. So, he also recognizes that "if part of what happened to me up there was about impairment, another part was about desire, my desire to climb mountains" (Clare 2009: 8). The extraordinariness of mountain climbing is something that comes from his childhood in rural Oregon where he was abandoned by his mother and sexually abused by his father and his father's friends; he developed a connection with nature as his refuge, but also as his affirmation of existence in the face of those who sought to make his subjectivity invisible or valueless.

Where does the freedom lie in this story? What is that freedom? Certainly, hiking would seem to "free" him from the negative experience of abuse, and his accomplishments might even be said by some to "free" him from the limits of his disability. However, Clare recognizes that desires come out of and are mediated by experience, and we need to be self-critically aware of them and the cost they can exact. Hence his desire to climb Mt. Adams is motivated by his love of climbing; but it also, he recognizes, comes from a fear of his body's limitations. Thus, reflecting on how others react to his story, he notes that they offer rationalization, such as the wetness and the weather, for the supposed failure, and suggest that he would have made it had the weather been better – that his body could have overcome the mountain had conditions been different. But "I never once heard, 'You made the right choice when you turned around'" (Clare 2009: 10). That is, the interpretation of his experience as a failure of his body, rather than the success of his judgment, layers over his experience to reinforce a shaping of his desire and its relation to his body. Supercrip, he suggests, can be a trap. Self-awareness, and positive liberty's second-guessing of oneself, yields a different way of understanding his relation to his body, to the mountain, to the conditions. "Post-revolution," he proffers, "I expect there will still be literal mountains I want to climb and can't, but I'll be able to say without doubt, without hesitation, 'Let's turn around here. This one is too steep, too slippery for my feet'" (Clare 2009: 13). Clare's self-awareness of the limits of his body and how that has shaped his desire creates a more open space for the positive liberty conception, one that recognizes the body as a term of both constraint and possibility to desire, subjectivity, and imagined futures. The positive liberty that disability can yield is a conception of freedom in which desire and subjectivity are seen as social constructions through time and space, culture, and bodies, contingent and ever-emerging.

CHAPTER 10

Positive Freedom and Paternalism

Horacio Spector

According to a standard account, liberalism is committed to the rejection of legal paternalism. The usual tenet is that paternalistic interferences with people's free choice violate their right to individual autonomy. Liberals assume that individual autonomy has "lexical priority" over individual well-being. This assumption makes the right to individual autonomy absolute. Therefore, even if paternalistic interference greatly enhances the well-being of an individual, it is impermissible. Because individual autonomy outweighs individual well-being, paternalistic interferences should be banned in a liberal polity. However, the fact is that paternalistic policies are common currency in most liberal democracies, and liberal governments claim or at least assume that those policies are not inimical to liberal principles.

Legal measures that discourage or ban such choices as smoking, consuming drugs, and gambling, or that encourage or require wearing a helmet when riding motorcycles, using seat belts in cars and buses, and purchasing health insurance, are generally justified on the basis of those interventions' expected contribution to people's own good. One way of looking at such interventions, which can be deemed *utilitarian*, is that they increase people's well-being or welfare, sometimes by eliminating or reducing self-inflicted harm. Another way, which can be called *positive libertarian*, is that such interventions are sometimes necessary to promote people's positive freedom. Basically, positive freedom is an individual's effective power to conceive, choose, and perform courses of action that realize his idea of a meaningful life. On this view, paternalistic interferences can be justified as necessary ways of maximizing individuals' positive freedom.

Suppose Congress passes a law that levies a special tax on the interstate commercialization of certain drugs in order to deter their consumption.

I am grateful for helpful comments to Larry Alexander and Guido Pincione.

This policy curtails free choice in removing the option of buying drugs without the duty to pay the special tax. (I assume that the commercialization of those drugs was totally free before the new law.) However, many people would think that this policy does not disrupt but rather advances the positive freedom of would-be consumers. Rather than a measure oriented to people's well-being, it can be just a way of augmenting their positive liberty. In fact, it seems natural to claim that drug addictions reduce people's positive freedom through the formation of psychological constraints on behavioral patterns that would otherwise enhance their capacity to lead a meaningful life over time. In this chapter, I will suggest a positive freedom-enhancing justification for the state to apply paternalistic interventions. More specifically, I will defend a *positive libertarian* approach to paternalism.

I focus on *legal* or *state paternalism*, that is, paternalistic policies adopted by state action through legal rules, directives, or standards. A definition of legal paternalism will be helpful. I will say that government *A* acts paternalistically toward citizen *S* with respect to *S*'s choice if (1) *A* nudges or causes *S* to make a choice *C* that he would otherwise not probably make on his own by raising the costs of some other alternatives open to *S*, removing them from *S*'s set of legally permissible options or restructuring *S*'s formalized decision-making procedure, (2) without *S*'s ex-ante actual consent, and (3) with the intent or (implicit or explicit) claim that *C* will protect, ensure, or enhance *S*'s interests, well-being or positive freedom more effectively than an alternative choice that *S* would probably make in the absence of *A*'s paternalistic action (or similar action by *A* or others).

My argument is twofold. First, I will argue that paternalistic interventions do infringe the right to direct one's life, and that, therefore, the scope of this right cannot be redefined to conceal the conflict. However, the fact that there is an unavoidable conflict between individual sovereignty and paternalism does not mean that paternalism is necessarily unjustifiable. My second claim is that, since the right to direct one's life is not absolute, it can be outweighed by considerations related to an individual's positive freedom. Especially, the state can sometimes justifiably prevent an individual from losing positive freedom by intervening in his choice set or choice procedure.

I also contend that the conflict between the right to direct one's life and the state's prerogative to engage in paternalistic actions to protect one's own positive freedom is parallel to the conflict between individual rights and the state's prerogative to enhance social welfare. It is generally recognized that *sometimes* it is permissible to infringe an individual's right when the net gains in overall welfare exceed a certain amount. For instance, in Trolley cases, it is morally permissible for the driver or the bystander to turn the trolley toward one person as the only way to save the lives of a sufficiently greater number of others. By the same token, it seems sometimes permissible for the state to redirect economic threats in order to minimize overall harm (Pincione 2007). The trade-off between a right and the maximization of social welfare is struck by weighing the moral urgency of the right and the moral importance of increased social welfare. One version of this view rests on *threshold deontology*, a variety of deontological theory that allows the infringement of moral constraints when doing so is necessary to prevent social or collective losses that exceed a certain threshold. Threshold deontology presupposes that rights and public goals can be ranked along a cardinal scale of moral urgency or importance.

I will argue that, similarly, the right to direct one's life can be balanced against an individual's positive freedom. Thus, the argument that justifies the state's authority to infringe a moral right to maximize social welfare could also be used to justify an intrusion on someone's individual autonomy when this is needed to increase his positive freedom. The protection of an agent's positive freedom is a permissible moral goal, and, sometimes, this goal can offset the right to direct one's life. Paternalistic infringements of that right are not justified on the basis that such infringements do not infringe rights when their scope is properly demarcated. Instead, I acknowledge that paternalistic actions set back individuals' autonomous choices, but I nonetheless claim that such interferences are justified because, on some occasions, positive freedom considerations outweigh the right to sovereign individual choice.

I will deploy my argument in this sequence. In Section 10.1, I discuss traditional and contemporary forms of weak paternalism. The latter are founded on empirical findings in the field of behavioral economics. All forms of weak paternalism argue that permissible paternalistic interferences do not really curtail individual autonomy. I reject the definitional strategy of specifying the right to self-direction in such a way that paternalistic interferences become autonomy-respecting. In Section 10.2, I show that the right to positive freedom can sometimes be justifiably infringed. In Section 10.3, I distinguish between the *interpersonal* and the *intrapersonal* maximization of positive freedom. In the following section, I argue that paternalistic actions (not necessarily weak paternalistic actions) are justifiable if their positive freedom gains exceed a certain threshold ratio. Though I do not establish the magnitude of this threshold, I suggest that it is comparable to the threshold that governs interpersonal welfare maximization. I conclude in Section 10.5.

10.1 Autonomy-Respecting Forms of Paternalism

Legal paternalism has been classified in diverse ways. Joel Feinberg proposed an influential distinction between strong and weak paternalism (Feinberg 1980: 118–123). *Strong paternalism* allows interventions with individuals' choices if such interventions can cause them greater benefits or spare them greater harms. On this view, an individual's "own good" is a sufficient ground for legitimating interferences with people's choices. This is the kind of paternalism that Mill famously rejects in *On Liberty* by stating that "[h]is own good [the good of any member of a civilized community], either physical or moral, is not a sufficient warrant" to interfere with his liberty of action (Mill 1978[1859]: 9). By contrast, *weak paternalism* is mediated by a voluntariness standard. According to weak paternalism, "the state has the right to prevent self-regarding harmful conduct only when it is substantially nonvoluntary or when temporary intervention is necessary to establish whether it is voluntary or not" (Mill 1978[1859]: 118). Thus, weak paternalism only allows interventions that prevent someone from making a choice that is not under his full voluntary control. On this view, an agent's choice is not under his full voluntary control if it is caused by coercion or manipulation rather than by his deliberative processes, or those processes are vitiated by false information. Given that coercion or lack of information can impact someone's choice to different degrees, the difference between weak and strong paternalism might be considered as one of degree (Alexander 2008: 95–96).

Since nonvoluntary choices do not properly express an individual's autonomous choice, Feinberg alleges that weak paternalism respects the "inviolable sovereignty of the individual person over his own life" (Mill 1978[1859]: 125). The concept of *inviolable* sovereignty is missing in the strong paternalistic argument. For strong paternalists, the justification of paternalistic interventions resides on the greater good that the state can allow persons to enjoy by thwarting or impeding their judgments and choices. Weak paternalism tries to reconcile some interventions with individual sovereignty in the guise of a right to direct one's own life. On this view, the state does not violate individual sovereignty in pursuing a justifiable paternalistic policy in as much as it does not thwart or impede a person's voluntary choices. Yet the truth of this claim depends on how we understand the notion of voluntary choice.

Donald VanDeVeer describes weak paternalism in this way: "[t]he central idea is that although we may be justified in invasively deflecting an agent away from a self-harming outcome toward which he moves as a result of a 'nonvoluntary choice', we cannot nudge him toward an outcome which is foreign to his own, permissible, basic ends or goals" (VanDeVeer 1986: 87). He adds: "If we justifiably can substitute our judgment for that of the competent person it must be to nudge him back onto a path compatible with his own goals and values" (VanDeVeer 1986: 87). VanDeVeer claims that this characterization is too broad because it sanctions interferences that the subject might object to even if he were informed and unimpaired. The problem with weak paternalism is that it focuses on the actual causal sequence of a choice to establish its voluntariness, and the fact that a choice is not voluntary does not entail that the agent would not have made a fully voluntary different choice with identical content. For instance, a Jehovah's Witness who refuses a blood transfusion because he is confused or terrified might still object to it even if his choice was made in a fully voluntary way. For this reason, VanDeVeer defends paternalism in terms of individualized hypothetical consent. His appeal to hypothetical individualized consent is expressed in what he calls the "Principle of Autonomy-Respecting Paternalism." According to this principle, *A*'s paternalistic interference, *X*, with a generally competent subject, *S*, is justified if and only if (1) *A*'s doing *X* involves no presumptive wrong toward *S* or others, or (2) *A*'s doing *X* does not wrong those other than *A* or *S*, and either (1) *S* has given currently operative valid consent to *A* to do *X*, or (2) *S* would validly consent to *A*'s doing *X* if *S* were aware of the relevant circumstances, and *S*'s normal capacities for deliberation and choice were not impaired (VanDeVeer 1986: 88). Like other defenders of weak paternalism, VanDeVeer says that paternalistic interferences are justifiable only if they are autonomy-preserving in a defined way.

Richard Thaler and Cass Sunstein endorse a different variety of weak paternalism, which was originally proposed by Gerald Dworkin (1983). Interpreting Mill's anti-paternalistic argument in *On Liberty*, Dworkin argued that while sometimes it may be permissible for the state to restrain individuals' freedom for their own collective good, "[i]t is because coercing individuals for their own good denies their status as independent entities that Mill objects to it so strongly and in such absolute terms" (Dworkin 1983: 27). This argument against paternalism would allow paternalistic restraints in cases in which "irrational propensities" ("deficiencies in cognitive and emotional capacities and avoidable and unavoidable ignorance") can cause people to choose and act in nonautonomous, irrational ways. In those cases, the justification of paternalistic measures should be argued for "in terms of what fully rational individuals would accept as forms of protection" (Dworkin 1983: 29).

In a similar vein, Thaler and Sunstein make the case for the moral justification of governmental modifications of such decision-making procedures that, if left untrammeled, would incline individuals to make choices that are detrimental to their own good (either individual or collective). The core of this form of paternalism, which they call *libertarian paternalism*, is not to constrain individuals' freedom of choice but rather to induce them to make desirable choices by reformulating the method of choice in ways that, according to the findings of modern behavioral economics, can rectify their irrational decisional propensities. Thaler and Sunstein's appeal to behavioral economics to justify the paternalistic reshaping of decision-making procedures is a valuable contribution. They indicate diverse ways in which individuals can be nudged into doing some actions without restricting their profile of alternatives. For instance, they focus on such cognitive biases as the framing effect, loss aversion, present bias, and affect heuristics (i.e., emotion-driven decisions).

The interesting feature of this variety of weak paternalism is not its redefinition of the concept of voluntariness but rather its endorsement of paternalistic policies that eschew barriers or impediments to action and nudge individuals into courses of action that enhance their well-being by changing the *choice architecture*, that is, the way in which options are framed or structured (Thaler and Sunstein 2008, 2014). Unlike traditional weak paternalists, Thaler and Sunstein do not defend interventions that make it costly or impermissible for agents to pursue certain options, but rather those that modify the choice procedure. For instance, a libertarian paternalist would recommend reframing an agent's options in such a way that she is given the possibility to opt-out of a retirement program, instead of being asked to opt-in. Like other weak paternalists, Sunstein alleges that his paternalistic prescriptions are not violative of liberalism's commitment to individual autonomy (Sunstein 2019).

Though insightful, Thaler and Sunstein's argument leaves many reasonable paternalistic policies unexplained. In effect, the range of permissible paternalistic measures according to Thaler and Sunstein does not include many policies that are regarded as unexceptional in most liberal democracies. For instance, some municipal laws ban swimming in contaminated public waters. These laws remove that option from the permissible set of options of individuals, yet it's difficult to figure out how those municipalities could protect swimmers by modifying their choice architecture. Suppose municipalities require individuals who want to swim in those areas to fill in and sign a special form by which they declare that they disclaim public authorities' responsibility. It's very dubious that such procedural manipulation would serve to promote the goal of public safety as efficiently as the simple expedient of prohibiting swimming in those waters. It's very easy to imagine other examples. It is plain that we must often engage in non-libertarian paternalistic actions to protect individuals' well-being. If so, what's the point of restricting permissible paternalism to the procedural manipulation of the choice architecture? Legal paternalistic interventions that cause individuals to choose certain alternatives infringe on the right to autonomous choice. However, infringements on individual rights are sometimes morally justified.

10.2 The Right to Positive Freedom and Moral Justifications

Positive freedom is traditionally contrasted with negative freedom (Berlin 1969b; Spector 2010). To start with, negative freedom is narrower than positive freedom. In principle, free agency can be affected by a diversity of constraints (i.e., difficulties, impediments, and barriers). Constraints may be "positive" or "negative" factors. Negative freedom is typically curtailed by *positive factors* (e.g., acts of interference). Positive freedom can be diminished by positive *or negative factors* (e.g., lack of material means to execute an action).

Constraints can also be "external" or "internal." While *external constraints* characterize the environment or setting in which an agent acts, *internal constraints* are primarily grounded in the agent's mental makeup or her bodily constitution. Ideals of negative freedom only exclude external constraints imposed by others' *acts* (for instance, force and threats). By contrast, ideals of positive freedom often rule out all or most kinds of external and internal constraints (either negative or positive). Thus, an individual's positive (or negative) freedom may be diminished by threats, barriers, obstructions, and other forms of interference effectuated by other people, including the government. However, a widespread conception of positive freedom, which equates it with *power* or *opportunity*, requires the absence of *both* external positive and negative factors (Arendt 1961: 143; Macpherson 1973; Taylor 1979; Crocker 1980; Gewirth 1982: 311–117; Baldwin 1984; Sen 1985: 169–221, 1987, 1993, 1999; Christman 2005a: 79–88). At the outset, I have understood positive freedom according to this conception.[1] Therefore, positive freedom is reduced by poverty,

[1] Other conceptions of positive freedom are more robust in that they also exclude internal constraints of various kinds. Internal constraints encompass psychological, cultural, intellectual, physical, and economic difficulties that prevent an individual's real opportunity to choose and carry out various alternatives or plans of action. I will not consider these conceptions of positive liberty in this chapter.

because lack of money reduces an individual's power or capability to perform valuable courses of action.[2] Positive libertarians contend that social circumstances can increase or decrease positive freedom. Accordingly, we can understand the *right* to positive freedom as a set of liberties, claim rights, powers, and immunities that protect an individual's effective power to conceive, choose, and perform courses of action that realize his idea of a meaningful life.

The *right to self-direction* is basically the right to direct one's own life *without* the interference of other people. This right is an important aspect of the *right to positive freedom*. Therefore, the right to self-direction is entailed by the right to positive freedom (Spector 1992: 97–98). Insofar as the right to positive freedom includes the right to self-direction, this right is in tension with legal paternalism. Clearly, paternalism infringes people's right to direct their lives according to their own judgments. For instance, if the state imposes on the public the obligation to vaccinate against a disease, it infringes their right to direct their lives. (I assume that the option of refusing vaccination counts as a form of directing one's life.) However, the infringement might be justifiable for various reasons. The vaccine may prevent the disease and eradicate the virus that causes it. If the state intervention is morally justifiable as a form of protecting someone's right to positive freedom, it does not violate the right to self-direction. Only unjustifiable infringements can be considered right violations.

To be sure, the conflict between the right to direct one's life and the state's claim to enhance an individual's good by nudging or prodding him into making a certain choice can be settled by specifying the right to self-direction. Specification of rights proceeds by demarcating their scope through the introduction of exceptions or qualifications (Thomson 1976: 10–11; Feinberg 1978: 98–104). The trick is to redefine the right to direct one's life in such a way that it accommodates a bundle of permissible paternalistic interferences. Once we redefine the reach of the right, it is no longer at odds with permissible legal paternalism.

Infringements of rights are sometimes morally justifiable. Thus, most moral rights admit justifications such as self-defense, defense of others, and lesser-evil justifications. Similarly, the right to self-direction is not absolute: it sometimes allows paternalistic interferences. The obvious example is Mill's bridge example. Even though Mill says that "in the part which

[2] I am not preempting Gerald Cohen's argument that lack of money reduces negative freedom as well (Cohen 2011b). The distinction between negative and positive freedom can be blurred by understanding the notion of interference in an expansive way.

merely concerns himself," an individual's "independence is, of right, absolute," he acknowledges that there are cases in which the government can permissibly prevent individuals from performing actions that will certainly harm them. Thus, Mill says that

> if a public officer or anyone else saw a person attempting to cross a bridge which had been ascertained to be unsafe, and there were no time to warn him of his danger, they might seize him and turn him back, without any real infringement of his liberty; for liberty consists in doing what one desires, and he does not desire to fall into the river. (Mill 1978[1859]: 9, 95)

In this case, the justification *undercuts* the right to self-direction by specifying its content or scope in such a way that the right *permits* the officer's stopping the pedestrian before he steps into the bridge. However, if the question is the justifiability of the paternalistic interference, specifying the right to self-direction begs the question. Rather than justifying the conclusion that the interference is permissible, the specification of the right presupposes the permissibility of the interference.

Moral justifications do not undercut rights but rather rebut them by appealing to the greater good that is sought by the justification. Justifications are rebutting defeaters. Typically, they include a *proportionality constraint.* Rights can be permissibly infringed only if the moral urgency of the good sought is reasonably stronger than the moral weight of the infringement. If the moral urgency of the appeal to the good does *not* significantly exceed the moral importance or weight of the right infringement, the infringement is unjustifiable. For example, if by turning the trolley the bystander can save only one person at the cost of causing the death of another, his throwing the switch is probably impermissible.

Moral justifications that appeal to the greater good are generally *standards.* Standards are formulated in vague terms such as "reasonably," "proportionately," and so on, which can be applied to concrete situations only by exercising evaluative judgments. In moral justifications, a ratio qualifies the extent to which the good pursued by the infringement must exceed the intrinsic disvalue of the infringement. If the good to be obtained is *reasonably* or *proportionately* greater than the moral evil caused by the infringement, the act is permissible. However, vagueness in moral justifications can be interpreted as holding at the linguistic level (*semantic vagueness*), as showing a lack of knowledge (*epistemic vagueness*), or as reflecting indeterminacy at the level of the normative content (*normative vagueness*). If the vagueness is normative, the vague formulation figuring in the standard mirrors the normative indeterminacy. Then the moral proposition is by necessity a standard. However, if the vagueness is semantic or epistemic, it would be possible, in principle, to discern or find the rule that lurks behind the standard. Thus, the standard might be just a vague formulation of a precise rule that either applies or does not apply to a concrete situation.

10.3 Interpersonal and Intrapersonal Maximization

An infringement of the right to self-direction can be analogized to infringements of moral constraints. Moderate strands of moral deontologism hold that such infringements are justifiable if they are necessary means to achieve a greater overall good. Deontologists disagree about the conditions of justifiability. For instance, some deontologists require that the bystander in Trolley situations not intend the killing of the innocent person trapped on the sidetrack. Other deontologists focus on the trade-off between the moral costs and the moral gains (i.e., the greater good achieved). Thus, threshold deontologists claim that compliance with moral constraints becomes optional when the evil caused by the compliance reaches a certain threshold. If by respecting someone's right to freedom an agent will cause great human suffering, infringing the right becomes permissible (or perhaps obligatory given certain conditions) (Nozick 1974: 30; Thomson 1990: 153; Ellis 1992; Brennan 1995; Alexander 2000; Zamir and Medina 2010). On this view, the proportionality constraint is interpreted as a *threshold condition*. When the condition is met, the infringement is permissible; otherwise, the moral balance between the gain and the loss is impermissible. Though in ordinary morality, the proportionality constraint is often expressed in fuzzy terms, threshold deontologists say that this kind of vagueness is semantic or epistemic; objectively, they claim, there is normative *determinacy*: a moral rule sets up a precise threshold for each justification.

To define the threshold condition, we need a cardinal scale that allows proportional comparisons between the moral weight of both rights and welfare. Then, if a welfare-based goal requires encroachment on a right, we must determine the *ratio* between the moral urgency of the greater good that is sought (*G*) and the moral weight of the right infringement (*I*). We can state the threshold condition in simple mathematical terms:

$$\frac{G}{I} \geq K. \qquad (10.1)$$

By convention, we can bracket the negative and positive signs of all real numbers. If the ratio is equal to or greater than a certain threshold (*K*), the infringement is justifiable; otherwise, it is impermissible – a *violation* of the right. Alternatively, the formula can be read as stating that the ratio of the value of the greater good G to the disvalue of I, that is, $G{:}I$, is equal to or greater than K. If an agent wants to assess whether the achievement of a greater good justifies curtailment of a moral right, she ought to establish the ratio between the seriousness of the right infringement and the moral importance of the good to be caused (or the evil to be avoided). The ratio must be equal to or greater than K for the trade-off to be *proportionate* (permissible); otherwise, it is impermissible.

Though the bridge example illustrates rights specification, Mill gives other examples that can be understood as *moral justifications* to infringe the right to self-direction. He says, approvingly, that an engagement by which a person sells himself or allows himself to be sold as a slave is null and void, that is, unenforceable by law or opinion (Mill 1978[1859]: 101). Likewise, he holds that it is permissible for the state to tax stimulants or prohibit *public* gambling houses to discourage individuals from using stimulants "beyond a very moderate quantity" or engaging in addictive gambling (Mill 1978[1859]: 99–101). While using stimulants and gambling may impose risks on oneself and others (for instance, family members), selling oneself into slavery has adverse consequences in terms of one's positive freedom. Mill asserts that "by selling himself for a slave, he [an individual] abdicates his liberty; he foregoes any future use of it beyond that single act" (Mill 1978[1859]: 101). If the state were to enforce the slavery contract, it would commit a sort of inconsistency. On the one hand, it would support positive freedom by granting individuals freedom of contract but, on the other hand, it would betray positive freedom by facilitating the enforcement of an individual's abdication of his liberty. Unlike other libertarian views (Alexander 2013), a positive libertarian theory of paternalism cannot permit indentured servitude.

Now if an appeal to the greater good can justify the infringement of an individual's moral right, why could it not be also permissible to infringe an individual's right of self-direction by actions that increase his overall positive freedom? In fact, the prohibition of the self-enslavement contract is an instance in which it is permissible to infringe the seller's right of self-direction as a way of maximizing his overall liberty (in the long run). The right to self-direction is a side-constraint; therefore, it rules out interferences with an individual even if such interferences maximize his positive freedom over time. Just as moral rights generally ban the maximization of overall well-being, the right to self-direction bans the intertemporal maximization of an individual's positive freedom. Now, the right to self-direction is based on the deontological respect for positive freedom as a component of individual autonomy (Spector 1992: 97–98). Thus, it is self-defeating to prohibit infringing *S*'s right to self-direction when the infringement will effectively produce a *sufficiently greater* amount of *S*'s overall freedom. It's not maximization, but rather *proportionate maximization* that threshold deontologists require for the infringement to be justifiable.

Actually, paternalistic interferences that enhance the addressees' positive freedom are more reasonable than those paternalistic actions that increase their physical or moral well-being. Since the right to self-direction protects positive freedom, the intertemporal maximization of positive freedom may sometimes justify the infringement of that right. Treating the right to self-direction in a different way would be arbitrary. Why should *interpersonal* good-based considerations have a justifying force that *intrapersonal* positive libertarian considerations lack? In particular, why would it be impermissible to infringe *S*'s right to self-direction when doing so is necessary to avoid a disproportionate loss of *S*'s own positive freedom?

My positive libertarian case for paternalism rests on threshold deontologism. Thus, I will assume the threshold formulation of the proportionality constraint in greater-good justifications. The symmetry between the interpersonal and the intrapersonal justification of rights infringements suggests the following analogical argument:

> It is permissible for government *A* to infringe *S*'s right to self-direction for the overall good when the ratio between the infringement and the overall good is equal to or greater than threshold *K*.
>
> If it is permissible for government *A* to infringe *S*'s right to self-direction for increasing the overall good when the ratio is equal to or greater than *K*, then it is also permissible for government *A* to infringe *S*'s right to self-direction for increasing *S*'s own good when the ratio is equal to or greater than *K*.
>
> Therefore, it is permissible for government *A* to infringe *S*'s right to self-direction for increasing *S*'s own good when the ratio is equal to or greater than *K*.

This reasoning is intuitive because the analogy expressed in premise 2 can hardly be rejected. Generally, compensation is not possible when we permissibly infringe on *S*'s right to self-direction for increasing the overall good. However, things are different in the intrapersonal case. In effect, premise 2 could be recast as an *a fortiori* argument, since the moral reason to infringe an agent's right to self-direction with full ex post compensation is stronger than the moral reason to infringe an agent's right to self-direction to maximize the aggregate good. In effect, the right to self-direction can be taken as a *property title* or as a *liability title* (Calabresi and Douglas Melamed 1972: 1089–1093). On the former interpretation, no one may infringe *S*'s right to self-direction without *S*'s prior consent. On the latter, it is sometimes permissible to infringe *S*'s right to self-direction if *S* receives full ex post compensation. The reasoning assumes that the right to self-direction is a liability title.

Another way of making the same point is to say that the *principle of personal separateness* is not affected if the self-direction loss and the welfare gain accrue to the same individual. In interpersonal cases, when someone's good is sacrificed in order to maximize the aggregate good, the principle of personal separateness provides a pro tanto moral reason against performing the maximizing action. However, the separateness principle is inapplicable to justifiable paternalistic interferences. In fact, in performing those interferences we sacrifice someone's good for the purpose of enhancing his own good. However, the compensation is *less than perfect* if the paternalistic action infringes on *S*'s right to self-direction in order to maximize *S*'s own *good*. That is, the incommensurability between utility and self-direction prevents perfect compensation. Infringements on the right to self-direction should be compensated by self-direction gains. However, it is not easy to conceive self-direction gains. At first blush, the concept of self-direction is not scalar or quantifiable. However, given that positive freedom is subservient to the right to self-direction, it is easier to justify infringing *S*'s right to self-direction as a way of maximizing *S*'s positive freedom than to justify infringing *S*'s right to self-direction as a way of maximizing *S*'s good. Therefore, we can strengthen the analogical argument by substituting "*S*'s positive freedom" for "*S*'s own good" in premise 2:

> 2. If it is permissible for government *A* to infringe *S*'s right to self-direction for the overall good when the ratio is equal to or greater than *K*, then it is also permissible for government *A* to infringe *S*'s right to self-direction for increasing *S*'s overall positive freedom when the ratio is equal to or greater than *K*.

The new premise avoids the problem of comparability between self-direction and utility by placing gains and losses on the scale of positive freedom. This strategy echoes Mill's account of indentured servitude. Mill grounds his rejection of the slavery contract on the fact that by making it, the seller annihilates his own freedom, the very reason that warrants his freedom of contract. By reducing losses and gains in the intrapersonal case to a single value dimension, we can justify losses in terms of self-direction as a way of maximizing positive freedom, which in turn is essential to exercise the right to self-direction. Thus, it becomes plausible to extend greater-good (and lesser-evil) justifications to paternalistic actions.

10.4 Threshold Positive Libertarianism and Paternalism

The positive-freedom case for paternalism can be stated in this way. It is permissible to infringe *S*'s right to self-direction as a necessary way of increasing *S*'s positive freedom when the ratio between *S*'s *net* gain in positive freedom (*F*) as a result of government meddling with *S*'s self-direction powers (*I*) is equal to or greater than *K*. We can represent this principle with a formula similar to equation (10.1):

$$\frac{F}{I} \geq K. \qquad (10.2)$$

As is obvious, the extent of F and I cannot be determined without a method for quantifying positive freedom. This is not an easy task. Suppose we have two different legal systems, S1 and S2. S1 recognizes three liberty-types A, B, and C, and S2 recognizes those same three liberties plus the liberty-type D. Because the list of liberty-types protected in S1 is a proper subset of the list of liberty-types protected in S2, S2 protects greater positive freedom than S1. However, such comparisons are impossible when the legal regimes to be ranked involve logically independent sets of liberty types.

Various authors have proposed different ways to measure negative or positive freedom that do not appeal to the concept of set membership. For instance, Hillel Steiner computes negative freedom as a function of all the actions an agent is free or unfree to perform (Steiner 1983). Following Isaiah Berlin, Lawrence Crocker maintains that positive freedom must be measured in terms of the number of alternatives of actions, the probability of the agent's performing each action, the value of each action to the agent, and the variety or diversity of alternatives (Crocker 1980: 53–54). Elsewhere, I have argued for the exclusion of probability, diversity, and evaluative considerations from the computation of negative freedom (Spector 1992: 40–48). Similarly, Ian Carter disentangles the problem of measuring the extent of an individual's freedom from the problem of gauging the value of that freedom (Carter 1999: 140–146). He defends an account of negative freedom focused on the number of available sets of compossible actions and the probability of the availability of those sets, where the availability is diminished by such constraints as force and threats (Carter 1999: 239).[3]

For my purposes, all I need is a scalar approach to positive freedom. Now, I have defined positive freedom as the *effective power* to conceive, choose, and perform courses of action that realize an agent's idea of a meaningful life. A positive freedom account of paternalism must consistently measure positive freedom in terms of an individual's power to perform various alternative actions. Thus, I give up a negative approach to the measurement of freedom and adopt instead one based on the idea of powers and capabilities. Basically, this is the view offered by C. B. Macpherson and Amartya Sen. Macpherson identifies positive freedom with a person's *developmental powers*, that is, his ability to use and develop his capacities. He measures a person's power by the number of external impediments to that ability. This notion of overall positive freedom is not independent of the value of development powers, because not all powers are equally relevant to the computation of positive freedom. Macpherson says that "positive liberty is liberty to act as a fully human being" (Macpherson 1973: 42, 71, 105, 113). In the same vein, Sen defends a metric of *capabilities*. According to Sen, capabilities are substantive freedoms "to choose a life one has reason to value" (Sen 1999: 74). Sen explains the concept of capabilities in terms of *functionings*, which he understands as valuable aspects of living conditions that an individual successfully achieves. Sen defines a capability set as a set of alternative combinations of functionings that are feasible for a person. He adds:

> A person's "capability" [...] is thus a kind of freedom: the substantive freedom to achieve alternative functioning combinations (or, less formally put, the freedom to achieve various lifestyles). For example, an affluent person who fasts may have the same functioning achievement in terms of eating or nourishment as a destitute person who is offered to starve, but the first person does have a different "capability set" than the second (the first can choose to eat well and be well-nourished in a way the second cannot). (Sen 1999: 75)

Sen claims that the availability of alternatives to the actual plan of life a person chooses is valuable on its own (Sen 1985, 1987: 36). Thus, opportunities that an agent does not use have a value that is independent from the value of the highest-ranked option (Sen 1999: 76).

[3] Kramer disagrees with Carter in claiming that the measurement of freedom must rely on evaluative considerations (Kramer 2003: 428–441).

Macpherson and Sen converge on the position I adopt here. I think that positive freedom could be measured on the basis of the number of alternative actions an agent is capable of performing (n), the potential contribution of an action to the achievement of a valuable human functioning (v), and the degree of real power or capability the individual has to perform an action (p). We can summarize these factors in the following formula:

$$\sum_{i=0}^{n} v \times p. \tag{10.3}$$

To be sure, this formula is contestable, yet it illustrates how we can make sense of the extent of *S*'s overall positive freedom. When government *A* acts paternalistically toward citizen *S*, it causes gains and losses of *S*'s positive freedom that can be computed with the above formula (10.3). However, encroachments on individuals' right to self-direction are not merely justified by their ability to maximize their positive freedom. According to formula (10.2), justifiable infringements must provide a *proportionally greater* amount of positive freedom. That is, justifiable paternalistic actions must provide a sufficiently greater extent of positive freedom. Mathematically, this principle can be stated by requiring that the ratio between the positive freedom gain and the positive freedom cost of infringing the right to self-direction be equal to or greater than *K*.

K in formula (10.2) represents the moral urgency of the right to self-direction. The right to self-direction not only requires a compass of alternatives from which the agent is effectively capable of choosing but also the right to be fully in charge of one's life. The latter right implies anyone else's lack of authority to compel the agent to make decisions except in cases in which others' claims or collective interests are at stake. Positive libertarian paternalism allows governmental paternalistic interventions (either via public compulsory interventions or modifications of the choice architecture) if the difference between the marginal reduction of positive freedom caused by the paternalistic intervention and the resulting marginal increase of positive freedom is equal to or greater than *K*. Positive libertarian paternalism only allows interventions that increase *S*'s overall positive freedom beyond a moral threshold (that is, *K*).

The principle of personal separateness is not involved in a justifiable paternalistic intervention, for such intervention secures perfect compensation in terms of positive freedom. However, though paternalistic actions may yield a net gain in *S*'s overall positive freedom, they infringe *S*'s self-direction right, even if the infringement might be justified on the grounds that government's interference will probably advance *S*'s positive freedom better than the choices that *S* would make on his own. In turn, the right to self-direction follows the *principle of personal autonomy*. This principle expresses the value of making one's own choices. T. M. Scanlon disaggregates this value into three categories of reasons. First, he argues that choice is valuable in that it is instrumental in advancing an agent's future enjoyment (*instrumental value*). Second, he says that choice is valuable because the agent's choice represents his judgments and thoughts (*representative value*). Finally, Scanlon claims that choice is valuable in that it expresses the fact that the agent is a competent person who can make his own decisions (*symbolic value*) (Scanlon 1998: 252–253). According to Scanlon, paternalistic interventions should be assessed in terms of the extent to which they injure symbolic and representative values. For instance, it might be argued that labor regulations do not affect the representative value of autonomy because they don't diminish but rather enhance workers' capacity to act according to their judgments and thoughts; nor do they run afoul of the symbolic value of autonomy, for such regulations do not treat workers as incompetent agents but rather as individuals who need legal support to pursue their own judgments and thoughts (Scanlon 1998: 254). These examples are controversial, but they are helpful to illustrate the notions of representative and symbolic value.

Representative values are essential to personal autonomy. An autonomous choice expresses an agent's rational nature in his actual interaction with the world. It seems that instrumental values and symbolic values are parasitic on representative values. It's because an autonomous choice represents the agent's judgments and thoughts that an agent will more likely pursue his preferences by acting on his own. It is because of the representative value of the agent's autonomous choices that an agent is treated as a fool or a child if he is prevented from choosing in accordance with his judgments and reasons. An agent's rational nature causes him to respond to changes in his environment on the basis of reasons. Thus, the choices of an individual depend on the agent's rational nature and his environment. An agent is more likely to represent his judgments and thoughts if he can choose among a wider set of options. This is the representative value of choice. Generally, the wider the menu of alternatives open to the agent, the more fully his choices will represent his own rational nature rather than the environment in which he acts (Spector 1992: 97–98, 2013: 574–575; Kramer 2003: 431). Also, the richer the range of options open to the agent, the more likely he is to further his preferences and inclinations. This is the instrumental value of choice.

On the subjective side, the degree of positive freedom may impact the authenticity of the agent's preferences and judgments. Thus, an agent preference *P* is nonautonomous if he would not have formed *P* in the face of a *larger* compass of feasible options. One mechanism that leads to nonautonomous preferences is based on the capacity of human beings to adapt their preferences to their social or natural environment. *Adaptive preferences* are shaped by the lack of a larger set of feasible options (Elster 1983: 229–230). Though no society is viable without a diversity of constraints on human choice, some restrictions on the sets of feasible options may cause an agent to form preferences that cannot be considered his own in that he would have had different or even opposite preferences in the context of a richer set of feasible options. The richer the range of feasible options, the lower the probability that an agent's preferences are formed by adaptation. This means that the concept of *autonomous preferences* must be understood by reference to the concept of positive freedom.

As I said, justifiable paternalistic actions do not affect the principle of separateness because they yield a net gain of positive freedom. However, in interfering with an individual's autonomous capacity to make his own decisions, government infringes his right to self-direction. Since agents' self-direction powers are protected by moral constraints, paternalistic actions do infringe the autonomy principle. The weight of this principle corresponds to the moral urgency of the right to self-direction in formula (10.2), represented by *K*.

Just as threshold deontologism resolves the conflict between an individual's rights and the overall good, positive libertarian paternalism resolves the conflict between the positive freedom of an agent's current time-slice self and his overall positive freedom (future selves included). Both moral views establish a threshold above which a reasonable trade-off is permissible. In this way, positive libertarian paternalism borrows from threshold deontologism the idea of a reasonable trade-off between competing moral considerations.

There is also an informational similarity between intrapersonal and interpersonal maximization. In effect, informational constraints beset both the interpersonal maximization of utility and the intrapersonal maximization of positive freedom. Defenders of paternalism generally assume that government (or a private third party) *knows* that a possible action by *S* will maximize *S*'s overall good. Similarly, positive libertarian paternalism must assume that government has proper knowledge about the positive freedom's advantageous consequences of its interferences. But in realistic scenarios, the government often lacks proper information about an agent's judgments or thoughts. Government failures are common in social policy, and legal paternalism is no exception. The absence of perfect information introduces a degree of uncertainty that must be taken into account by discounting *F* (the positive freedom gain) by the likelihood of governmental error.

Despite the similarities, there is an important disanalogy. Interpersonal maximization justifies coercing an individual in order to respect other people's *moral claims*. The conflict holds between an individual's moral rights and the requirement to maximize the overall good. When the agent is not prepared to fulfill his maximization duties on his own, a third party (the state) is justified to forcefully sacrifice an individual for the sake of the overall good. *Moral autonomy* is congenial with the moral permission to enforce those duties an individual is not voluntarily disposed to discharge. By contrast, in a case of pure paternalism (i.e., an intrapersonal case), other people's claims are not relevant. Therefore, the moral permission to deprive an agent of his freedom to act in accordance with his judgments and thoughts cannot rest on other people's claims.

How should we assess *K* in formula (10.2) as compared with *K* in formula (10.1)? In interpersonal cases, the government may claim the authority to maximize the overall good because no single individual's incentives are generally aligned with the furtherance of this goal. In contrast, in intrapersonal cases, individual agents generally need no one else to align their choices with their own interests. Moreover, if they fail to do so, other people's claims or interests are not frustrated. Therefore, there is no need for the government to act by proxy in the furtherance of people's individual interests. If government *A* infringes *S*'s right to self-direction, even as a way of producing a significant gain of *S*'s positive freedom, *A* disregards the principle of personal autonomy. This is a reason to think that *K* in formula (10.2) has a higher value than *K* in formula (10.1). On the other hand, whereas utility-maximizing policies infringe the principle of personal separateness, paternalistic interventions do not offend personal separateness because the same individual gets the ensuing costs and gains. The fact that intrapersonal paternalistic interventions do not infringe the principle of personal separateness is a reason to think that *K* in formula (10.1) has a higher value than *K* in formula (10.2). We have two opposite effects: one flowing from the principle of personal autonomy, the other from the principle of personal separateness. It is plausible to suggest that both effects cancel each other out, and that, as a corollary, *K* in formula (10.2) is comparable in magnitude to *K* in formula (10.1). This means that *A*'s paternalistic intervention toward *S* is permissible only if it will very likely cause a significant net gain of *S*'s overall positive freedom.

10.5 Conclusion

I have argued that positive libertarianism can justify a governmental paternalistic intervention in someone's choice if this intervention will in all likelihood produce a significant gain of his overall positive freedom. The degree to which the intrapersonal gain in positive freedom must exceed the positive freedom loss caused by the intervention depends on the moral urgency of the right to self-direction. The magnitude of K cannot be specified, but the positive libertarian case suggests that its value is very high. It's only in cases where an agent's free or unimpeded choice will irreversibly endanger his overall positive freedom in a way or to an extent that will compromise his personal autonomy over time that the government is morally justified to infringe his right to self-direction. Libertarian paternalistic interventions (advocated by Thaler and Sunstein) stand a better chance of being justified because the degree of their meddling with people's self-direction powers (I in formula 10.2) is very low. According to the *positive* libertarian argument, it is of secondary importance whether government A nudges or causes citizen S to make a positive-freedom enhancing choice C by raising the costs of other alternatives open to S, excluding them from S's set of legally permissible options or restructuring S's choice architecture. *The justification lies in the substantial relative gain of positive freedom caused by the interference.* Thus, the positive libertarian approach to paternalism is a variety of strong paternalism.

CHAPTER 11

Beyond Positive and Negative Liberty
Habermas and Honneth on Political Freedom

Maeve Cooke

Many contemporary political theorists agree that the distinction between negative and positive liberty is questionable.[1] Leaving aside those at the extremes, even theorists who explicitly embrace a negative conception rarely deny that their negative understanding has positive elements (Pettit 1997a, 2009).[2] In a similar vein, those who place themselves – or, more likely, are placed by others – in the positive camp tend to question the usefulness of the negative versus positive distinction (Wellmer 1998; Honneth 2014).[3] Nonetheless, the distinction continues to serve as an important frame of reference. It is widely acknowledged that it articulates a fundamental difference in modern approaches to the question of political freedom, even if the terms "negative" and "positive" are seen as not always helpful. In his essay "What's Wrong with Negative Liberty?" Charles Taylor makes both these points (Taylor 1985a: 221–229). His opening paragraph endorses the view that "there are two . . . families of conceptions of political freedom abroad in our civilization" (Taylor 1985a: 211); the bulk of the essay shows that the two families are not well characterized in terms of a crude negative versus positive distinction. Indeed, he destabilizes

[1] Following Isaiah Berlin, I refer to negative liberty in a general sense as the absence of an external obstructing or interfering agency and positive liberty as a rationally self-determining agency (Berlin 1969b).

[2] An example here is Phillip Pettit, who from the beginning has placed himself on the negative side of the divide (Pettit 1997a), while arguing that freedom as non-domination represents an alternative path to traditional negative conceptions of freedom as absence of interference. Freedom as non-domination, which Pettit construes as freedom from *arbitrary* interference, clearly has positive components. Arbitrary interference impacts a person's ability to make deliberative choices, or the options that fall within the domain of their choice, and hence, prevents them from exercising a key component of personal agency. Pettit acknowledges this implicitly when he describes it as an alienating experience (Pettit 2009).

[3] The widespread suspicion within contemporary political theory of positive conceptions is not conducive to self-identification as a positive theorist. As Charles Taylor observes, advocates of a negative conception tend to pin the crudest version of the positive version on their opponents – while themselves asserting the crudest version of the negative conception (Taylor 1985a: 214).

the distinction by showing that an exclusively negative view of freedom is incoherent. With the exception of the extreme views of theorists such as Thomas Hobbes and Jeremy Bentham, even proponents of negative liberty embrace the modern Western, "post-Romantic" view of the self as a purposive being with distinctive interests that are the basis for each self's particular form of self-realization (Taylor 1985a: 216–217; cf. Taylor 1989a). Accordingly, their negative view of freedom as the absence of external impediments inevitably involves evaluative discrimination as to what counts as an impediment; if it did not, their position would be incoherent, failing to fit with their (perhaps unacknowledged) view of the self as a purposive being. Crucially, such evaluative discrimination must be construed "positively" in that human subjects, in working out for themselves what their deep purposes are, inevitably make reference to an "external authority"; in consequence, they are no longer "the final arbiter of [their] being free/unfree" (Taylor 1985a: 222). In other words, it can never be ruled out in principle that the subject is wrong about what it truly wants (Taylor 1985a: 223).

Taylor describes these processes of discrimination among deep purposes as strong evaluations (Taylor 1985a: 220). In *Sources of the Self*, he develops this idea at length (Taylor 1989b). Strong evaluations constitute evaluative roadmaps for particular subjects at a given time. Such roadmaps determine the significance and relevance for subjects of particular ways of behaving and acting and of particular ways of living their lives. Strong evaluations involve an orientation to the good. When subjects ask questions such as "Do I want to be the person I am now?" or "Do I want to pursue my present path in life?" they position themselves reflectively in relation to ideas of the good. "The good" is that which is picked out as comparably higher in a qualitative distinction and in this sense a "higher good" (Taylor 1989b: 63). Higher goods depend on "constitutive goods" (Taylor 1989b: 91–107). Examples of such goods include God, history, reason, art, and nature. Constitutive goods define the subject's value-directed relationship to the world; accordingly, they are an integral element of their identities as strong evaluators. They command moral allegiance and as such are "moral sources." The process of strong evaluation thus calls for openness to experiences in which the power of moral sources makes itself present in a full-bodied way to human subjects (Cooke 2006: 135). Its receptive aspect demands in turn flexibility, open-mindedness, sensitivity to others, and imaginativeness. Nonetheless, strong evaluation is a form of self-determination: the point of critical reflection by subjects on the validity of their deeper purposes is to ascertain *for themselves* what kind of person they would like to be and what paths they should pursue in order to be that kind of person, and to take *responsibility* for their evaluative judgments.

Taylor's discussion makes a further influential contribution to contemporary thinking about political freedom. It suggests that the negative versus positive distinction should be recast as one between "individualist" and "communalist" approaches of freedom, to adopt the terminology used by Albrecht Wellmer in the essay "Models of Freedom in the Modern World" (Wellmer 1998: 3–37). Individualist approaches see individual freedom as always potentially threatened by others, be these governments, corporations, or private persons. Communalist approaches view individual freedom as *social* freedom, as realizable only in interaction with others within a society of a certain type. While he does not expand his thoughts on the matter in this particular essay, Taylor clearly favors (what Wellmer calls) a communalist approach.[4]

I agree with Taylor that a distinction along communalist and individualist lines is a more fruitful one for contemporary political theory. Furthermore, I agree with his analysis of the incoherence of purely negative conceptions. I take my lead from him in favoring a conception of freedom that is in a broad sense communalist, while moving beyond any crude negative versus positive distinction. I advocate a universalist conception of political freedom that dynamically integrates the valid insights of communalist and individualist approaches. I see the task of further developing this kind of conception as a challenge for contemporary political theory. In other writings, I elaborate my thoughts on the shape and substance of such a conception. In the present essay, I seek to show what can be learned, positively and negatively, from the normative accounts of freedom offered by Jürgen Habermas and Axel Honneth, whom I see as engaged in a similar endeavor. I argue that neither of their accounts of political freedom articulates a convincing version of the required conception; nonetheless, each contributes in important ways in doing so.

Wellmer, drawing on Taylor's work, identifies one strong reason for favoring a communalist approach to freedom in the political public sphere: the implausible picture of human agency underlying individualist approaches, which take isolated individuals, characterized by certain natural rights and goal-oriented rationality, as their starting point (Wellmer 1998). Rejecting this picture, communalist theories argue that the "notion

[4] Taylor develops his thoughts on his communalist position in several other essays, for example, Taylor (1989b).

of a human individual existing outside society and rationally pursuing his or her own contingent purposes is not only a fiction (as the individualist would agree) ... but an inappropriate and noxious fiction" (Wellmer 1998: 5). They see human subjects as essentially social individuals: their individuality is the product of, not the precondition for, their socialization within particular cultures, traditions, and institutions.[5] This implies that relations between human subjects are the very condition of individual freedom, not a limitation on it.

In addition to the questionable anthropological premises of the individualist view, there are epistemological reasons to be suspicious of it. Wellmer, again following Taylor, points out that the individualist view has close affinities with the objectivistic, mechanistic, and physicalistic tradition of modern science which has served to legitimate the modern capitalist economy; communalist views, by contrast, have almost invariably been critical of it (Wellmer 1998: 6–7).

Wellmer finds the communalist rejection of the anthropological premises underlying the individualist approach persuasive and welcomes the communalist suspicion of the epistemology associated with it. However, this does not lead him straightforwardly to support a communalist position on freedom. Rather, he endorses Hegel's assertion, arising from his critique of Romantic utopias of reconciliation, that no communal freedom is conceivable in the modern world that is not based on the institutionalization of an equal negative freedom for all (Wellmer 1998: 25). His conclusion is that the modern universalist understanding of freedom "entails a normative dualism of 'negative versus positive' (i.e., communal) freedom" and that, in consequence, a "dialectical tension is built into the universalist idea of freedom itself" (Wellmer 1998: 35).

Wellmer's use of the term "universalist" is apposite. It captures an important feature of the particular kind of communalist freedom that theorists such as Taylor envisage, when they seek to conceptualize freedom beyond any crude negative versus positive distinction. This is inclusiveness in principle of all human others in the spheres of social interaction within which freedom is realized. In the following I adopt this terminology. Accordingly, I describe the challenge for contemporary critical theory as the task of developing a universalist conception that dynamically integrates the communal and individual moments of freedom. This dynamic aspect,

[5] I endorse the basic features of the communalist approach to agency. Nonetheless, the claim that individuality is the product of socialization seems to me too strong. I hold that individuality is produced *in significant measure* by way of socialization processes.

too, is well captured by Wellmer when he speaks of dialectical tension. At certain points in his essay, however, Wellmer suggests a *contest* rather than tension, reflecting the tendency within modern political theory to think of freedom in terms of a competition between two rival conceptions, in which one conception invariably wins. For example, he writes: "the rights of negative freedom are, in a certain sense, rights even *against* the demands of communal rationality" (Wellmer 1998: 28). On a benign reading, this formulation simply asserts the right to dissent and to act as a dissenter. It does not question the mutual dependence and equal normative weight of communal and individual freedom. However, it could also be read as asserting the normative primacy of individual freedom. As Habermas makes clear in *Between Facts and Norms*, his major work on law and democracy, this position would be a cause for concern (Habermas 1996).

One of the main concerns of Habermas's book is to show that "private" and "public" autonomy are co-original. Co-original means that they mutually presuppose one another and are normatively of equal weight (Habermas 1996: 82–131). In Wellmer's terminology, I take Habermas's co-originality thesis to assert an evenly balanced, dialectical relationship between the individual ("private") and communal ("public") moments of a universalist idea of freedom.

Habermas criticizes Kant, Jean-Jacques Rousseau, and their respective successors in the liberal and civic-republican traditions for setting up a competition between private and public autonomy.[6] Invariably, one mode of freedom wins the contest: private autonomy in liberal theories and public autonomy in civic-republican ones. There are significant costs in each case. When private autonomy wins, democratic government is restricted by primordial natural or moral rights. A significant cost here is the freedom gained through collective self-legislation, expressed in the idea that citizens are free only if they can see themselves as the authors of the law to which they are subject. When public autonomy wins, the self-determination of individuals is subordinated to the principle of collective self-realization. A significant cost here is the freedom gained through legally recognized individual rights, in particular the right of individual citizens to challenge the law when it is perceived as fundamentally hostile to their self-determining agency. Given these costs to freedom when one pole of the dialectical relationship is asserted at the expense of the other, Habermas seeks to eliminate the competition between private and public autonomy.

[6] The competition is not always intended or acknowledged.

I align myself with his basic aim but argue that he fails to achieve it. To see this, we must look more closely at his co-originality thesis and what he means by private and public autonomy.

Habermas's co-originality thesis has two key components. It asserts, (i) private and public autonomy are evenly balanced and (ii) they mutually presuppose one another. At first glance the first component is relatively straightforward: "the private autonomy of citizens must neither be set above, nor made subordinate to, their political autonomy" (Habermas 1996: 104). I take Habermas to mean that we need an account of the relationship between private and public autonomy in which neither has normative priority over the other – normatively they must be of equal weight. However, if we probe what it could mean for neither to have normative priority, we soon see that it calls for a particular reading of the second component. Although a weaker and a stronger reading of this component is possible, only a stronger reading will meet the requirement of even balance. On the weaker reading, Habermas asserts the reciprocal *dependency* of private and public autonomy; on the stronger reading, he asserts their reciprocal *constitution*.

The weaker reading is compatible with several of his formulations of the co-originality thesis, such as when he writes that private and public autonomy "mutually complement" each other (Habermas 1996: 99, 106), are "mutually dependent," or "mutually presuppose" each other (Habermas 1996: 84). In this reading, private autonomy is a necessary condition of public autonomy in the sense that only agents whose equal legal status is guaranteed by a system of rights could engage in political deliberation. Conversely, public autonomy is a necessary condition of private autonomy in the sense that legal recognition of each citizen as a bearer of rights must be secured through the exercise of public autonomy, typically leading to a system of subjective rights.

However, Habermas's criticisms of Kant, Rousseau, and their respective successors in the liberal and civic-republican traditions for failing to show the internal (conceptual) connection between private and public autonomy point toward a stronger reading of his position. He describes his aim as reconciling private and public autonomy at "a fundamental conceptual level" (Habermas 1996: 84) and as showing their "internal" relationship (Habermas 1996: 104). By internal relationship, I take him to mean that private autonomy is itself an element of public autonomy and public autonomy is itself an element of private autonomy: each is part of the very meaning of the other. Or, put differently, each moment of freedom reciprocally constitutes the other in significant respects. His remark that private and public autonomy "mutually interpret" each other (Habermas 1996: 100) and his reference to their "dialectical relationship" (Habermas 1995: 130) can be read in this way. Not only is there textual evidence for the stronger reading; only the stronger reading would suffice for the purpose of a mutually constitutive and evenly balanced relationship. For, if private and public autonomy were not related in this way, there would be no *freedom-related* reason against asserting the normative priority of the one over the other. The mere dependency of private autonomy on public autonomy (e.g., in the form of the legal recognition of citizens as moral agents or as bearers of rights) is readily compatible with the idea that it is genetically and normatively prior to public autonomy. This is why the relationship between the two moments of freedom must be construed as mutually constitutive (in significant respects) and evenly balanced. In order to judge whether Habermas succeeds in showing this, we must consider carefully what he means by private and public autonomy.

Up to now, I have used the term private autonomy as synonymous with individual freedom. However, in the case of Habermas's theory, this is misleading. Although his use of the term is ambiguous, it is clear that he does not straightforwardly embrace an individualist approach, in which freedom is understood as the absence of any external impediment or interference. Indeed, in his writings prior to *Between Facts and Norms*, Habermas understood individual freedom as moral autonomy in a revised Kantian sense. His revised conception of autonomy is part of a more general dialogical rearticulation of Kantian moral theory. This is what has come to be known as discourse ethics (Habermas 1990). Like Kant, Habermas limits morality to the class of universally justifiable normative judgments, leaving aside matters of "the good life:" he regards particular needs, desires, and values as ethical matters that are distinct from moral questions; this is because the answers to ethical questions are inescapably context-bound and thus are not susceptible to justification on grounds of their universalizability.

Like Kant's moral philosophy, too, Habermas's discourse ethics is deontological, cognitivist, universalist, and formalist. It is *deontological* in the sense that it attributes an imperative, binding force to moral norms that is analogous to the unconditional character of truth claims. It is *cognitivist* in the sense that it answers positively the question of whether we can rationally justify normative statements, whereby rationality has a context-transcending meaning. It is *universalist* in the sense that it is construed in terms of universalizable interests. Finally, it is *formalist* in the sense that the distinction between valid and invalid norms is not made

on the basis of their particular content but is rather decided in a process governed by a formal principle of universalization (Habermas 1990: 160). This principle, "U," requires valid moral norms to be universalizable, in the sense of being acceptable to everyone and equally good for everyone.

Habermas conceives moral autonomy as a form of freedom that involves rational acceptance of the validity of particular moral norms: it is self-determination on the basis of moral *insight*. Again, there is an evident analogy with the Kantian view – autonomy for Kant, too, requires the self ("autos") to be governed by law ("nomos") that is moral.

However, there are also some important differences between Kant's moral philosophy and Habermas's discourse ethics, and by extension, between their respective conceptions of moral autonomy (Habermas 1990: 203–204). Most importantly for present purposes, discourse ethics is *dialogical* in a double sense. First, norms are valid only if they could be vindicated by an agreement reached among participants in real argumentations (guided by idealizing suppositions). By contrast, Kant assumes that individuals can test the validity of their maxims of action "monologically," in isolation from others. Furthermore, the validity of moral norms is dialogical in the sense that it is dialogically *produced*: the validity of moral norms is not just *tested* in an (idealized) procedure of argumentation, it is *generated* within an (idealized) procedure of argumentation. This is Habermas's thesis of immanent transcendence. According to this thesis, transcendence is generated *within* human practices of communication and is thus "innerworldly" (Habermas 2008: 92–93). In Kant's case, by contrast, the validity of moral norms is not produced by way of argumentation but is genetically prior to and normatively independent of it.

In line with his dialogical rearticulation of Kant's theory of moral validity, Habermas also offers a dialogical reinterpretation of moral autonomy. In his account, moral autonomy, like moral validity, is produced dialogically. More precisely, it is generated within intersubjective deliberations about the validity of moral norms. This means that moral autonomy, for Habermas, is genetically and normatively a social construct.[7] In contrast to Kant, for whom moral autonomy is primordial and belongs inalienably to every human being, moral autonomy for Habermas has no pre-social justification. Thus, it cannot be used to ground pre-political natural rights that place restrictions on the exercise of popular sovereignty.

[7] It should be noted that normative priority does not follow automatically from genetic priority. In his discussion of Kant, who attributes both genetic and normative priority to moral autonomy, Habermas sometimes writes as though the one entails the other.

This point is crucial for Habermas's account of law and politics if he is to avoid the normative prioritization of private autonomy, and corresponding downgrading of public autonomy, that he criticizes in the case of liberal traditions.

In *Between Facts and Norms,* Habermas speaks primarily of private autonomy when referring to individual freedom. Confusingly, however, private autonomy sometimes means moral autonomy and sometimes subjective freedom of choice [*Willkürfreiheit*]. One reason for the confusion is that on some occasions he adopts a legal-theoretical perspective; here, the theorist adopts a functional, objectivating, perspective on the law. On other occasions, he adopts a moral–theoretical perspective; here, the theorist adopts the subjective perspective of agents who are subject to the law.

To further confuse matters, he tends to switch between these perspectives without making clear that he is doing so (Peters 1994; Cooke 1999). Thus, in the initial part of his discussion, he emphasizes that he is not attempting a normative justification of law, but rather offering a functional explanation that follows Kant's account of the legal form (Habermas 1996: 111–112). His professed concern to offer a functional explanation fits with his Kantian view that the legal form abstracts from the capacity for moral autonomy and that free choice (*Willkür*) is a sufficient source of law-abiding behavior. However, in apparent contradiction to his self-professed functionalist approach, he then elaborates his co-originality thesis under the heading "A Discourse-Theoretical Justification of the System of Basic Rights." Consistent with a justificatory enterprise, he appears to adopt a subjective perspective in this part of his discussion (Habermas 1996: 118–131).

A further complication is that his normative justification of the system of rights appeals to an idea of private autonomy characterized in language evoking ideas of self-ownership and self-sufficiency that are closely associated with standard liberal interpretations of autonomy. Thus, he describes private autonomy as *freedom from communicative freedom*, by which he means discursive freedom, the forms of freedom acquired by agents in intersubjective processes of deliberation. It is freedom from the obligations of communicative freedom: "the negative freedom to withdraw from the public space of illocutionary obligations to a position of mutual observance and influence" (Habermas 1996: 120). To be sure, formulations such as these could be taken to express the objectivating standpoint of modern law. However, this reading runs counter to his express intention to offer a *justification* of the system of basic rights. Moreover, he is clearly adopting a subjective rather than objectivating perspective when he writes that the agent "who simply decides as she wishes is not concerned whether the reasons that are decisive *for her* could also be accepted by others" (Habermas 1996: 119–120). Or again, when he writes: "Legally granted liberties entitle one to *drop out of* communicative action, to refuse illocutionary obligations; they ground a privacy freed from the burden of reciprocally acknowledged and mutually expected communicative freedoms" (Habermas 1996: 120). Remarks such as these, which express a subjective perspective (*lack of concern*, freedom from the *burden*) conjure a picture of private autonomy indistinguishable from the liberal conception targeted by his co-originality thesis.

What does Habermas mean by public autonomy? For Habermas, again following Kant (and Rousseau), public autonomy is the freedom acquired when citizens understand themselves as both the authors and the addressees of the law (Habermas 1996: 120, 454). He claims, however, that discourse theory enables us to make better sense of this intuition than either Kant or Rousseau. For this purpose, he introduces, in a first step, a general discourse principle, which states: "Just those action norms are valid to which all possibly affected persons could agree as participants in rational discourses" (Habermas 1996: 106). In contexts of democratic deliberation, where rational discourses are concerned with action norms in legal form, the discourse principle takes on the specific character of a principle of democracy; democratic legal norms are justified by calling on moral, ethical-political, or pragmatic reasons; in consequence, their validity (legitimacy) is determined not by the moral principle of universalizability, "U," but by the principle of democracy (Habermas 1996: 108). According to the principle of democracy, "only those statutes may claim legitimacy that can meet with the assent [*Zustimmung*] of all citizens in a discursive process of legislation that in turn has been legally constituted" (Habermas 1996: 110). Public autonomy is the freedom of citizens when they collectively agree to laws in a public and democratic way.

There is an evident analogy between Habermas's conception of public autonomy and his conception of private autonomy qua moral autonomy. It shares its principal dialogical features: it is a genetically and normatively *social* form of freedom, with no pre-political origins; it is constitutively *intersubjective*, coming into existence by way of interactions between human subjects in processes of deliberation; it is *processual*, a form of freedom that is generated within processes of deliberation. In addition, public and moral autonomy are construed cognitively by Habermas. Just as individual human subjects acquire moral autonomy by way of a discursive process that enables them to bind themselves freely to insights of practical reason, they acquire public autonomy by way of a discursive process that enables them to bind themselves freely to formal principles regarding the exercise of power; these likewise are understood as insights of practical reason (Habermas 1996: 121; 2003, 77–79).

However, the *analogy* between public autonomy and private autonomy qua moral autonomy is not sufficient for the purposes of Habermas's co-originality thesis. This, as we have seen, requires him to show the *mutually constitutive connection* between the two moments of freedom. In order to meet this challenge, he has to demonstrate that public autonomy is an element of the very concept of private autonomy and vice versa.

If private autonomy is construed as moral autonomy, Habermas will be unable to do this. This is due to the contrast he draws between political and moral autonomy. He defines public autonomy in terms of discursively generated insight into the general rational acceptability of interests within a specific legal-political institutional context. Moral autonomy, by contrast, is defined in terms of discursively generated insight into the universalizability of interests, whereby no human subject may be excluded in principle from participation in the discursive process. Due to this fundamental difference in operating principles – in the one case, a context-dependent principle and in the other, a context-transcending one – the valid outcomes of collective law – and decision-making processes cannot contribute directly to the constitution of moral autonomy. At most, they may change the interests of individual subjects *prior* to their participation in moral deliberations, which are processes in which moral autonomy is generated, but such changes are not part of the generative process itself. The following thought experiment illustrates my point.

Think of a new, democratically generated law prohibiting the sale of animal flesh for human consumption. The law is based on an agreement reached by citizens who engage in legal-political deliberations, drawing on a complex interplay of pragmatic, ethical-political, and moral reasons. As such it results from the exercise of political autonomy as construed by Habermas. According to his distinction between legal-political deliberations and moral deliberations, citizen agreement on the validity of a law does not mean that this law is deemed to be universalizable, in the sense of rationally acceptable to everyone, everywhere; it means that it is deemed to be rationally acceptable to all citizens within a particular jurisdiction. Let us imagine that the new law impacts profoundly the everyday behavior and life-orienting evaluations of citizens, giving many of them reasons to live their lives significantly differently and leading them to see the relationship between humans and other animals in a new way. Such profound ethical identity transformations entail cognitive shifts: changes in perception of "deep purposes" (Taylor). For example, those who undergo them may now, for the first time, embrace a vegan way of life as a deep purpose; this will, in turn, affect their other deep purposes and the particular interests they have in connection with them. As a result of the ethical transformations set in train by the new law, therefore, the set of particular interests that individual subjects bring with them into their moral deliberations will be quite different from the set they would have brought with them previously. For Habermas, however, the intersubjective, discursive process that generates moral autonomy *starts* with the particular interests that subjects bring within them into moral deliberation. The transformation of interests *within* the deliberation is part of the discursive process: through the exchange of reasons individual subjects test the universalizability of their particular interests and modify or abandon them in light of this requirement. In generating moral autonomy, as Habermas conceives of it, only such discourse-*internal* transformations of interests are relevant. Transformation of interests that takes place *prior* to moral deliberation has no bearing on the generative process (Cooke 2013). Put differently, our thought experiment shows that public autonomy may impact profoundly ethical identity, and by extension, ethical autonomy, but it does not contribute directly to the generation of moral autonomy.

However, Habermas avoids this difficulty when he construes private autonomy not as moral autonomy but as subjective freedom of choice (*Willkür*). As we have seen, private autonomy in this sense grants individual subjects the freedom to drop out of communicative relationships with other subjects and, within certain limits, to pursue their wishes independently of the approval of others. In Wellmer's formulation, it grants "the right to be – within certain limits – selfish, crazy, eccentric, irresponsible, deviant, obsessive, self-destructive, monomaniac, etc" (Wellmer 1998: 24). In modern democracies, such freedom is typically protected by a system of subjective rights. Accordingly, Habermas casts his thesis as an argument for the conceptual connection between public autonomy and a system of rights. This runs as follows. The legal code establishes certain very general basic rights. These basic rights remain "*unsaturated* ... They must be *interpreted and given concrete shape* by a political legislature in response to changing circumstances" (Habermas 1996: 125). More precisely, the particular rights granted to citizens must be decided by citizens themselves by way of formally organized public processes of intersubjective deliberation nourished and enriched by informal opinion-making processes in "an open and inclusive network of overlapping, subcultural publics" that constitute a "wild" complex (Habermas 1996: 307). In other words, public autonomy constructs the particular rights that serve to secure private autonomy.[8] But even this thesis, however convincing, does not amount to an argument for the mutually constitutive, evenly balanced connection between public and private autonomy. This is because it is readily compatible with the standard liberal view that rights are a protective shell for an *antecedently defined* idea of private autonomy. Worryingly, given his critique of this liberal view, Habermas appears to affirm it when he refers to the law as a shield or "protective mask" that is held up over the physiognomy of persons to protect their freedom of choice from interference by others (Habermas 1996: 531–532, n. 42[9]).

In sum, Habermas's co-originality thesis offers an insight important for the endeavor to develop a universalist conception of political freedom in which there is a dialectical integration of its individual and the communal moments. It shows that such a conception calls for a mutually constitutive, evenly balanced connection between these two moments. Although his account of their relationship does not succeed in meeting this challenge, its failure is instructive, for it casts light on what is needed for success. The element missing in Habermas's theory is a conception of private autonomy that depends on public autonomy not only formally for protection, but also substantively for its development through interaction with the ethically inflected prescriptions and recommendations of democratically generated laws and ordinances. If public autonomy is to play a significant role in *constituting* private autonomy, as required by the co-originality thesis, private autonomy cannot be sealed off from the possibility of substantive change through the exercise of public autonomy. The problem is that Habermas seems to seal it off: to all appearances, the substantive quality of private autonomy is independent of the process of collective self-legislation. Let us now turn to Axel Honneth's account of political freedom. We shall see if it more successfully integrates the individual and communal moments.

Honneth's name for a universalist idea of freedom that integrates both individual and communal elements is social freedom. Here he adopts the terminology of Frederick Neuhouser in his discussion of Hegel's idea of

[8] Habermas treats the internal connection between popular sovereignty and human or civil rights as synonymous with the internal connection between public and private autonomy (Habermas 1996: 104). I argue that it is not (Cooke 2020a).

[9] Habermas attributes this view to Hannah Arendt but provides no textual evidence for his claim.

freedom in the *Philosophy of Right* (Neuhouser 2000: 5–7; Honneth 2014: 43). The distinctive feature of Honneth's account is that freedom cannot be realized, in the Hegelian sense of actualized in social reality, "without taking into account the institutional forms that enable its realization" (Honneth 2014: 41). His guiding intuition is the Hegelian concept of concrete freedom: "We restrict ourselves gladly in relating ourselves to an other, but in this restriction know ourselves as ourselves" (Hegel 1965: 228). In other words, he embraces Hegel's idea of freedom as being "with oneself in the other" (Honneth 2014: 44). Put differently again, Honneth conceives of freedom in Hegelian terms as a dialectical relationship between the "I" and the "We."

Like Hegel, Honneth anchors freedom in three complexes of social institutions, understood both as action systems and as ethical spheres [*sittliche Sphären*], within which subjects can grasp each other as the other of their own selves (Honneth 2014: 44). Freedom becomes real within each institutional complex when "we encounter each other in mutual recognition and can understand our own actions as a condition for the fulfilment of others' aims" (Honneth 2014: 124). The three action systems/ethical spheres that make up the institutional order are: (i) personal relationships (ii) the capitalist market economy and (iii) the political public sphere. In each, one indispensable element of individual agency takes shape and is realized intersubjectively: in the sphere of personal relationships, individual needs and characteristics; in the sphere of the capitalist market economy, particular interests and abilities; in the political public sphere, individual aims of self-determination (Honneth 2014: 131). Each of these spheres is grounded on its own self-referential norms, which in turn are linked to forms of social freedom with their own independent logic (Honneth 2014: 329–330).

On Honneth's distinctive reading of Hegel, social freedom is an internally differentiated concept, within which the forms of social freedom institutionalized in each of the three ethical spheres interact dynamically. The three spheres are connected with one another in a reciprocal relation analogous to the relation actualized in concrete freedom: each sphere realizes its distinctive normativity only when it grasps the other spheres as the other of itself (Honneth 2014: 330). In the dynamic interaction between the three components, the social freedom institutionalized in the political public sphere has a special role, since it produces political and legal principles for the other spheres of freedom. Thus, "democratic will-formation is the active centre of the entire institutional order" (Honneth 2014: 329).

My focus for present purposes is Honneth's idea of social freedom in the political public sphere (as shorthand, "political freedom"). Given that social freedom, for Honneth, occurs within three institutional complexes, each with its own self-referential norms and distinct form of freedom, my question is: What is the distinctive form of the social freedom generated in the political public sphere? We know that it realizes the individual aim of self-determination; moreover, that its realization involves relations of reciprocal recognition with an other. How should we understand this relationship?

Honneth's conception of political freedom is similar to Habermas's in several respects. In both cases, freedom is construed as a relationship between individual self-determination and collective self-legislation. For both, too, the political public sphere is a social space in which citizens arrive at generally acceptable beliefs through deliberative discussions; these beliefs determine the principles to be obeyed by the legislature in accordance with the rule of law (Honneth 2014: 254). Connected with this, both theorists agree that democratic procedures are not merely instruments for problem-solving, but rather the context for democratic will-formation within communicative processes in which participants seek to reach a common understanding about what ought to be done; this entails reflection on what aims and values are worth striving for (Honneth 2014: 269). In addition, in both accounts, collective self-legislation by way of formal law- and decision-making processes is nourished and enriched by discussions and political struggles in the informally organized public sphere (Honneth 2014: 253).

Notwithstanding these significant points of convergence, there are some noteworthy differences between Habermas's and Honneth's accounts of political freedom. One difference is Habermas's connection of autonomy with rational insight. Honneth does not make this connection.

For Habermas, the point of the exchange of reasons in intersubjective deliberations is to arrive at a mutual understanding that is construed cognitively as a rational achievement: participants seek outcomes that are rationally valid according to standards that have some independence of the context of deliberation. Honneth makes no such connection between deliberation and rational insight through the exchange of reasons. Instead, he leaves the question of the epistemic dimension of critical reflection to one side. While he does not reject Habermas's claim that autonomy is dependent on rational insight, he does not endorse it either. We gain the impression that the epistemic quality of the outcomes of critical reflection is unimportant for the realization of social freedom in the political public sphere. Indeed, Honneth takes Émile Durkheim to task for over-emphasizing the cognitive role of the public sphere and, in his discussion of John Dewey, warns against the narrowness of epistemological approaches to the justification of democracy[10] (Honneth 2014: 269, 271).

A second noteworthy difference has to do with their respective understandings of the social preconditions of political freedom. Honneth criticizes Habermas for downplaying the importance of the social preconditions that enable political law and decision-making processes. Habermas makes it a matter of "fortunate co-incidence" whether the social conditions enabling political will-formation actually obtain (Honneth 2014: 379, n. 381). Against this, Honneth asserts an internal connection between the social freedom generated through democratic will-formation and the forms of social freedom that have their homes respectively in the sphere of personal relationships and the economic market. He describes these forms of freedom as preconditions [*Voraussetzungen*] for the freedom of democratic self-legislation, making clear that he means necessary conditions: "If the conditions of social freedom are not realized in personal relationships and on the market, then the social relations that enable citizens to take part in the process of democratic will-formation ... will be absent" (Honneth 2014: 254). Importantly for Honneth, the conditions of social freedom are realized only when they are embodied in everyday habits and practices. Thus, the social conditions for social freedom in the political public sphere will be met only when individual subjects *learn* to be free according to the norms distinctive for personal relationships and the economic market and conduct their everyday lives in these spheres accordingly. Otherwise, as Honneth illustrates by way of a normative reconstruction of the historical development of the democratic public sphere, (Honneth 2014: 255–304) they are likely to be excluded from the democratic processes within which they come to be politically free (Honneth 2014: 229–330). Put differently, the forms of free agency constituted in the spheres of personal relationships and the economic market are indispensable elements of the free agency constituted in the political public sphere. Using the language employed in the previous section, we could say: Freedom in the political public sphere is internally related to freedom in the other two spheres.

[10] My claim is not that he is wrong to criticize Durkheim for neglecting the promise of freedom inherent in the democratic public sphere or to commend Dewey for expanding his theoretical gaze beyond epistemology to encompass cooperative interaction. My point, rather, is that he appears to distance himself from their cognitivist approaches.

This casts some light on free agency in the political public sphere, but does not yet tell us what is distinctive about it vis-à-vis agency in the other spheres. Social freedom, as we know, occurs in a reciprocal movement between the "I" and the "We." In the political public sphere, this takes the specific form of a movement between individual self-determination through the pursuit of particular aims, on the one side, and collective self-legislation in democratic processes, on the other side. Accordingly, we could expect Honneth to offer an account of their mutually constitutive connection: how individual self-determination is itself an element of collective self-legislation and vice versa. But he does not.

Let us consider his position more closely. We have seen that he construes collective self-legislation along broadly Habermasian lines. We now need to see what he means by individual self-determination. In doing so, we will notice a third difference between Habermas and Honneth: to all appearances, Honneth does not embrace Habermas's processual, dialogical understanding of individual self-determination.

The idea of individual self-determination is surprisingly underdeveloped in Honneth's account. It is surprising since Honneth's commitment to the ethical value of individual freedom, and concern to make sense of its social dimension, provides the normative framework for *Freedom's Right*.

The opening page of part l proclaims:

> Of all the ethical values prevailing and competing for dominance in modern society, only one has been capable of leaving a truly lasting impression on our institutional order: freedom, i.e., the autonomy of the individual. (Honneth 2014: 15)

He characterizes the idea of autonomy as the idea that the value of human subjects lies in their capacity for self-determination and refers to the "enormous gravitational force" exerted by this idea (Honneth 2014: 15–16). Its force derives from the fact that the idea of individual freedom establishes a connection between the horizon of the individual and the normative framework of the social order as a whole (Honneth 2014: 15–16).

The first part of his book is devoted to showing the limitations of the dominant traditions within modern political theory in which individual freedom is interpreted respectively as legal freedom and as moral freedom. The second part of the book elaborates the three components of his alternative Hegelian conception of social freedom. Since the norm of freedom proper to the political public sphere is the "aim of self-determination," we would expect him explicitly to address the question of individual autonomy in the second part; he does not.

It is nonetheless possible to piece together a picture of what Honneth means by individual freedom by drawing on his discussion of negative freedom, which is the basis for the institutional complex he calls legal freedom, and on his discussion of reflexive freedom, which is the basis for the institutional complex he calls moral freedom. In each case, Honneth brings out their limitations, and identifies their pathologies, while acknowledging the "kernel of intuitive truth" at their heart (Honneth 2014: 22).

The kernel of truth that Honneth discerns in the Hobbesian view of negative freedom is the importance of securing "a protected free-space for egocentric action, unimpeded by the pressures of responsibilities towards others" (Honneth 2014: 22–23). Accordingly, Honneth describes "[n]egative freedom [as] an original and indispensable element of modernity's moral self-understanding" (Honneth 2014: 29). Legal freedom is also deemed indispensable. Despite its limitations and pathologies (Honneth 2014: 81–94), he argues that the idea of a protected free space must be applied in all three of the ethical spheres that interact dynamically in his account of social freedom (Honneth 2014: 61).

The idea of reflexive freedom, too, has a kernel of truth. Freedom in this sense focuses on the subject's relationship-to-self: "according to this notion, individuals are free if their actions are solely guided by their own intentions" (Honneth 2014: 29). Like legal freedom, moral freedom is deemed indispensable. Despite its limitations and pathologies (Honneth 2014: 104–120), he argues that social institutions can function as sites of social freedom only if moral freedom is institutionalized: "if we have the officially certified opportunity to examine [a particular] institutional setting in light of our own intentions and beliefs and even to depart from it if necessary"[11] (Honneth 2014: 61).

Thus, we can extrapolate from his discussion an idea of individual freedom with two indispensable components. First, independence, in the sense of the subject's capacity to explore the meaning and aims of its individual life while suspending all existing role obligations and attachments. Second, reflective evaluation by the subject of the meaning and aims of its life from the point of view of whether it can affirm them "as its own." In both cases, freedom depends on *retreat* from established social practices. Importantly, Honneth accounts for the value of both kinds of

[11] In Honneth's account, reflexive freedom is a norm integral only to the political public sphere; it is not one built into the spheres of personal relationships or the capitalist market (Honneth 2014: 331).

withdrawal from social praxis in terms of the value of social freedom. Independence and self-reflexivity have a merely dependent and potential character unless they are *reconnected* with institutions within the social world (Honneth 2014: 65–66).

The challenge for Honneth is to show that the subject's reconnection with social praxis is motivated by an interest in freedom itself. If it is not, we have arrived at a picture of individual freedom that is readily compatible with the individualist view we encountered initially. Put differently, the autonomous subject's independence and self-reflexivity do not in themselves provide reasons to claim that freedom is realizable only in interaction with others within a society of a certain type; nor do they provide reasons to deny that individual freedom is always potentially threatened by others, be these governments, corporations, or private persons.

Honneth does not confront this challenge in the case of the political public sphere. Indeed, he does not clearly acknowledge it. Moreover, his discussion of the relationship between the "I" and the "We" in this particular sphere is significantly out of step with his discussion of the relationship in the other two spheres.

There is a striking contrast between his account of the relationship between the "I" and the "We" in the public political sphere and the two other spheres. In the two other spheres, he explains the relationship by way of "objective" anthropological considerations, which drive the individual subject to see its relationship with an other as the fulfillment of its aims: it is not a question of a decision or resolve on its part. In the case of the "We" of personal relationships, the individual subject is propelled by its "natural" desires; in the case of the "We" of the economic market, it is driven by objective constraints of survival (Honneth 2014: 278). If in each case freedom is taken to mean self-realization, in the sense of actualizing individual potentialities, we can say that for the "I," connection with the "We" is an element of its own freedom. By contrast, in the case of the "We" of democratic engagement, the individual subject must first *resolve* to do so (Honneth 2014: 278). Here, connection with "an other," and social praxis in general, is not an element of its very freedom, but depends on a motivation that is *external* to freedom. While Honneth is alert to the problem of motivation connected with the need for resolve, he does not indicate that he sees it as a potential threat to the very *concept* of social freedom in the political public sphere. Instead, he treats it as a problem endemic to the *historical phenomenon* of social freedom in this particular sphere.

In his normative reconstruction of the democratic public sphere, he shows how in various historical conjunctures, lack of motivation to participate in the democratic process seriously damages the social conditions that enable social freedom. Drawing on Dewey, he refers to the problem as political apathy (Honneth 2014: 272) and its solution as political solidarity. Dewey, like Durkheim before him, knew that citizen readiness to put commitment to the common good ahead of their own personal aims, "springs from the binding force of solidarity ... which obligates the members of society to feel responsible for each other and make the necessary sacrifices" (Honneth 2014: 292). In the same vein, Dewey observes that the "exercise of [their] individual freedom [requires citizens to] put the pursuit of the common good ahead of [their] own private aims and act in cooperation with others to improve the conditions of social life" (Honneth 2014: 292). This leads Honneth into an extended discussion of the kind of political culture that would nourish and enrich such feelings of solidarity. However, the very language in which he articulates the importance of solidarity awakens the suspicion that a conflict between the "I" and the "We" is built into the concept of social freedom in the political public sphere (*readiness* to prioritize commitment to the common good, *obligation* to feel responsible for others and *make sacrifices*). In sum, Honneth's formulation of the motivational problem in terms of political apathy and solidarity is in tension with his own account of social freedom. Contrary to what he suggests, the problem is not just depoliticizing *political cultures*, which destroy the "moral resources that could enable a democratic citizenry to withstand in solidarity the various misdevelopments [Honneth] has diagnosed" (Honneth 2014: 328). The more fundamental problem is the lack of an inherent motivation by self-determining subjects to engage in collective processes of self-legislation, for this calls the very concept of social freedom into question.

Our discussion has uncovered a deficiency in Honneth's account of social freedom in the political public sphere: it fails to show the *internal* – mutually constitutive – connection between individual self-determination and collective self-legislation and, thus, between the "I" and the "We." In the previous section, I argued that Habermas's theory, too, fails to show this, although for different reasons. In conclusion, I suggest that Habermas and Honneth can learn from each other's strengths and weaknesses and that contemporary political theory can learn from the strengths and weaknesses of both. For the sake of brevity, my remarks concentrate on what can be learned from their accounts of freedom as individual self-determination – the individual moment of freedom – leaving aside the question of what can be learned from their accounts of freedom as self-legislation – the communal moment of freedom.

Habermas can learn from Honneth's emphasis on the social preconditions of freedom in the political public sphere, especially his attentiveness to the need for individual subjects to learn the meaning of social freedom through prior and parallel learning processes in the other institutional spheres. Honneth is right to say that in the spheres of personal relationships and the economic market, subjects learn through everyday habits and practices what the mutual dependency of "I" and "We" means; without this kind of socialization, they are unlikely to be able to engage in democratic political processes as subjects on an equal footing. He is also right to say that Habermas underplays the importance of such socialization.

Furthermore, Habermas can learn from Honneth that the counterpart to communal freedom (public autonomy) is neither moral autonomy nor subjective freedom of choice, but an *ethically inflected* mode of individual self-determination. To be sure, Honneth's account of individual self-determination is seriously underdeveloped. However, extrapolating from his remarks on independence and self-reflexivity, I suggested that we can form a picture of autonomous agents who independently explore the meaning and aims of their particular lives and assess them reflectively from the point of view of their ethical validity.

This picture fits well with Taylor's account of post-Romantic selves as strong evaluators: as subjects who critically reflect on the validity of their deeper purposes in order to ascertain *for themselves* what kind of person they would like to be, and what paths to pursue in order to be that kind of person. At first glance, it may seem troubling that Taylor makes evaluative discriminations dependent on an "external authority" – on an agency external to the subject. However, I hold that he is right to do so, on condition that the word "authority" is understood in a sufficiently differentiated way and also given a cognitivist interpretation.[12] However, the cognitivist component is missing in Honneth's account of self-determination. This makes no reference to standards of validity in a truth-related sense, which transcend the assignments of meaning and value of particular human subjects in particular socio-cultural contexts. Here,

[12] I propose a conception of ethically self-determining agency in which particular assignments of meaning and value raise validity claims that call for intersubjective assessment, while referring to ideas of the good that go beyond practices of intersubjective assessment. These ideas of the good can be described as "external authorities." Importantly, I differentiate between nonauthoritarian and authoritarian authorities (Cooke 2020b).

Honneth can learn from Habermas. First, from Habermas's dialogical interpretation of moral (and political[13]) autonomy, which builds a cognitivist moment into the very concept of freedom; this allows him not only to make *change for the better* in a truth-related sense part of the very concept of autonomy; it also allows him to make the quality of the change dependent on an agency external to a given subject (for Habermas, the other participants in moral deliberation constitute this "authority"[14]). Second, Honneth can learn from Habermas's connection of autonomy with *dialogically dependent* rational insight, which enables him to offer a nonauthoritarian interpretation of the "external authority" to which the agent's evaluative discriminations refer (Cooke 2020c).

The shortcoming of Habermas's account of autonomy is that he does not extend it to an *ethically* self-determining agency (Cooke 2021). Lacking an account of ethical autonomy, he cannot explain how collective self-legislation can contribute constitutively to the substantive quality of individual freedom. By this, I mean that he is unable to explain how the results of collective self-legislation, in the form of laws, ordinances, regulations, and other prescriptions and recommendations, can change the "deeper purposes" of individual agents, for the better (or the worse) in a truth-related sense, in a way that affects the very substance of their freedom (Cooke 2020a, 2020b).

11.1 Conclusion

From the point of view of an idea of freedom that moves beyond any crude negative versus positive distinction, contemporary political theory has much to learn from the work of Habermas and Honneth. Their respective accounts of political freedom are illuminating and instructive although, in the end, unsatisfactory. We can learn negatively from their lacunae and blind spots and move beyond either approach, while taking on board their clear vision of a form of political freedom in which the individual and communal moments are constitutively connected in an evenly balanced way. Our examination of the two authors has shown how difficult it is to make sense of this mutually constitutive connection. Nonetheless, it has allowed us to pinpoint a weakness common to both accounts: their

[13] There is a transformative element built into Habermas's conception of public autonomy as well.

[14] I agree with Habermas that discursive interaction contributes constitutively to the development of autonomy, but disagree with his further claim that the rightness of evaluative judgments is *determined* discursively. See Cooke (2013); Cooke (2020c).

inadequate conceptualizations of the individual moment of freedom. It has also enabled us to see that a dynamic integration of the individual and communal moments of freedom demands a particular conception of individual self-determination. It calls for a conception of ethically inflected, self-determining agency, in which agents engage critically with the validity of their own "deeper purposes," which are permanently open to change for the better in a truth-related sense.[15] Further elaboration not just of this, but also of the communal moment of freedom, is an important task for contemporary political theory.

[15] The corresponding view of the communal moment of freedom is one of collective self-legislation by way of legal-political institutions whose "deeper purposes" are permanently open to challenge by engaged individuals and groups who have good reasons to disagree with their authoritative prescriptions and recommendations. I have not been able to consider this aspect of freedom in the public political sphere here. I elaborate my thoughts on both the individual and communal moments of freedom in Cooke (2019), Cooke (2020b), and in a book currently in preparation.

CHAPTER 12

Property and Political Power
Neo-feudal Entanglements

Rutger Claassen

12.1 Introduction

Over the course of the twentieth century, many philosophers have argued in favor of a liberal–egalitarian accommodation of capitalism, in which the liberty of the market is to be combined with an egalitarian distribution of property. We can see this accommodation as a position between "pure capitalism" on the one hand and a socialist overthrow of capitalism on the other hand. In the words of Gerald Gaus, a pure capitalist system is based on "maximally extensive feasible property rights" (Gaus 2010). Property here refers to private property. In the classical liberal tradition, the protection of private property rights has been defended as the basis for a flourishing capitalist economy. Theorists of positive freedom, among others, have been prominent in arguing for the liberal–egalitarian accommodation. They have argued that an egalitarian distribution of private property is necessary to give every citizen equal positive freedom. To lead an autonomous life, every citizen needs control over some private property. Call this the "positive freedom argument" for liberal egalitarianism.[1]

The liberal–egalitarian accommodation to capitalism has come under threat in the last decades, as documented by a renewed widening of inequalities in wealth and income (Piketty 2014; Atkinson 2015). In this chapter, I will argue that this predicament requires us to look at one important precondition of the positive freedom argument. This precondition I call the

I would like to thank John Christman, Igor Shoikedbrod, Dick Timmer and Huub Brouwer for their written comments on previous drafts, as well as audiences at the HDCA Conference, the OZSW Conference, and the (Il)liberal Democracy-group at Utrecht University. I thank the Dutch Research Council (NWO) for their financial support under grant no. 360-20-390.

[1] While I do think this is the most convincing argument, I acknowledge also arguments from negative or republican freedom could be used to defend the "liberal–egalitarian accommodation." To the extent that this is so, the remainder of the chapter is also of interest to those who are more convinced by these arguments. Personally, I believe that republicans implicitly accept, or should accept, a positive view of freedom (Claassen 2018a: 226–229; Claassen and Herzog 2019).

depoliticization of private property. Private property is conceived as a purely private phenomenon, which has no effect on the exercise of political power. As long as the liberal–egalitarian accommodation works, this precondition is easily taken for granted. However, whether this precondition is met is a contingent matter; and perhaps it can never be fully achieved. Whatever of that, in today's world, it is seriously eroded. Defenders of the positive freedom argument, therefore, need to turn their attention to the problem posed by the relation between private property and political power.

After presenting the positive freedom argument (Section 12.2), the remainder of the chapter takes up this challenge. To start up the discussion, I first present Rafe Blaufarb's account of the history of the French Revolution's attempt to abolish feudalism. He shows how the disentanglement of private property and political power was central to that revolution. This disentanglement itself can be defended normatively in terms of the ideal of (individual and collective) positive freedom. However, as Jeffrey Winters argues, this disentanglement has failed. His research shows that liberal–democratic societies in name are oligarchies in reality. In democratic oligarchies, oligarchs refrain from protecting their property rights themselves, and rely on the impersonal structure of the bureaucratic state instead (Section 12.3). Building on these accounts, I then propose a reorientation of the positive freedom argument, in three respects. Key to this reorientation is the introduction of a conception of property as "discretionary property," which gives its holders what I call "investment autonomy." Only discretionary property can be used as capital, which can be invested to give its owner political power (Section 12.4). Where this happens, we face neo-feudal entanglements under the cloak of overtly liberal–democratic structures of government; or a *re-politicization of private property*. I give two examples of such contemporary neo-feudal analogs of feudal structures: that of oppressive labor relations and lobbying activities (Section 12.5). Section 12.6 concludes.

12.2 Property in the Positive Freedom Tradition: The Liberal–Egalitarian Accommodation

In this section, I will give a reconstruction of the positive freedom argument in favor of liberal egalitarianism.[2] This argument can be summarized as an

[2] I generalize here about the tradition of positive freedom, which contains authors who have, as far as they considered property, come to a variety of positions (Reeve 1986: 107–108). My reconstruction here is based on positive freedom authors like T. H. Green ([1931] 1999: 168–169), Macpherson (1973), Christman (1994: 167), and Gewirth (1996: 173). Although less clearly in the positive

answer to three questions, all relating to property: first, what is property? Second, which form should property take? Third, who should hold how much property?[3]

(1) The definition of property. In the property literature, one definitional question is about whether property should be seen as a "right to a thing" or as a "right against other persons." The positive freedom argument combines both and defines property as a right against others with respect to a thing. Property is not simply a thing, although we sometimes speak this way when saying "This house is my property." Nor does property simply refer to a relation between a person and the object of property. Crucially, property denotes a triadic relation, where the authority of the holder of property over the object is secured against claims of others to the same thing. Moreover, this "thing" can be highly intangible, such as a share in a company or an intellectual property right (Cohen 1927: 12; Macpherson 1973: 127; Christman 1994: 16). Lawyers define the substance of this authority by distinguishing a bundle of rights, the so-called incidents of property, such as the right to use, manage, and destroy the object, the right to enjoy the income, the right to alienate, etc. (Honoré 1987).

Property rights generate two types of power for the owner, which are both, like property itself, private powers, situated in the private sphere. On the one hand, an owner has a power-to: a power to do things with the object as she likes, such as to consume it or sell it. This power is purely personal, only relating the object to its owner. On the other hand, an owner also has a power-over: a power over others, to the extent that they lack the powers-to that the owner has with respect to the object. The authority of the owner is defined by the fact that he/she can enjoy the object to the *exclusion* of others. This second power is social, in that it gives the owner power over the behavior of others, who are to refrain from interfering with her enjoyment of the object. Still, this social dimension is situated in the private sphere, between citizens. Neither of these powers is public, or political.

(2) The form of property. The second question is: which forms should property take? Usually, private property (held by individuals), public

freedom camp, many writers on property also put such a similar argument forward (e.g., Munzer 1990: 90–98; Lomasky 1987: 120; Waldron 1988: 295). See also the writings on property-owning democracy, quoted in-text. For my version of this argument, see (Claassen 2015). In the legal literature, one can think of positive freedom-inspired authors like Alexander (2009), and Dagan and Dorfman (2017).

3 See (Claassen 2018b) for an overview of these questions, with two additional dimensions of property which I leave out of consideration here: who is the legitimate subject of property? Which are the legitimate objects of property claims?

property (held by the state), and common property (held by groups of citizens) are seen as the main alternatives. The positive freedom argument focuses on private property.[4] However, positive freedom is exactly defined (as self-mastery, self-determination, or autonomy), the argument always has the same instrumental structure. A certain measure of control over a domain of private affairs is a necessary condition for the capacity to lead an autonomous life. Take, for example, Joseph Raz's conception of autonomy, which consists of the three components of (1) independence, (2) inner mental abilities, and (3) an adequate range of options (Raz 1986). Property gives one independence, since one does not have to ask permission from others for making a certain move with respect to one's property holdings. Jeremy Waldron has put this with exemplary clarity where he states:

> The element of exclusive use which property rights involve is often justified on the basis of its connection with freedom and privacy. If every resource is publicly controlled or in principle available for use by all on equal terms (. . .) the use of material resources by an individual will in every case count as an other-regarding action (. . .). And since every action involves the use of some material resources (if only the land to stand on to perform it), it would follow that individuals were answerable to others for each and every action they performed. This, it may be argued, would be intolerable: such complete answerability would be morally exhausting and individually debilitating. (Waldron 1988: 295)

Property also gives one an adequate range of options, to the extent that the domain of one's property holdings is sufficiently large. The domain in which one can make independent decisions also allows one to make choices of one's own with respect to several dimensions of a good life: one's housing, clothes, food choices, etc. Most controversially, property also helps with the development of one's inner reflexive abilities, the abilities, in Rawls's terminology, to formulate and revise a life plan. These capacities for autonomous deliberation are key to the positive freedom tradition. Thus, John Christman argued:

> The material conditions of one's life have a direct effect on the opportunities and options which, in turn, constrain the development of one's tastes and character. If there is no television around me, for example, or if the books I can read are all Zane Grey Westerns, then these conditions will affect directly the values and attitudes that I will come to have. One's

[4] In this focus, the positive freedom tradition does not diverge from the rest of political philosophy, which overwhelmingly focuses on the justification of private property.

immediate environment, of course, had the most direct effect on this process, but other conditions of one's life, such as social arrangements, leisure activities, work setting, and access to political life, will all play a basic role in the lifestyle that one must adopt as one's own. What is necessary for minimal autonomy, then, is that individuals have a degree of control over, or approval of, the general aspects of these material conditions. (Christman 1994: 167)

Christman continues the argument by saying that this in turn will involve some property over some objects. Like Waldron, however, Christman also accepts that for some objects, full property rights may not be necessary (e.g., one may also rent one's apartment), while for other material conditions access to publicly owned facilities may be enough (e.g., health care and educational facilities). In the end, what is important is having "control rights," which he defines as that part of the bundle of rights which allows a person to "manipulate, develop, perhaps destroy, and consume" (Christman 1994: 167) resources.[5] While these are not full liberal ownership rights, they still are rights to a set of exclusive, unconditional controls granted to the individual: she does not need the permission of others to exercise these rights. This is true as much for her right to get medical treatment as for her right to a private living space. Control rights in Christman's theory stand in contrast to income rights, which he defines as the rights to alienate or make productive use of one's resources (Christman 1994: 128). These latter rights are exercised in a social context (most often that of the market), and here one cannot assume such a direct link between autonomy and control. Hence, Christman argues, for these rights separate principles of distributive justice are justified.[6]

(3) The distribution of property. The third question is: how should property be distributed? Who should hold how much property? Positive freedom is an egalitarian political ideal: it requires a political structure guaranteeing the basic conditions of positive freedom to all citizens. This equality of positive freedom requires that all citizens do not just have a formal right to own whatever property they are able to acquire, but an actual bundle of some property holdings (wealth). With "some" property, I refer to a threshold level of property; a sufficientarian, not a perfectly equal distribution of property. Whether the threshold level should be very minimal or rather generous can be debated. In contrast to this, some

5 Christman largely follows Reich in conceptualizing these welfare rights as "new property rights." See Christman (1994: 172) and Reich (1964).

6 For a criticism of the distinction, see Attas (2006).

egalitarians defend narrowing the *range* between the wealthiest and the poorest as a precondition for positive freedom (either in addition to a threshold or as a self-standing principle). However, I think this does not necessarily follow from the argument so far. Positive freedom (e.g., as characterized by Raz's three dimensions of autonomy) requires a personal domain of control that is *sufficiently* large, not necessarily equally large as one's neighbors.

In theory, a sufficientarian distribution of property can be the outcome of a market economy in which all individuals trade freely (perhaps supplemented with voluntary philanthropic activities). However, very often market economies lead to unequal outcomes, so that active government intervention is needed as a correction to achieve this aim. Property egalitarianism can be implemented through welfare state mechanisms, such as public delivery of essential services (health, education) and the tax-and-transfer system. It can also be implemented through a program of "property-owning democracy," in addition to welfare state measures (Rawls 2001; O'Neill and Williamson 2012; Thomas 2017). Either way, the distributive role of government is legitimate because the "income rights" part of the property bundle has – as we saw – a less direct connection to positive freedom, compared to the "control rights" part. To fund access for all to control rights over some objects, everyone's income rights need to be relativized. Positive freedom defenders hence need to balance their commitment to an egalitarian demand for redistributing property with other prerequisites of positive freedom, such as, most notably, the economic freedoms (like the freedom of contract), which underlie a market economy.

In conclusion, the positive freedom tradition defends a powerful philosophical argument for the liberal–egalitarian accommodation to capitalism. Like classical liberals, positive freedom defenders endorse a private property-based market economy, protected by government. Unlike them, they also endorse government-enforced measures to distribute property (more) equally than the market would. Let's now turn to the tacit precondition of this argument, the depoliticization of property.

12.3 Back to History: The Great, but Fragile Demarcation

The revolutions of the eighteenth century have been decisive moments in the establishment of liberal–democratic regimes in the Western world. They are also revolutions in the history of property. I take my lead from two books, which provide contrasting but ultimately complementary perspectives on the problem of property, in the context of discussing the French Revolution and the American Revolution, respectively. Blaufarb in his *The Great Demarcation* (2016) argues that the French revolutionaries attempted to break the feudal entanglements of private property and political power and establish a "great demarcation" between both. Winters, in his *Oligarchy* (2011), shows how the American revolutionaries were trying to shelter the property holdings of the wealthiest from popular control. He argues that the great demarcation in reality was meant to provide a cloak for the continued political power of property. On closer inspection, it turns out to be a very fragile demarcation.

Blaufarb's book is a close study of a decisive moment in the French Revolution and its aftermath.[7] The moment was the so-called Décret du 4 août, adopted by the revolutionary *Assemblée Nationale* in the night of August 4, 1789. Just a few weeks after the downfall of the Bastille, and under pressure from peasant riots all over France, the Assemblée in this decree solemnly declared that it "hereby completely abolishes the feudal system" (article 1). The nineteen articles of the decree dictate the abolishment of personal serfdom, Church and noble privileges, manorial courts, ground rents, and other feudal practices. Blaufarb argues in his book that this historical event should be understood as a constitutional moment; not, or not just, a socio-economic moment in a bourgeois revolution (as Marxist scholars have argued). He details the juridical debates in the decades before the Revolution, and how the decree builds on these debates and decides the matter on behalf of the anti-feudal side in the debate.

What was at stake, Blaufarb argues, was a rearrangement of the relation between private property and political power. The feudal regime blurred the relation between them, from both sides of the divide. In the "private" sphere, property often gave rise to political power. Landholding – which was the predominant form of holding property – followed the rules of the tenurial system. Landed property, the so-called fiefs – were divided in a hierarchical chain all the way up from the Crown, through several layers of Lords, to simple tenants at the bottom. Each of them was subordinated to the higher strata, through bonds that were not simply proprietarian, but enmeshed with personal dependencies. Subordinates had to swear loyalty to their lords (the *seigneurs*), perform menial tasks, pay dues, and be subjected to their civil and criminal jurisdiction (Blaufarb 2016: 4).

[7] The analogy with feudalism is something one rarely encounters in contemporary political philosophy. An exception, which inspired my own approach, is Freeman (2001).

On the other hand, in the "public" sphere, political power under the *Ancien Régime* was treated as a piece of private property, in the form of the so-called *offices vénales*. These were a creation of the monarchy from the sixteenth century onwards, which, under fiscal stress, had started to sell public offices in the bureaucracy, courts, and military for money. A true market for these offices arose, they could be bought and sold, given as part of a dowry, used as collateral on a loan, etc. (Blaufarb 2016: 2). Sovereignty was thus fractured and divided into countless pieces held by private persons as their property. Of course, the King himself also held his public power as personal property, although he could not sell this office, but only bequest it to his heirs. The venal offices can be seen as a radical extension of this personifying logic all across the public sphere.[8]

The revolutionaries wanted to do away with this state of affairs and create a great demarcation, Blaufarb argues. The realm of private property should be purged from elements of political power, while at the same time the pieces of the realm of public power should be reassembled into one unified, truly public power. For what reason? As Blaufarb points out, the underlying motive of the revolutionaries was to create a domain of free and equal citizenship on the one hand, and a domain of popular sovereignty on the other hand (Blaufarb 2016: 13). Here things become interesting for the tradition of positive freedom. These twin ideals are, in contemporary terminology, those of individual and collective positive freedom.

Isaiah Berlin famously discussed both of these forms of positive freedom, without at all times making a sound distinction between them (Berlin 2002; see also Macpherson 1973: 109). However, both are important for the set-up of a modern, post-feudal society which the French revolutionaries had in mind. On the one hand, in the private sphere, people could become independent citizens, being freed from relations of subordination to others through their possession of individual, absolute property rights. On the other hand, by having a public sphere of unified sovereign power, purified of private interests, citizens could collectively exercise power over themselves. Put differently, the *ontological* split between a pure private and a pure public domain is a necessary condition for the realization of the two *normative* ideals which the revolutionaries allocated to these spheres: individual and collective positive freedom. Blaufarb's historical narrative suggests that the fates of individual freedom

8 In addition to privately held office, the public sphere was affected by property in another way. The Crown was an important landowner itself, owning countless royal domains. Blaufarb in the final parts of his book discusses how difficult it was to get rid of these domains.

and collective freedom hang in the balance together. If the revolutionaries were right, then realizing these normative ideals requires a specific institutional program of purification, of making sure political power was not tainted with propietarian elements and vice versa. Such a constitutional relation between property and power is the precondition of the liberal–egalitarian accommodation.[9]

Although this ontological split is a necessary condition, however, it may not be a *sufficient* condition. Blaufarb himself suggests as much, with respect to the public sphere. For within a few years after the French Revolution, Napoleon's dictatorship showed that the newly formed unified sovereign power, taken out of the hands of feudal lords, could also be used for authoritarian purposes (Blaufarb 2016: 11). I would add that the same is true on the other side of the divide, where the purification of property from feudal rights and obligations does not guarantee equal freedom for all.[10] The risk is that under the cover of an overtly liberal–democratic regime, private property continues to (1) exercise political power itself (in the private sphere) and (2) influence political decision-making (in the public sphere). To understand our contemporary problems in maintaining the demarcation of property and political power, I will now turn to Winters's work, which provides a comparative study of different political regimes, modern and premodern, under the perspective of wealth-holding.

Oligarchs are defined by Winters as "actors who command and control massive concentrations of material resources that can be deployed to defend or enhance their personal wealth and exclusive position" (Winters 2011: 6). Oligarchy refers to the "politics of wealth" by oligarchs, and Winters describes this politics as one of "wealth defense": the use of resources for protecting (1) existing property holdings (this Winters calls "property defense") as well as (2) the income streams deriving from them ("income defense") (Winters 2011: 6–7). Winters explains how oligarchs can pursue wealth defense either by ruling themselves directly, like warlords, sultans, or dictators, or by defending their wealth indirectly, in a situation where others rule. His conviction is that all existing and past

9 In contemporary theories of justice, this theme of "sphere separation" has been stressed by Walzer (1983).

10 Blaufarb's book catalogs in great detail the problems the revolutionaries encountered in the years after 1879 to actually make the Great Demarcation work. It turned out to be a juridical quagmire to resolve the competing claims of lords and tenants, and to purify the public domain from proprietary influences (I will come back to these matters in Section 12.5).

societies are to some extent oligarchies. The difference is that in modern democratic societies, wealth defense is pursued indirectly.

From this perspective, the revolutions of the eighteenth century can be interpreted as a transition from one form of oligarchy to another. Oligarchies and democracies are not mutually exclusive regime types, and oligarchy persists under conditions of democratic decision-making. To explain why this transition can be advantageous to oligarchs, Winters stresses what he sees as an essential link between property and violence (Winters 2011: 21). Large wealth inequalities always cause social conflict. Hence wealth needs to be protected, ultimately by force. When oligarchs rule directly, they have to hire others to protect their wealth. When they accept a democratic state, they surrender political authority to an impersonal government and disarm. In exchange, they get secured property rights. It is now the state who – largely at the expense of the (upper-) middle classes who pay the lion's share of taxes – protects everyone's property rights, including those of the oligarchs (Winters 2011: 24). Their property defense thus guaranteed, oligarchs can focus on income defense. This can be described as an implicit bargain. On noneconomic issues, the public can decide freely, and oligarchs may differ in their political views as well. However, on issues linked to the protection of wealth, on which oligarchs agree, democracy must bow to their interests. In Winters's words, "democracy and oligarchy can coexist indefinitely as long as the unpropertied classes do not use their expanded political participation to encroach upon the material power and prerogatives of the wealthiest" (Winters 2011: 11).

Of course, this strategy has its preconditions; and ideology is an important one. Theories of democracy and property together need to legitimize this bargain. Under the guise of "equality" and "the rule of law," everyone's property is protected against assaults. The fact that this is more advantageous to those who own a lot cannot be read from the face of the law. Winters notes how across different sorts of regimes from antiquity to today large-scale redistribution has most of the time successfully been constructed as illegitimate.[11] One particularly influential argument was raised in the context of the eighteenth century American adoption of the US Constitution, also in 1789. In the years before, the newly independent country suffered a severe economic recession as a backlash of the war with England. Rich American landholders had lent to the state governments to

[11] The rare moments of such ideological justifications broke down, oligarchs fell back on a violent defense of their property claims (Winters 2011: 21, 25).

sponsor the war and also financed mortgages for farmers on a large scale. To protect their interests, they pushed the government to tax the general population to pay off their debts to them; while at the same time they used the court system to push farmers to pay off their mortgages. This led to fierce struggles, judicial and violent, between debtors and creditors, which played out differently in different states (Winters 2017: 178–184).

In this setting, a decisive theoretical argument was made by James Madison, Alexander Hamilton, and others, which echoed earlier statements of the problem of oligarchy by Aristotle, Montesquieu, and others (Winters 2017: 176–177). This argument was that the rich formed a minority, which, like all minorities in a democracy, needed to be protected against the tyranny of the majority. The Founding Fathers believed that there will always be rich and poor classes in a free country; inequality is the price of freedom. To obtain a stable democracy, the interests of both classes have to be protected, and this requires in particular a defense of the wealth of the rich (Winters 2017: 184–186). This argument is widespread in the history of political philosophy. It is not only found in Aristotle and other prerevolution writings, but also, strikingly, in John Stuart Mill's mid-nineteenth century liberalism. When discussing the class interests of "manual laborers" and "employers of labor," Mill explicitly defended that "these two classes (. . .) should be, in the arrangements of the representative system, equally balanced, each influencing about an equal number of votes in Parliament" (Mill 1991: 300).[12]

The practical effect was that a constitution was passed which in several respects protected the interests of the rich in the defense of their wealth. It put the right to print money and the right to pass bankruptcy laws in the hands of the federal government, thus putting these weapons beyond the reach of the states. It created a Senate with a limited membership, in which the interests of large landholders would be represented. Finally, a powerful Supreme Court was created, not directly accountable to the people. Its power to constitutionally protect the rich would appear over time, up until today's *Citizens United* ruling (Winters 2017: 187). On top of this, Winters recounts, has come the twentieth-century development of what he calls an "Income Defense Industry": the army of professional lawyers, consultants, bankers, and others who help wealthy clients to escape taxation and pursue other means to protect their income (Winters 2011: chapter 5). We may add to this the property qualifications which, until

[12] The reverse claims in the history of philosophy, emphasizing the danger the rich pose to political stability, are given by Machiavelli, Jefferson, and Tocqueville (Winters 2011: 29–30).

the twentieth century, were imposed on the eligibility to vote, which prove how resistant the thought was, even in a modern context, that property is a prerequisite for exercising political power.

What should we take away from all of this? Whereas the French Revolution, in Blaufarb's rendering, provided the blueprint for a modern, liberal state in which private property and public power are neatly separated, the American Revolution, in Winters's account, shows how beneath the surface a structure is created which serves the interests of those holding property. Both accounts supplement each other. The Revolutions provide us with a normative blueprint of liberal democracy and at the same time open up the question of whether this Great Demarcation isn't a Fragile Demarcation, which can never be realized, given the interests of the wealthy. The philosophical question is how to conceptualize this conundrum. If, as Winters suggests, ideology plays a role here, what are the obstacles in our *theories* of property which make it so difficult in practice to withhold political power from private property?

12.4 Discretionary Property and the Autonomy to Invest in Political Rule

The problem of private property's political power suggests a threefold reorientation, compared to the standard argument, presented in Section 12.2. In this section, I will outline this program of reorientation, with a focus on one of the three elements: the conception of property itself.

(1) Collective positive freedom. Today, discussions of positive freedom are almost invariably about individual positive freedom. The collective concept is most often set apart, when discussed at all (Christman 1991). This does not mean that there is no attention to the social constitution of individual positive freedom; indeed the extent to which one can only be free as an individual under the right social condition is very much a part of the debate (see "Introduction" to this volume). Still, this is different from a focus on collective positive freedom.[13] The relative neglect of collective freedom is also apparent in the property literature, although there are exceptions (Macpherson 1973; Gould 1988). The standard argument described in Section 12.2 is focused on connecting

[13] Democratic theory is all about collective freedom and here there are discussions about the relation between both types of freedom. Is there an intrinsic argument for democracy, from the point of view of individual freedom? Or is there an instrumental link, in the sense that more democracy enhances respect for individual freedoms? (Claassen 2018a: chapter 7). Are private and public autonomy "co-original," as Habermas has suggested? (Habermas 1996).

the constitutive elements of individual positive freedom to private property. What the historical account developed earlier suggests is that collective positive freedom is a precondition to having individual positive freedom. For without a domain of collective freedom, in which political power is exercised impartially, sheltered from the undermining influence of private property, no domain of individual freedom can be guaranteed (in addition, this may also require a revaluation of collective, either common or public, forms of property, as conditions for both individual and collective freedom itself, see (Claassen 2018a: 178–185)).

(2) The conception of property. Second, a reconceptualization of the conception of property itself is necessary, showing how and under which conditions property can become a source of political power under ostensibly liberal regimes.[14] As we saw in Section 12.2, property rights give owners two kinds of private power (control over objects, control in the sense of exclusion of others). What does it mean to say that property is, or generates, *political* power? The locus classic for the claim that property is a form of political power is Morris Cohen's "Property and Sovereignty," where he argued that "dominion over things is also imperium over our fellow human beings" (Cohen 1927: 13). In his view, property amounts to the exercise of "political sovereignty." In defense of this claim, Cohen makes a comparison between feudal lords and modern captains of industry. In his view, both had the power to "command the services of large numbers who are not economically dependent," and both had the power to "determine what we may buy and use." These phenomena give an illustration of property's political power, indeed. However, what is lacking is a property-theoretical explanation of how this comes about.

The first step to such an explanation is to make a distinction between property that is used as capital and property that is not used as capital. The history of conceptualizing capital is split between one tradition which sees capital in materialist terms and another one in process terms. According to the former, capital is a stock of material objects, such as factories and machineries, which can be used to generate new wealth when mixed with land and labor. Capital in this sense refers to "capital goods," which are to

[14] Despite the fact that the political effects of wealth-holding have recently got some more attention in political philosophy, work on this remains scarce. From a liberal perspective, see Christiano (2010, 2012), J. Green (2016), and Robeyns (2017). The literature on property-owning democracy, despite being focused on the undermining of democracy ('the fair value of the political liberties') by inequalities in property (Rawls 2001: 139), does not address the problem in property-theoretic terms (O'Neill and Williamson 2012; Thomas 2017). Neo-republicans come closer to the issue as I conceive it here (e.g., McCormick 2006, 2011; Rahman 2017; Thompson 2018).

be distinguished from consumer goods, since the former, but not the latter are a means of production. The alternative tradition holds that capital is an investment fund. As Jonathan Levy states: "Capital is property capitalized – a legal asset assigned a pecuniary value in expectation of a likely future pecuniary income" (Levy 2017: 494).[15] In this view, anything can become capital when it is assigned a pecuniary value in search of future profits. Land and labor (slaves!) have certainly functioned as capital in the past, as have machines and financial assets. Capital is property invested in an uncertain future (Beckert 2016: 201). I will here follow this process definition of capital.

This definition, with its reference to the future income, zooms in one of the two parts in the bundle of property rights which Christman distinguished. When owners start using their assets not for personal use, but for generating income in the future, they exercise a specific part of their property rights: their income rights. The political power of property arises only in this context. It is not because others are excluded from simultaneous access to the objects that I own (my nonpolitical power), but because I make use of my property to generate income, that I can wield political power. Put differently, property as an object of control is different from property as a resource mobilized for investment. Thus, for a different (but complementary) reason than Christman's, I would endorse a development of property theory in which these two parts of the property bundle are radically separated. Their impact is different; hence the analysis must be different.[16]

Not all property, however, can be converted into capital. The next step, I propose, is to introduce a concept of "discretionary property." We can think of this on an analogy with Robert Goodin's concept of "discretionary time," which is the time available for use after one has spent time on generating a socially accepted standard of living. Such discretionary time generates "temporal autonomy" (Goodin et al. 2008). Similarly, it is a prerequisite for capital investment to have property discretionarily available, i.e., property not needed to cover one's basic living expenses. Let the latter level be indicated by a socially accepted standard-of-living, and discretionary property defines whatever property holdings one has above this line. Having property available above the standard-of-living as

[15] This follows an institutionalist tradition that includes Veblen and Commons. I encountered the reference to Levy in Pistor (2019: 12), who makes use of the same tradition.

[16] A closely related distinction is the one between "personal property" and property in "the means of production." However, that distinction has physicalist overtones; as if some types of objects essentially are one or the other. It is the type of use made of property that is crucial.

discretionary property, gives its holder "investment autonomy," i.e., the ability to transform one's property holdings into capital. This gives discretionary property a different, political potential, which nondiscretionary property does not have. This potential is concealed on the surface. Just as time as an abstract quality always looks the same, the visible money and material goods held by two persons do not show by themselves how they are discretionary resources for the one, but not for the other person. When we pierce through this illusion, we realize that both types of property require a differential treatment. Inequalities between individuals in terms of investment autonomy are at the source of their differential ability to exercise political power.

(3) Equality in distribution. Third and finally, this necessitates a reorientation in the positive freedom defenders' take on inequality. The analysis in Section 12.2 earlier revealed the need for a sufficiently large domain of control to become positively free. This can roughly be equated with the level of the standard of living just mentioned. The argument here suggests going beyond this requirement, and mandates an egalitarian range: a maximum ratio of the highest to the lowest wealth holdings. The reason for this is that inequalities in investment autonomy can be converted (if the analysis in the following section is convincing) into differences in political power. These differences, when too large, undermine the liberal dichotomy, the Great Demarcation between private property and public power, to which defenders of positive freedom should remain wedded. To put this bluntly, imagine a two-person world in which the standard of living is at 10. Now imagine person A holding resources at level 11, person B at a much higher level, say 40. While both can access a private domain of control, B can invest resources into private and public means of buying political power, while A cannot. In the end, B will come to dominate A. Hence, a much further going equalization of control over resources between the A's and B's of this world is needed, although it is difficult to say how much exactly (Claassen 2018a: 185–191).

In this section, I have proposed a reorientation of the positive freedom theorist's argument about property, in several respects. Discretionary property, available as capital freed up for investment, can in principle be used to generate political power, also under liberal-democratic conditions. But *how* does that happen? This will be the topic of the final section.

12.5 From Feudalism to Neo-feudal Entanglements

Several authors have proposed theoretical models for understanding the links between private property and political power (Lindblom 2001;

McCormick 2006; Christiano 2012). Most of these accounts only look at the public sphere (the political arena), i.e., one of the two sides of the Great Demarcation. I propose we need a unified account of the emergence of political power on *both sides* of the divide. These are complicated empirical processes. For example, on the public side, we have to look at lobbying, campaign finance, threats of relocation, funding of think tanks and media outlets, etc. Nonetheless, I think it is fruitful to systematize these phenomena as a matter of property theory.[17] To make this plausible, I will in this section once more return to the birthplace of the Great Demarcation, and argue that contemporary "neo-feudal" entanglements of private property with political power can be seen as close cousins of the original feudal entanglements. I use two examples, one on the private side, and the other on the public side of the private/public divide.

As mentioned earlier, with the official abolishment of the feudal order, the great demarcation was not yet established. A key debate in the years after 1789 turned on the compensation measures that, many believed, were required to implement a non-feudal order. For the Decree of August 4 required every landowner to be bought out by the tenant who wanted to acquire his land in full ownership. Some opposed this, but the revolutionary Assemblée initially held on to the position that the creation of absolute ownership rights without compensation would be an unjust expropriation of the lords, whose collecting of feudal dues provided their main source of revenue. However, this position provoked a strong backlash from peasants and their spokesman in the Assemblée, who complained that the right to become full owner would be meaningless, because almost nobody could pay the nationally determined rate of compensation, which was meant to reflect the full price of land had it been on an open market (Blaufarb 2016: 72).

To complicate matters, the legislation dealing with these procedures made a distinction between two types of lord–tenant relation: those which were based on contract and those which were based on force and domination. Feudal dues were considered to be contractual, unless proven otherwise, and hence apt for compensation (Blaufarb 2016: 70–71). As the Revolution progressed, the opposition against this system increased, and in 1793 it was overturned by an approach that presumed that all

[17] For an account that shows more systematically how this political power of capital is shaped in a variety of legal dimensions (see Pistor 2019). Also see theories of "extractive power" (Thompson 2018; building on Macpherson 1973), "value extraction" (Mazzucato 2018), and "rent-seeking" (Stiglitz 2012: 119–127) in the economy.

feudal contracts were invalid, because tainted by histories of domination (Blaufarb 2016: 82). This reversal of the burden of proof was fiercely opposed by those defending the lords' interests, as an illicit form of expropriation.[18] This shows that already at that time, there was an acute awareness that the feudal property relations represented an ambiguous legacy: sometimes lord–tenant relations could be based on legitimate exchanges of promises, but other times they could be cover-ups for illegitimate exercises of power. It also shows that there is no politically neutral approach to solving such property disputes. Each of the approaches chosen over time has its own political winners and losers.

A very similar ambiguity holds for the current-day labor contract. Is it an expression of voluntary will or a source of oppression? All sides of the debate today grant that labor contracts – as much as the feudal land contracts – create a relation of authority. This insight is the starting point of the economic theory of the firm, which argues that firms come into existence because it is more efficient to create relations of authority between employers and employees than have spot-market contracts between them for every separate act of production (Coase 1937; Singer 2018). However, many economists hold that employment contracts are voluntarily undertaken, which renders the submission to authority unproblematic. This is attacked by critics. For example, Elizabeth Anderson criticized two economists holding this point of view as follows:

> Alchian and Demsetz appear to be claiming that wherever individuals are free to exit a relationship, authority cannot exist within it. This is like saying that Mussolini was not a dictator, because Italians could emigrate. ... Perhaps the thought is that where consent mediates the relationship between parties, the relationship cannot be one of subordination. That would be a surprise to the entire social contract tradition, which is precisely about how people can consent to government. (Anderson 2017: 55)

Such an insistence on the continuing fact that the labor relationship is a hierarchical one is a prerequisite for the argument which many Marxists have made, and which Anderson subsequently also makes, that workers most of the time face very high exit costs, and thus should be understood as facing a contract which is more coercive than voluntary (Anderson

18 The search for ending the divided domain, and creating absolute property rights, may seem to reveal a wish to do away with any bundle-splitting; making any tenant-relation impossible. However, I read the history as focusing on creating *just* property rights, i.e., non-affected with political rights/duties, which can include freely contracted forms of fragmentation of property rights.

2017: 56). To the extent that this is true,[19] labor relations are exercises of *political* power in the private sphere, just as much as feudal land contracts were. They give employers regulatory capacity with respect to many aspects of their workers' lives, which workers cannot (easily) escape. The contractual nature of the labor contract conceals this continuity with the *Ancien Régime*.

Let's now turn to the public sphere. Interestingly, venal offices were already contested during the *Ancien Régime*. For example, Rousseau condemned the phenomenon in his *Discourse on Political Economy*, saying "venality [is] pushed to such excess that reputation is reckoned in cash, and the virtues themselves are sold for money" (Rousseau 1997: 19). Interestingly, such a suspicion of venality had already led one of the most famous lawyers during the *Ancien Régime*, Charles Loyseau, to create a new doctrine, in which the property in the office is split. The officeholder, who has bought the office from the state, should be understood as having a right "in" an office but not "to" that office, Loyseau claimed. He has a merely usufructuary right while the state retained the property right to the office (Kaiser 1994: 306). This is quite a remarkable construction, resembling the idea of contemporary democratic theories that office holding is the only temporary grant of power that always remains tied to a giver (the state itself). The latter retains this power and will give it to others at some future point in time. The distinction gives a flavor of legitimacy to venality by suggesting that the property right remains where it belongs, in public hands. Of course, this construction could not save these offices from critique. Even if offices are merely usufructuary rights both under feudal and democratic regimes, the meritocratic nature of gaining political power through elections is different from the commercial nature of buying and selling offices. Nonetheless, the discussion shows how subtle the understanding of these offices can be.

A not-so-different thing is going on when rich individuals or corporations buy political power by donating to politicians. Here too, the suggestion is that political power truly remains in the hands of politicians, despite receiving donations from private individuals. In this area, and also in the area of lobbying, explicit contracts (quid pro quos) are condemned as instances of corruption. However, despite this danger of corruption, the practices themselves are allowed, albeit to different degrees in different

[19] This extent is variable, even under a capitalist economy, depending on the exit options welfare states give to workers. Welfare states can de-commodify labor, i.e., decrease this dependency, by providing alternative sources of income (Esping-Andersen 1990).

countries. The rationale for this is that democracies rely on input from private parties (both financial and in-kind) to the political process. In a democracy, groups of citizens are allowed political participation, and hence need to be able to fund their political activities. All of this should be different once one of them gains office, however; from that moment onwards, past influences should not play any role. Hence the liberal-democratic system puts private parties and political actors in a fundamentally ambiguous situation to each other. Campaign donations may have been made out of genuine enthusiasm for a candidate, without expecting a return. They may also have been made with the implicit expectation of a return. If the labor contract is an *incomplete* contract, this is an *implicit* contract. In both cases, political power can nest in the structure undercover, without revealing its true nature.

Both before and after the Great Demarcation, theorists wrestled with these boundary-crossings between property and political power. From feudal land to modern labor, from venal office to lobbying, the entanglements remain, albeit now concealed under the official private/public distinction which prohibits the influence of private property on political power.

12.6 Conclusion

This chapter has argued that defenders of egalitarian property arrangements (among whom, many defenders of positive freedom) have to pay more attention to the great but fragile demarcation on which their argument for such arrangements relies. The demarcation is built on a purification of private and public spheres which is constantly undermined. Capitalist legal-political arrangements themselves leave space for such undermining dynamics, where discretionary property is invested in political rule. We are left with Winters's sobering assessment, that the transition to liberal-democratic societies may well have been a cost-reducing device for oligarchs searching to protect their property. The big question for defenders of positive freedom is to see how this liberal order can be made truly egalitarian. This would require a fortifying of the great but fragile demarcation. This chapter has analyzed that problem is some depth. However, this opens up many competing ways to deal with the problem, which need to be addressed in future research.

CHAPTER 13

Public Reason, Positive Liberty, and Legitimacy

Chad Van Schoelandt

> No greater freedom can be imagined for a man than absolute, blind submission to an unjust law.
>
> G. A. Cohen (1991)

13.1 Introduction

The public reason tradition holds that authoritative laws or social moral rules must be justified *to* the people subject to them. The rules must be justified on the basis of reasons that members of society have or can reasonably access, particularly reasons deriving from their own beliefs and values on sincere reflection, not merely reasons that may exist inaccessibly to them.[1] This tradition incorporates multiple ideas of freedom. Most prominent for most theories of public reason are forms of negative liberty – freedom in the sense of not being interfered with by another. The basic idea is that people are free and equal, so each should be allowed to choose for themselves unless there is sufficient justification for someone to interfere. Public reason views hold that there is a presumption of liberty such that an individual does not need to justify her private actions but does have to justify interfering with, coercing, or making moral demands on others. In Gaus's (2011: 344–345) example, Alan does not have to justify his splitting of pebbles on the public beach but Betty must justify interfering with Alan's pebble splitting.[2] In a similar vein, Rawls (2005: xliv, 68) endorses liberty insofar as he holds that exercises of coercive political power specifically require public justification.[3] As Kevin Vallier (2014: 31)

[1] For elaboration of this form of justification-to and discussion of what sorts of rules fundamentally require public justification, see Van Schoelandt (2015). For a general introduction to public reason, see Gaus and Van Schoelandt (2015).

[2] Gaus gets the example from Benn (1988), though I am here interested in Gaus's use of this case as part of a public reason account.

[3] For discussion, see Neufeld and Van Schoelandt (2014).

notes, this presumption of liberty in the public reason tradition is specifically a presumption of *negative* liberty.

Despite the prominence of negative liberty, the public reason tradition also considers positive liberty. Following Bringhurst and Gaus (2018: section 1), I here understand positive liberty in terms of reasoned control as part of free agency or living a free life.[4] One can see this sort of positive liberty in Immanuel Kant's moral philosophy with its emphasis on the autonomy of acting in accordance with reason in contrast to the heteronomy of following one's mere inclination without reason's regulation.[5] Following one's unrestrained desires, on such an account, is a form of unfreedom. The core Kantian idea is that true liberty involves compliance with the laws one gives oneself. In this way, morality, instead of being a constraint on one's liberty, is a prerequisite and foundation of one's liberty.

The public reason tradition focuses on the laws (or social moral rules) that members of society impose upon each other.[6] Though laws constrain negative liberty, the legal system is compatible with or even conducive to the members of society treating each other as free and equal persons if and only if the laws are publicly justified to each member. Publicly justified laws help each member live in accordance with her own reason and values, and thus a publicly justified legal system helps members realize positive liberty. Such laws are an important foundation of liberty.

Positive liberty is realized in laws supported by one's reason, rather than purely arbitrary or merely externally imposed laws. One might plausibly think that liberty requires laws to realize justice. G. A. Cohen (1991) humorously claims that the greatest freedom is realized in submission to an *unjust* law while satirizing what he sees as a particularly German understanding of freedom as submission rather than following one's desires. One does not live a free life through blind submission to unjust laws, and it would seem paradoxical for someone to suggest that unjust laws are a source of positive liberty.

The fact that positive liberty seems grounded in *just* laws raises an important difficulty for public reason theorists. Put bluntly, public reason

[4] This is not the only form of positive liberty one may be concerned with. Alternatives include liberty as power, as discussed by Gaus (2000: chapter 5), or freedom-to, as discussed by Schmidtz and Brennan (2010: 3–4, 10–11). See also the "Introduction" to this volume.

[5] Sensen (2017) provides an insightful discussion relating Kant and the public reason tradition.

[6] Throughout this chapter, I discuss laws since most public reason theorists focus on them. On a number of views, however, including my own, laws are secondary to the social-moral rules to which members of society hold each other accountable. On this sort of social morality, see Gaus (2011: chapter IV), Strawson (1961, 1962), Van Schoelandt (2018).

theorists must hold that submitting to unjust laws can realize positive liberty. As this chapter explains, public reason theorists have come to recognize that the exercise of reason in a free society generates divergent views about justice.[7] Members of society reasonably disagree about justice, so we cannot expect that any society will be fully just from each member's perspective. In light of this, theorists have turned their attention from ideals of a fully just society to institutions that each member can recognize as *legitimate* even if not fully just.[8] On public reason accounts, legitimate laws warrant voluntary compliance even if members of society may also work to reform the laws in hopes of making them more just. With this transition, public reason theorists must clarify whether positive liberty is being abandoned along with justice or how positive liberty is realized through unjust, though legitimate, laws.

This chapter will consider three public reason approaches for positive liberty within a society that is, from an individual's perspective, legitimate though not fully just. The Values strategy holds that shared justificatory values are sufficient for liberty despite disagreement about which institutions best realize those values. The Political strategy holds that legitimate laws go a long way toward supporting members' positive liberty though a member would realize even more liberty were she to live in a society that was fully just from her perspective. The Civil strategy holds that the members of a merely legitimate society must rely more on nonpolitical supports for positive liberty, such as the development of personal virtue and participation in voluntary associations. This nonpolitical strategy thus does not give up on achieving positive liberty, but instead emphasizes alternative approaches to liberation. The Shared Social World strategy holds that in conditions of reasonable pluralism reason directs us to live according to the rules we can reasonably share with others rather than demanding compliance with the rules we might find ideal. Positive liberty, then, is realized by members living under rules that each may recognize as legitimate, even if the society does not satisfy their ideals of justice.

13.2 Well-Ordered Societies

The public reason account of positive liberty is most straightforward when we consider what Rawls (1999: section 69; 2001: section 3) calls a well-

[7] The society need not even be particularly free for disagreements to emerge, for even the totalitarian regimes of the twentieth century produced dissidents and significant ideological divisions.

[8] Gaus and Van Schoelandt (2017) discuss the development of Rawls's thought regarding disagreement about justice.

ordered society. Such a society is characterized by the members effectively governing their society in accordance with a shared conception of justice. The laws of such a society are justified to each member since each member reasonably endorses the governing conception of justice to which the laws conform. The members make moral demands on each other and coercively enforce laws, but these are only the demands and laws that each member herself reasonably endorses. In such a society, then, each member can recognize that the laws are in accordance with her own reason and thus facilitate, rather than detract from, her ability to live as a free person. With this sketch in view, it is worth considering what the members of a well-ordered society agree and disagree about.

13.2.1 Disagreement

Even in the most ideal of cases, members of society deeply disagree about wide-ranging issues. People reason under what Rawls (2005: section II.2) calls the burdens of judgment, including the facts that moral concepts are often vague, values must be weighed, evidence is often conflicting, and our overall assessments are influenced by our differing life experiences.[9] Public reason theorists accept the enduring fact that sincere exercise of reason leads people to diverse and conflicting moral, religious, and philosophic views, including views about how to live a good life. Briefly, there is reasonable pluralism of comprehensive views. This disagreement is centrally important since it limits what laws are justifiable to the diverse members. For instance, laws imposing adherence to a particular religion are not justifiable to the members of society insofar as they reasonably disagree about religion. Such laws would impose on people the requirements of another's reason rather than the requirements of their own reason. Public reason theorists, such as Gaus (1999: 7–9), hold that laws that are not publicly justified are authoritarian. Imposing laws based on one's reasonably rejected comprehensive views fail to treat others as free and equal. Public reason theorists are thus interested in what institutions can be justified to members of society given their reasonable pluralism of comprehensive views.

13.2.2 Agreement within Well-Ordered Society

Despite their deep disagreements in comprehensive views, members of a well-ordered society agree on a conception of justice. It is worth detailing

[9] Besson (2005: pt. 1) insightfully discusses in considerable detail the sources of reasonable disagreement. Muldoon (2016, 2017) provides valuable insights regarding perspectival diversity.

what this agreement includes. For a simple example, consider a society well-ordered by Rawls's (2001) conception of justice as fairness. Though the members have deep diversity in their comprehensive doctrines, each endorses justice as fairness. Most centrally, that means they all agree that the appropriate principles for governing their society are the principle of liberty, fair equality of opportunity, and the difference principle and that a prior principle has absolute priority over any later principle. Since that conception is itself open to diverse interpretations, we must further assume that the members share the same interpretation of justice as fairness. For instance, they all interpret the difference principle as including leisure among its relevant goods. In the same vein, members of a well-ordered society agree about the scope of application of the principles, such as whether and how the principles of justice regulate families.[10] Of course, for us, nothing hangs on *which* interpretation they share, or even *which* conception of justice they share, so long as they share one.

Beyond the principles of justice, members also agree to a set of political values and a free-standing justification of the principles from those values. For justice as fairness, the members share a conception of themselves as free and equal citizens with a sense of justice and the capacity to form and revise a conception of the good, and from this conception, they construct a procedure in which representatives under a veil of ignorance in an original position select the principles of justice as fairness over alternatives such as utilitarianism.

The members of society also agree that the society in fact satisfies their shared conception of justice. Though many theorists do not emphasize the difficulty here, assessing whether a society does so is not a simple matter. Typically, we expect agreement that a society satisfies a given conception of justice to rest on the members' agreeing about the effects of policies in the complex social system. For instance, the members must agree on whether the economic system satisfies the difference principle. Assessing that requires a variety of judgments, including assessing the index of different goods (income, prerogatives, etc.) relevant to the principle. Even more difficult is that such assessment requires comparing the actual system to possible alternative systems. The difference principle, after all, requires *maximizing* the prospects for the least well-off, so it requires that the least well-off have prospects at least as great as this class would under any relevant alternative. Every member of such a society well-ordered around justice as fairness agrees that the society satisfies that requirement.

[10] For defense of one interpretation regarding families, see Neufeld and Van Schoelandt (2014).

This is not particular to the difference principle, for other principles of justice raise similar issues. For instance, within justice as fairness, fair equality of opportunity requires assessing the effects of policies on opportunities and assessing which qualitatively different opportunities may be relevantly equal. Assessing the fair value of political liberties, as part of the principle of liberty, requires assessing the effectiveness of diverse members' political liberties, including whether differences in wealth can be converted into differences in political power. Alternatives to justice as fairness would likewise require difficult empirical assessments. For instance, utilitarianism requires comparisons to unimplemented alternatives and the capabilities approach requires assessing the effects of policies on the different capabilities.[11] Likewise, a Nozickean entitlement theory requires assessing the justness of the actual history of property holdings, including determining such difficult issues as whether past injustices were properly rectified, whether the Lockean Proviso to leave enough and as good was satisfied (requiring comparisons to counterfactual circumstances), and which risky behaviors may be prevented (and with what forms of compensation).[12] The general point here is that a well-ordered society, in requiring members to agree that their society satisfies their shared conception of justice, requires the otherwise highly diverse members to agree about a wide range of complex empirical issues.

13.2.3 Positive Liberty in a Well-Ordered Society

It is worth emphasizing that the conditions of well-orderedness involve a reasoned recognition of the requirements of justice. The focus is not on a society that merely happens to satisfy the requirements of some understanding of justice thought to be independent of the reason and values of the members of the society, such as an esoteric Platonic ideal. Instead, the society is structured in accordance with standards supported by the reason and values of the members of that society. The institutions thus only demand from a member what her reason supports. For each member, the laws compel her to act as her own reasoning would lead her to see as the right way to act, and these laws are conducive to promoting the good as she

[11] On the capabilities approach, see Nussbaum (2001) and Sen (1993).

[12] On such entitlement theories, see Nozick (1974) and Mack (2018). Lomasky (2005) argues that one can get rather different results from the entitlement theory than Nozick defended in light of the actual history of extensive injustice. Otsuka (2005) defends a highly egalitarian view based on an alternative interpretation of the rights to acquire external property.

understands it. In such a case, we may even say that the coercive governmental apparatus merely compels the members to be free.

It is worth contrasting this with flatly unjust institutions, particularly institutions imposing laws that are not justified to the members of society. As Gaus puts it, rules that are not publicly justified are authoritarian. To command obedience to unjustified rules is to subjugate members to the reason and values of those possessing power, rather than to treat those members as free and equal. Institutions that are not publicly justified are not supportive of members' positive liberty. Minimally, such institutions restrict the negative liberty of the individual without improving her positive liberty, and very often they detract from her positive liberty by compelling her to act against her own reason and values.

The essential point here is that the laws of a well-ordered society, unlike laws that are not publicly justified, enhance the positive liberty of the members of society insofar as those laws merely compel them to act in ways supported by the reason and values of the members themselves. Compliance with such laws is thus a form of autonomy instead of heteronomy.

13.2.4 Furthering Positive Liberty within a Well-Ordered Society

Note that even in a well-ordered society the government does not exhaust the conditions of positive liberty. One cannot expect any government to be alone sufficient for the members of society to have the fullest degree of positive liberty. Any liberal regime leaves the members large personal jurisdictions within which to act at their own discretion. While these personal jurisdictions include discretion over some issues that may be essentially irrelevant to an individual's positive liberty, such as which brand of cola to drink, the jurisdictions also include discretion over profoundly important decisions about the member's life. A member of a liberal society has significant discretion over how she develops her talents, what occupation she pursues, whether to have a family, which, if any, religion to practice, and an indefinite variety of other decisions relevant to her values. Moreover, the powers of government coercion have practical limits. Liberal, or even totalitarian, governments are not able to compel motivation or feeling, but acting from the right motives and with the right feelings is necessary for the fullest liberty.

In a free society, an individual at times will need to exercise self-control, choose prudentially, and work to reflect on her values and live with integrity. Living within just institutions does not negate the need for individual effort to achieve freedom.[13] While a just society creates valuable opportunities for its members, it is still up to each member to pursue and realize those opportunities. Though a just society may mitigate certain temptations, individuals still face and have to withstand temptations. Within a member's particular circumstances, she may use widely varying strategies to facilitate her self-control, such as undergoing therapy or using precommitment devices.[14] Overall, then, even a member of a well-ordered society must struggle to realize a greater degree of positive liberty.

Note that it is not the case that there is simply the government and the isolated individual struggling for liberty. Within liberal societies, the non-governmental social environment can greatly affect an individual's positive liberty. I will particularly emphasize the wide range of social institutions in which an individual chooses to participate. People participate in all manner of activities and associations to promote their values and facilitate their ability to live in accordance with their reason. We should recognize the importance of such association within free societies.

Consider alcohol as a classic example from discussions of positive liberty. T. H. Green saw alcohol as dangerous for freedom and defended legislation to restrict access to alcohol as a way to help promote people's freedom. Let us suppose that the fully just well-ordered society allows access to alcohol subject to various regulations. Furthermore, suppose that Abraham is a member of society who endorses the overall legal regime permitting alcohol consumption while also holding that alcohol poses serious dangers and can be destructive of freedom. Abraham may even suffer from alcoholism and feel that his alcoholism drives him to act against his values. In such a case, Abraham may have many options within civil society to help him live according to his values and to abstain from consuming alcohol. For instance, he may join a religious group that prohibits alcohol consumption, a temperance society promoting voluntary abstinence from alcohol, or the straight-edge subculture within the punk scene.[15] Such associations employ various means to reinforce Abraham's commitments, including social pressure or requirements for penance.

[13] T. H. Green (quoted in Nicholson 1985: 519) said that "no one could be made directly good by another."

[14] There is tremendous variety in the strategies and techniques individuals may employ to enhance their ability to live in accordance with their values. Contrast, for instance, the techniques and strategies of Boice's (1990), Baumeister and Tierney's (2012), and Wilson's (2016). As Nietzsche (1978: 235) highlights, we have wide-ranging options regarding how to tend our mental gardens.

[15] T. H. Green was himself a member of multiple temperance associations, including at least one that required its members to pledge abstinence from alcohol (Nicholson 1985: 519).

Moreover, he may join an organization such as Alcoholics Anonymous for strategies and mentorship, make friends with teetotalers, frequent dry establishments, and make many other decisions to support living in accordance with his values. Abraham's positive liberty derives not merely from government policies and personal will power but also from the voluntary associations that support his ability to live in accordance with his values.

Beyond helping with restraint, voluntary associations also help individuals engage in the positive behaviors and ways of living that they value. For instance, collective undertakings of charitable works may help some members do the positive acts that their conceptions of the good support. Many individuals may believe that it is important to engage in charitable or community-supporting acts yet may not so act if left to do so in isolation. Elvira may find community service valuable, but the force of inertia and the salience of other obligations may stand in her way. In light of this, she may choose to attend a university, such as Tulane University, that prioritizes and requires community engagement. Though no law compels Elvira to engage in such activities, she can opt into institutions with requirements and opportunities to help her act on her own values. Even outside of institutions with requirements, some members of society join groups that organize charitable activities that are salient, enjoyable, and social for their members. A member of society may at times not act according to her own reason because she is distracted or acting on other projects, so being a part of a group that organizes activities even without imposing requirements can help her act on her values.

As a final illustration here, note that many of the supporting activities of members of a liberal society are market activities. Within a market, members can purchase and contract for wide-ranging goods and services to help them live according to their own values. For instance, many individuals concerned about their nutrition and exercise hire a personal trainer to provide additional accountability, subscribe to a service providing healthy meals to reduce the temptation of deviating from their nutrition plan, purchase planners and programs to help them track progress and get positive reinforcement, or even contract to incur penalties should they fail to meet their goals. Likewise, many commercial gyms offer group classes to provide professional guidance along with the social aspect of the activity that is encouraging for many people. These programs provide valuable support for people who may be much less successful acting in isolation. In the same vein, many people join forums to discuss their challenges, exchange advice, and receive expert feedback for pursuing their goals. People develop and use many services and tools to live by their reason and values and thus to enhance their liberty.

The important point is that members create, join, and participate in a tremendous variety of associations of diverse types within civil society. Diverse members of society cooperate in living according to their values. Moreover, the members of society are able to continuously change these associations and to create new associations to fit their needs and circumstances. The members are thus not limited to the associations that exist at one time and may continue to innovate within civil society.

To take a step back and emphasize the general point, even in a well-ordered society positive liberty requires much more than government. Though the government may provide important support for aspects of positive liberty, the members of society must still make choices and work, both individually and within voluntary associations, to live in accordance with reason and their own values.

13.3 Unraveling of Well-Orderedness

The public reason account of positive liberty is fairly straightforward if the social institutions are in accordance with a shared conception of justice. Though a well-ordered society does not guarantee the fullest possible positive liberty, such a society would significantly support the positive liberty of its members. This account, however, faces the fundamental problem that we must expect disagreement about matters of justice. All of the burdens of judgment that generate disagreement in comprehensive conceptions also apply to conceptions of justice, so there will be reasonable disagreement about justice much like the reasonable disagreements about moral, philosophic, and religious matters. This section discusses the forms and extent of reasonable disagreement about justice, while the next section discusses ways that public reason theorists may approach positive liberty given such disagreement.

13.3.1 The Many Points of Disagreement

One way a society can fail to be well-ordered is for its members to disagree about whether the society satisfies the conception of justice they share. In such a case, the members of society agree on the conception of justice, such as justice as fairness, but disagree about whether their society satisfies that conception. As noted previously, for members of society to agree that a society satisfied a conception of justice would be a considerable achievement given the range and complexity of judgments involved. It seems likely that members will disagree about what laws are required by a conception of justice and how well existing laws stack up to the requirements of justice.

We may include here the fact that members may disagree about whether the society satisfies a given conception of justice because they interpret that conception differently. For instance, members may come to favor different policies in light of different specifications of the index of goods within the difference principle.[16] Even with substantial agreement about a conception of justice, then, members of society reasoning under the burdens of judgment will often disagree when interpreting and applying that conception of justice.

Going back a step, we should expect people to disagree about the appropriate conception of justice. Even people that agree about the general structure of the derivation of principles of justice may disagree about the actual output of the derivation. Though some theorists defend Rawls's claim that agents in the original position would select justice as fairness, others plausibly argue that Rawls's own apparatus would instead select alternative principles, such as utilitarianism or libertarianism.[17] Even if members of society agree on a procedure for selecting principles of justice, under the burdens of judgment the members will come to conflicting conclusions about the best conception of justice. Disagreement about the principles of justice, of course, tends to generate further disagreements in assessing their society.

This potential for disagreement does not uniquely afflict the Rawlsian original position of contracting situation. Other specifications of the contracting situation are open to divergent output. Moreover, alternatives to the social contract model face similar issues. For instance, appeal to what an impartial spectator would favor does not seem to prevent disagreement insofar as members of society may favor different forms of impartiality (Sen 2009: chapters 1 and 9) and may diverge in what they think any given form of impartiality more specifically requires. Likewise, attempts to derive natural rights seem open to significant disagreements or indeterminacies.[18]

[16] Philippe van Parijs (2003) discusses varieties of the difference principle.

[17] Motchoulski and Smolenski (2019) provide a recent defense of the selection of the difference principle within the original position. For a sense of the variety of conflicting views theorists argue is supported by the original position, compare Chung (2018), Doppelt (1981), Lomasky (2005), de Marneffe (1994), Moehler (2018: chapter 3), Okin (1991), and Tomasi (2012). See also Muldoon et al. (2014) on disagreement in the original position.

[18] For an insightful discussion of at least significant indeterminacy in a natural rights account, see Lomasky (1987, 1998) and Mack (2010).

More centrally, disagreements will emerge because members of society will disagree about precisely how to even specify a procedure for selecting principles of justice. There are alternative ways of specifying the original position, such as with different specifications of the information provided to the agents. One should expect that the highly diverse members of society under the burdens of judgment would favor competing ways of formulating this procedure and thus derive competing principles of justice. Moreover, Rawls (2005: xlix) notes that while he proposes using the original position to identify political principles, other people "will think that other ways to identify these principles are more reasonable." One must expect reasonable disagreement about whether any original position is appropriate, with many members of society endorsing competing procedures.

We have thus far been implicitly assuming that the members of society agree on the relevant justificatory values. People agreeing on values but reasoning under the burdens of judgment will still disagree about the procedures, principles, and particular policies they derive from those values. Going back even further, people will also disagree about which specific values are relevant for political justification. Some Rawlsians acknowledge reasonable disagreements about values (for example, Lister 2013: 131). Furthermore, that there will be such disagreements can be seen in the fact that Rawlsians themselves give conflicting lists of political values. For instance, Leland and van Wietmarschen (2017: 146) endorse "a set of basic liberal-democratic values, such as freedom, equality, the rule of law, and the idea of fair social cooperation, together with a set of uncontroversial political values such as security and efficiency." In contrast, Ebels-Duggan (2010: 63) includes "political values such as public health, safety, and protection of natural resources." Other theorists favor more limited lists, perhaps including merely freedom and equality. Importantly, these values are themselves open to highly divergent interpretations, so we should expect further disagreements among people supporting competing interpretations of values they share at some level of abstraction.

The overall picture, then, is that instead of a well-ordered society with agreement about justice despite the diversity of comprehensive doctrines, we should expect that members of a free society reasoning under the burdens of judgment will come to competing views about their comprehensive doctrines and justice. The disagreements run all the way through their views on justice, including reasonable disagreements about what values are relevant for justice, what procedures are best for formulating principles of justice, what principles would be selected by such a procedure, and what policies the appropriate principles of justice would favor.

13.3.2 *Injustice for All*

At this point, it is worth taking a step back to survey what may be expected in place of a well-ordered society in light of the burdens of judgment generating reasonable disagreement about justice. Several Rawlsian philosophers write as if a society can be expected to satisfy a single conception of justice, though some members of society will prefer an alternative conception.[19] For instance, in recognizing that there will be disagreements about justice, one might think that a sufficiently large plurality of a society may still unite around a conception and democratically impose it. Perhaps more people adhere to justice as fairness than to its competitors, so they will structure the society in accordance with justice as fairness, and should some alternative gain prominence the members may restructure the society in accordance with that alternative. One might then picture the members of society as divided in their support for a few different conceptions of justice while the society satisfies the most popular conception at any given time and switches between conceptions over time. That, however, is not a likely outcome.

Members of society work to implement policies in line with their competing conceptions of justice and their diverse empirical beliefs. Democratic policies are typically enacted by coalitions through compromise and political exchange, so it is often the case that even those in power will not find the policies entirely in line with their ideals. If the society has any sort of subsidiarity, federalism, or local governance, then the members may pursue their conceptions of justice at more local levels and thus institute different, perhaps even conflicting, policies within different jurisdictions. Over time, members will attempt to reform the institutions in a piecemeal process against considerable institutional stability. So, as a conception of justice gains in popularity, more of the laws may reflect adherence to that conception, but there is unlikely to be a swift switch from one conception to another. Instead of moving from compliance with one conception to compliance with an alternative conception, the society is more likely to slowly transition from one compromising hodge-podge of laws reflecting various conceptions that were previously held by an effective coalition toward an alternative hodge-podge of laws reflecting various conceptions that are currently held by an effective coalition.

[19] Along these lines, Neufeld and Watson (2018: 53) propose an alternative understanding of well-orderedness in which a society is well-ordered if it is in accordance with any member of a set of reasonable conceptions of justice.

In light of the earlier considerations, we see that any society we may realistically hope for is likely to be far from well-ordered. In a well-ordered society, all members reasonably agree that the society satisfies their shared conception of justice. With the burdens of justice generating disagreement about justice, many theorists have thought that a more realistic expectation is that society will satisfy the conception of justice of some plurality of the population, but even this is too optimistic. Instead, with vast disagreement about the requirements of justice, democratic processes are likely to produce mixes of policies that perhaps no member sees as fully just but instead represent compromises developed under path-dependent conditions. Thus, pluralism about justice is likely to result in every member of society reasonably holding that their society fails to conform to the conception of justice favored by her own reason.

13.4 Legitimacy and Positive Liberty

In light of the inevitable disagreements about justice, recent work in the public reason tradition focuses more on the possibility of the diverse members of society mutually recognizing their social institutions as legitimate, even though not fully just. Though public reason theorists differ in the details of the precise conditions of legitimacy, the general idea is that the laws may be legitimate as long as they are good enough, in the sense of being recognized as sufficiently reasonable or as at least superior to a relevant baseline.[20] Even though many, or perhaps all, members of society will reasonably see the merely legitimate laws as falling short of justice, the members may recognize the laws as good enough to be authoritative, an appropriate basis for making interpersonal moral demands, or permissibly enforced with coercive political power.

In light of the apparent connection of positive liberty to justice, it might be thought that the shift of focus to mere legitimacy involves abandoning concern for the positive liberty of the members of society. The remainder of this chapter lays out alternative approaches to positive liberty for public reason theorists concerned about social institutions that are publicly justified such that they are merely legitimate. These strategies are not necessarily exclusive or exhaustive. They are more or less independent strategies that public reason theorists may plausibly deploy to understand positive liberty.

[20] See, for instance, Gaus's (2011: section 16) discussion of the socially eligible set and Rawls's (2005: 137) discussion of the liberal principle of legitimacy for political coercion.

13.4.1 The Values Strategy

According to what I call the values strategy, legitimate laws support the positive liberty of members of society insofar as those laws are justified on the basis of values those members share. The basic idea is that though a member cannot recognize the laws as the optimal realization of her values, she may still recognize that the laws are justified by appropriate values. Consider, for instance, Quong's (2005) account, according to which members share support for a set of justificatory values, such as freedom and equality, though they may support different particular laws because they interpret or weigh these values differently. A member may still recognize the laws as legitimate even when she does not prefer them when she recognizes those laws are directed toward freedom and equality. She may understand the laws as only commanding that she act in accordance with her own values and thus as supporting her positive liberty, even if the laws are not optimal from her perspective.

This strategy faces significant limitations insofar as positive liberty seems to depend on the specifics of our values and reason. Consider different interpretations of a value. If a person is to live by her own values, she must be living as per her specific interpretation or conception of those values. We would not typically see it as living freely if someone lives per an interpretation she rejects of a value that she abstractly accepts. Similar problems arise when people disagree about which laws would realize their shared values. It does not seem to enhance a member's liberty to command her to comply with laws that she reasonably believes work against her values, even if other members reasonably believe the laws work for those values.

Furthermore, even when holding the interpretation of the values fixed, the balance matters. In an ordinary case, you would not say that an individual has positive liberty merely because she acts according to one of her values when in doing so she acts against one of her weightier values. She may regret succumbing to the temptation of eating excessive sweets because, despite valuing the enjoyment, the health costs outweigh the gustatory benefits. The fact that she values the enjoyment is insufficient for establishing that eating the sweets realized her positive liberty, and the fact that she rationally prefers to forgo the sweets in light of the balance of values suggests that succumbing to the sweet's temptation is a failure of her liberty. These considerations suggest that positive liberty is sensitive to the specification and balance of values, so the mere fact that laws are justified in terms of some balance of some interpretation of someone's values is insufficient to show that those laws support her positive liberty.

13.4.2 The Political Strategy

What I call the political strategy begins by holding that justice and positive liberty come in roughly corresponding degrees. In such a view, merely legitimate laws are not fully just but are relevantly close to justice. For instance, a supporter of justice as fairness may think that an incompletely just society still has a high degree of justice insofar as it gives special protection to freedom of speech and establishes considerable opportunities for its members. Insofar as the society realizes a high degree of justice, it is conducive to the positive liberty of its members. Though the society would not be well-ordered, the members significantly follow their own reason and values when they do their part in a political system that is from their perspective highly, though not fully, just.

Though those embracing this strategy hold that a merely legitimate society supports some degree of positive liberty, that degree is not as high as in a fully just society. Moreover, even between different legitimate yet not-fully-just societies, there is a greater degree of positive liberty in those that have more overall justice. This makes ongoing political reform a central project for liberation. For positive liberty, on this account, we should support legitimate institutions and continually advocate reforming them for greater justice. People may continually work to bring their society more in line with their values much as they may continually undergo therapy to further mitigate psychological impairments.

There is an important difference between the political strategy and the values strategy when it comes to guidance for members of society. In the values strategy, the fact that the laws are justified in terms of values the members of society share suffices for establishing the positive liberty of a member in the same way as would laws that were from her perspective fully just. On that view, there are no positive-liberty-based reasons for reform except insofar as ongoing reforms are needed to maintain legitimacy in changing circumstances. A more just society, according to the values strategy, would not sustain more liberty since legitimacy is already sufficient for ensuring that people are living according to their values. In contrast, the political strategy holds that bringing about more justice more fully liberates people. Moreover, while the values strategy suggests that the diverse members of society can essentially see themselves as working together to support the liberty of all, the political strategy implies that they essentially compete. Insofar as they disagree about what justice requires, each will see herself as promoting her liberty while others are actively, even if inadvertently, working to reduce her liberty by advocating less just policies.

13.4.3 The Civil Strategy

What I call the civil strategy holds, like the political strategy, that a merely legitimate society does not provide full liberty on its own. But, unlike the political strategy, the civil strategy focuses on supports for positive liberty outside of the political institutions. As Section 13.2.4 emphasizes, even in a well-ordered society one cannot expect the government to be sufficient for ensuring positive liberty. Private associations and personal efforts are necessary for someone to fully realize positive liberty even when living under just political institutions, especially insofar as those institutions remain liberal.

While voluntary associations are important even in a just society, one may expect it to be even more significant in a merely legitimate society.[21] Given the disagreements about justice, members of society may expect that political reform is of limited efficacy, particularly within moderate time horizons. The members may best promote liberty through efforts within civil society. Even though such efforts will typically not have the same scope as political reform, efforts within civil society can be extremely powerful for supporting positive liberty for many. Furthermore, the diverse members of society can contribute to many different efforts throughout the society and thus support the liberty of each through decentralized social processes.

Civil society presents a vast range of possibilities for people to combat temptations, create opportunities, develop themselves, coordinate, and cooperate. Such efforts can be through formal organizations or informal norms, geographically bounded or open, use or refrain from using negative sanctioning for enforcement, and operate as part of or outside of markets. Arrangements in civil society provide personal restrictions and facilitate activities of personal development, charity, mutual aid, and addressing collective action problems.[22] The members of a legitimate liberal society can form and participate in countless voluntary associations and practices to help themselves live according to their own reason and values. Importantly, the limited scope of these associations accommodates deep perspectival diversity. Any given association may have members that do

[21] One may read Rousseau as giving different strategies for pursuing liberty across his works, with *On the Social Contract* providing a collective, political strategy and *Emile* providing an individualist strategy to pursue when the collective institutions are not available.

[22] For discussion of mutual aid, see Beito (2000: chapters 1–3). Cornuelle (1965: chapters 5–6) and Ostrom (1990: chaps. 1 and 3) each provide important insights into addressing collective action problems through an independent sector and self-governance.

share relevant values supporting the association's activities, while reasonably dissenting members of society as a whole remain outside of that particular association and its demands.[23]

13.4.4 A Shared Social World

The final approach, which I call the shared social world strategy, emphasizes the way that a person's reason guides her in the circumstances of sharing a social world with diverse others. The fact of deep perspectival diversity is relevant for reasoning about how to live and influences what one's reason ultimately endorses. In this strategy, a person realizes positive liberty within a merely legitimate society insofar as her reason and values endorse the laws in light of the deep perspectival diversity of the society's members.

To illustrate the basic mechanics of this strategy, consider a simple case. Omnivorous Owen and Vegetarian Vera want to share a pizza. If Owen were ordering a pizza just for himself, given his gustatory values, he would order the works with extra pepperoni. However, Owen isn't getting a pizza alone. His values include valuing having the pizza with Vera and accommodating her commitments. In this social context, ordering the works with extra pepperoni would go against Owen's reason and values; it may be a heteronomous action driven by uncontrolled gluttony or thoughtless habit. So, though Owen's liberty would be realized with the works were he eating with other omnivores, within this social context Owen's positive liberty is realized through ordering a vegetarian pizza. Vera too may be compromising in her own ways; perhaps she prefers a simple cheese pizza when alone, but in this context, her reasoning supports a vegetarian combination to accommodate Owen.

The shared social world strategy extends commitments already present in the public reason tradition's views on justice. In that tradition, one must account for the reasonable pluralism of comprehensive doctrines when constructing an ideal conception of justice. Principles of justice are selected given reasonable pluralism about religious, philosophic, and moral matters.[24] The assumption of reasonable pluralism about comprehensive

[23] Gaus (1985) implies that public justification is required of the rules within civil association, but that these rules can be justified by appeal to the values of the members of those very associations. The rules do not need to be justified to all members of society as a whole.

[24] Views according to which justice functions to adjudicate conflicting claims make highly salient both the fact of disagreement and the fact that such disagreement influences what principles of justice are appropriate. See Van Schoelandt (2020).

doctrines is likely to affect what principles one endorses. One's reason endorses that conception of justice not in an unqualified way, but as the appropriate conception for a shared social world characterized by pluralism about the good. Different principles may be selected if we instead assumed agreement on a comprehensive view of the world. A well-ordered society provides positive liberty to its members only because the reason of a member is sensitive to the fact of perspectival diversity. When she reasons about how society should be organized, she is considering how a society with diverse views about the good should be organized. The shift to merely legitimate societies extends these considerations insofar as members reason about how society should be organized given the disagreements not only about the good but also about justice. The reason and values of the members direct the members to live in accordance with laws that each can endorse as adequate even if not optimal.

While it may seem paradoxical, this strategy implies that sometimes someone would fail to realize her own positive liberty were she to make society conform to her own conception of justice. Her conception may support positive liberty for all if realized in a well-ordered society. In a society with deep disagreement about justice itself, however, one's conception of justice may be entirely unacceptable for some other members. Imposing one's conception of justice on people that reasonably reject it seems to fail to treat those people as free and equal members of a cooperative system. A person's cooperative values give her significant reason to seek and support laws that all can endorse from their diverse perspectives even when this means forgoing making society conform to the conception of justice she would prefer in a more homogeneous society. Put bluntly, when we take deep perspectival diversity seriously, we see that sometimes positive liberty requires clear-eyed and well-reasoned submission to unjust laws.

Works Cited

Alexander, Gregory. 2009. "The Social-Obligation Norm in American Property Law." *Cornell Law Review* 94(4): 745–819.

Alexander, Lawrence. 2000. "Deontology at the Threshold." *San Diego Law Review* 37(4): 893–912.

2008. "Scalar Properties, Binary Judgments." *Journal of Applied Philosophy* 25 (2): 85–104.

2013. "Voluntary Enslavement." In Christian Coons and Michael Weber (eds.), *Paternalism, Theory and Practice*. Cambridge: Cambridge University Press, 231–246.

Allen, Amy. 1998. "Rethinking Power." *Hypatia* 13(1): 21–40.

2017. *The End of Progress: Decolonizing the Normative Foundations of Critical Theory*. New York: Columbia University Press.

Amundson, Ron. 2000. "Against Normal Function." *Studies in the History of Philosophy, Biology, and Biomedical Science* 31(1): 33–53.

Anderson, Elizabeth. 2017. *Private Government: How Employers Rule Our Lives (and Why We Don't Talk about It)*. Princeton, NJ: Princeton University Press.

Anderson, Joel, and Axel Honneth. 2005. "Autonomy, Vulnerability, Recognition and Justice." In John Christman and Joel Anderson (eds.), *Autonomy and the Challenges to Liberalism*. Cambridge: Cambridge University Press, 127–149.

Arendt, Hannah. 1961. "What Is Freedom?" In *Between Past and Future*. London: Faber & Faber, Chapter 4.

1963. *On Revolution*. New York: Viking Press.

1969. *On Violence*. New York: Harcourt.

Arneson, Richard J. 1985. "Freedom and Desire." *Canadian Journal of Philosophy* 3: 425–448.

Asch, Adrienne, and Michelle Fine. 1988. "Shared Dreams: A Left Perspective on Disability Rights and Reproductive Rights." In Michelle Fine and Adrienne Asch (eds.), *Women with Disabilities: Essays in Psychology, Culture, and Politics*. Philadelphia, PA: Temple University Press, 297–305.

Atkinson, Anthony. 2015. *Inequality: What Can Be Done?* Cambridge, MA: Harvard University Press.

Attas, Daniel. 2006. "Fragmenting Property." *Law and Philosophy* 25: 119–149.

Baldwin, Tom. 1984. "MacCallum and the Two Concepts of Freedom." *Ratio* 26: 119–149.
Baumeister, Roy F., and John Tierney. 2012. *Willpower: Rediscovering the Greatest Human Strength*, reprint edition. New York: Penguin Books.
Baynton, Douglas. 1996. *Forbidden Signs: American Culture and the Campaign Against Sign Language*. Chicago: University of Chicago Press.
2016. *Defectives in the Land: Disability and Immigration in the Age of Eugenics*. Chicago: University of Chicago Press.
Beauvoir, Simone de. 1976. *The Ethics of Ambiguity*, trans. Bernard Frechtman. New York: Citadel Press.
Beckert, Jens. 2016. *Imagined Futures: Fictional Expectations and Capitalist Dynamics*. Cambridge, MA: Harvard University Press.
Beito, David T. 2000. *From Mutual Aid to the Welfare State: Fraternal Societies and Social Services, 1890–1967*. Chapel Hill: The University of North Carolina Press.
Benhabib, Seyla. 2004. *The Rights of Others: Aliens, Residents, and Citizens*. Cambridge: Cambridge University Press.
Benn, Stanley I. 1988. *A Theory of Freedom*. Cambridge: Cambridge University Press.
Benn, Stanley I., and W. L. Weinstein. 1973. "Being Free to Act and Being a Free Man." In Richard E. Flathman (ed.), *Concepts in Social and Political Philosophy*. London and New York: Macmillan, 309–324.
Berlin, Isaiah. 1969a. "Introduction." In Isaiah Berlin (ed.), *Four Essays on Liberty*. New York: Oxford University Press, ix–lxiii.
1969b. "Two Concepts of Liberty." In Isaiah Berlin (ed.), *Four Essays on Liberty*. New York: Oxford University Press, 112–172.
1979. "From Hope and Fear Set Free." In Isaiah Berlin (ed.), *Concepts and Categories: Philosophical Essays*. New York: Viking Press, 226–260.
2002. "Two Concepts of Liberty." In Henry Hardy (ed.), *Liberty*. Oxford University Press, 118–172.
Besson, Samantha. 2005. *The Morality of Conflict: Reasonable Disagreement and the Law*. Portland, OR: Hart Publishing.
Bilgrami, Akeel. 2014. "Gandhi (and Marx)." In *Secularism, Identity, and Enchantment*. Cambridge, MA: Harvard University Press, 122–174.
2018. "Some Reflections on the Limits of Liberalism." *Social Scientist* 46(7–8): 3–20.
Blaufarb, Rafe. 2016. *The Great Demarcation: The French Revolution and the Invention of Modern Property*. Oxford: Oxford University Press.
Bohman, James. 2007. "Beyond Distributive Justice and Struggles for Recognition: Freedom, Democracy, and Critical Theory." *European Journal of Political Theory* 6(3): 267–275.
Boice, Robert. 1990. *Professors as Writers: A Self-Help Guide to Productive Writing*. Stillwater, OK: New Forums Press.
Bourdieu, Pierre. 1986. "The Forms of Capital." In J. G. Richardson (ed.), *Handbook of Theory and Research for the Sociology of Education*. New York: Greenwood, 241–258.

Bratman, Michael. 2000. "Reflection, Planning and Temporally Extended Agency." *The Philosophical Review* 109: 35–61.
Brennan, Samantha. 1995. "Thresholds for Rights." *Southern Journal of Philosophy* 33(2): 143–168.
Bringhurst, Piper, and Gerald Gaus. 2018. "Positive Freedom and the General Will." In David Schmidtz and Carmen Pavel (eds.), *The Oxford Handbook of Freedom*. New York: Oxford University Press, 40–58.
tenBroek, Jacobus. 1966. "The Right to Live in the World: The Disabled in the Law of Torts." *California Law Review* 54(2) (May): 841–919.
Burch, Susan, and Hannah Joyner. 2007. *Unspeakable: The Story of Junius Wilson*. Chapel Hill: University of North Carolina Press.
Calabresi, Guido, and A. Douglas Melamed. 1972. "Property Rules, Liability Rules, and Inalienability: One View of the Cathedral." *Harvard Law Review* 85(6): 1089–1128.
Carter, Ian. 1999. *A Measure of Freedom*. Oxford: Oxford University Press.
2019. "Positive and Negative Liberty." In Edward N. Zalta (ed.), *The Stanford Encyclopedia of Philosophy* (Winter 2019 ed.). http://plato.stanford.edu/entries/liberty-positive-negative/ (accessed September 29, 2020).
Chambers, Clare. 2008. *Sex, Culture, and Justice: The Limits of Choice*. University Park: Penn State University Press.
Christiano, Thomas. 2010. "The Uneasy Relationship between Democracy and Capital." *Social Philosophy & Policy* 27(1): 195–217.
2012. "Money in Politics." In David Estlund (ed.), *Oxford Handbook of Political Philosophy*. Oxford: Oxford University Press, 241–57.
Christman, John. 1991. "Liberalism and Individual Positive Freedom." *Ethics* 101: 343–359.
1994. *The Myth of Property. Toward an Egalitarian Theory of Ownership*. New York and Oxford: Oxford University Press.
2005a. "Saving Positive Freedom." *Political Theory* 33: 79–88.
2005b. "Autonomy, Self-Knowledge and Liberal Legitimacy." In John Christman and Joel Anderson (eds.), *Autonomy and the Challenges to Liberalism*. Cambridge: Cambridge University Press, 330–358.
2009. *The Politics of Persons: Individual Autonomy and Socio-historical Selves*. Cambridge: Cambridge University Press.
2012. "Can Positive Liberty Be Saved?" In Steven M. Cahn and Robert B. Talisse (eds.), *Political Philosophy in the 21st Century: Essential Essays*. Boulder: Westview Press, 155–168.
2014. "Coping or Oppression: Autonomy and Adaptation to Circumstance." In Andrea Veltman and Mark Piper (eds.), *Autonomy, Oppression and Gender*. New York: Oxford University Press, 201–226.
2015. "Freedom in Times of Struggle: Positive Liberty, Again." *Analyse &Kritik* 37(1/2): 171–188.
2020. "What If Anything Is Wrong with Positive Liberty? The Struggles of Agency in a Non-Ideal World." In Daniel Weinstock, Jacob T. Levy, and Jocelyn Maclure (eds.), *Interpreting Modernity: Essays on the Work of Charles Taylor*. Montreal, CA: McGill-Queens University Press, 95–113.

Chung, Hun. 2018. "Rawls's Self-Defeat: A Formal Analysis." *Erkenntnis*. https://doi.org/10.1007/s10670-018-0079-4 (accessed October 2020).

Claassen, Rutger. 2015. "The Capability to Hold Property." *Journal of Human Development and Capabilities* 16(2): 220–236.

2018a. *Capabilities in a Just Society. A Theory of Navigational Agency*. Cambridge: Cambridge University Press.

2018b. "Justice as a Claim to (Social) Property." *Critical Review of International Social and Political Philosophy* 21(5): 631–645.

Claassen, Rutger, and Lisa Herzog. 2019. "Why Economic Agency Matters: An Account of Structural Domination in the Economic Realm." *European Journal of Political Theory*, online first. DOI: https://doi.org/10.1177/1474885119832181.

Clare, Eli. 2009. *Exile and Pride: Disability, Queerness, and Liberation*. With a new introduction by David Spade. Boston: South End Press.

Coase, R. H. 1937. "The Nature of the Firm." *Economica, New Series* IV: 386–405.

Cohen, G. A. 1979. "Capitalism, Freedom and the Proletariat." In Alan Ryan (ed.), *The Idea of Freedom: Essays in Honor of Isaiah Berlin*. Oxford: Oxford University Press, 9–26.

1983. "The Structure of Proletarian Unfreedom." *Philosophy & Public Affairs* 12(1): 3–33.

1991. *The German Idea of Freedom*. University of Chicago. www.youtube.com/watch?v=ey-hYJM7B3I (accessed March 10, 2019).

2011a. *On the Currency of Egalitarian Justice, and Other Essays in Political Philosophy*. Princeton, NJ: Princeton University Press.

2011b. "Freedom and Money." In Michael Otsuka (ed.), *On the Currency of Egalitarian Justice, and Other Essays in Political Philosophy*. Princeton, NJ: Princeton University Press, 166–192.

Cohen, J. 2010. *Rousseau: A Free Community of Equals*. Oxford: Oxford University Press.

Cohen, Morris. 1927. "Property and Sovereignty." *Cornell Law Review* 13(1): 8–30.

Coleman, James S. 1990. *Foundations of Social Theory*. Cambridge: Harvard University Press.

Cooke, Maeve. 1999. "A Space of One's Own: Autonomy, Privacy, Liberty." *Philosophy and Social Criticism* 25(1): 23–53.

2006. *Re-Presenting the Good Society*. Cambridge, MA: MIT Press.

2013. "Violating Neutrality? Religious Validity Claims and Democratic Legitimacy." In C. Calhoun, E. Mendieta, and J. VanAntwerpen (eds.), *Habermas and Religion*. Cambridge: Polity Press, 249–276.

2019. "Nicht-Autoritäre Autorität: Beitrag zu einer kritischen Theorie der Politik'." In Ulf Bohmann and Paul Sörensen (eds.), *Eine Kritische Theorie der Politik*. Frankfurt am Main: Suhrkamp, 519–539.

2020a. "Private Autonomy and Public Autonomy: Tensions in Habermas's Discourse Theory of Law and Politics." *Kantian Review* 25(4): 559–582.

2020b. "A Pluralist Model of Politics." In V. Kaul and I. Salvatore (eds.), *What Is Pluralism?* New Delhi: Routledge, 139–154.

2020c. "Self-Efficacious Subjects: Rosa on Alienation and Its Antithesis." *Journal of Political Power* 3(3): 366–381.

2021. "Existentially Lived Truth or Communicative Reason? Habermas's Critique of Kierkegaard." *Constellations* 28(1): 51–59.

Cooper, John M. 2003. "Stoic Autonomy." In E. F. Paul, F. Miller Jr., and J. Paul (eds.), *Autonomy*. Cambridge: Cambridge University Press, 1–29.

Constant, Benjamin. 1988. "The Liberty of the Ancients Compared with That of the Moderns." In Biancamaria Fontana (ed.), *Constant: Political Writings*. Cambridge: Cambridge University Press, 303–307.

Cornuelle, Richard C. 1965. *Reclaiming the American Dream*. New York: Random House.

Crocker, L. 1980. *Positive Liberty*. Hingham, MA: Kluwer Boston.

Crowder, George. 2004. *Isaiah Berlin: Liberty and Pluralism*. Cambridge: Polity Press.

Dagan, Hanoch, and Avihay Dorfman. 2017. "The Human Right to Property." *Theoretical Inquires in Law* 18(2): 391–416.

Darby, Derrick. 2009. *Rights, Race and Recognition*. Cambridge: Cambridge University Press.

Davey, Laura. 2015. "Philosophical Inclusive Design: Intellectual Disability and the Limits of Individual Autonomy in Moral and Political Theory." *Hypatia* 30(1) (Winter): 133.

Davis, Leonnard. 2017. *The Disability Studies Reader*, 5th ed. New York: Routledge.

Dewey, John. 1927a/1916/1980. *The Middle Works of John Dewey, Volume 9, 1899–1924: Democracy and Education*, 1916. Collected Works of John Dewey. Ed. J. A. Boydston, P. Baysinger, and P. Levine. Carbondale: Southern Illinois University Press.

1927b. *The Public and Its Problems*. New York: H. Holt.

DiMatteo, Larry A. 1998–1999. "The History of Natural Law Theory: Transforming Embedded Influences into a Fuller Understanding of Modern Contract Law." *University of Pittsburgh Law Review* 60: 839–922.

Dimova-Cookson, Maria. 2003. "A New Scheme of Positive and Negative Freedom: Reconstructing T. H. Green on Freedom." *Political Theory* 31 (4): 508–532.

2019. "Where Does Real Freedom Begin? T.H. Green, P.P. Nicholson and the Necessary but Elusive Binaries of Freedom." in *Collingwood and British Idealism Studies* 25: 129–160.

2020. *Rethinking Positive and Negative Liberty*. London: Routledge.

Doppelt, Gerald. 1981. "Rawls" System of Justice: A Critique from the Left." *Noûs* 15(3): 259–307.

Dworkin, G. 1983. "Paternalism." In Rolf Sartorius (ed.), *Paternalism*. Minneapolis: University of Minnesota Press, 19–35.

2020. "Paternalism." In Edward N. Zalta (ed.), *The Stanford Encyclopedia of Philosophy* (Fall 2020 ed.), https://plato.stanford.edu/archives/fall2020/entries/paternalism/.

Dworkin, R. 1985. *A Matter of Principle*. Cambridge, MA: Harvard University Press.

2000. *Sovereign Virtue*. Cambridge, MA: Harvard University Press.

2011. *Justice for Hedgehogs*. Cambridge, MA: The Belknap Press.

2013. *Justice for Hedgehogs*. Cambridge, MA: Harvard University Press.

Ebels-Duggan, Kyla. 2010. "The Beginning of Community: Politics in the Face of Disagreement." *Philosophical Quarterly* 60(238): 50–71.

Edge, Matt. 2013. "A Theory of Freedom." *European Journal of Political Theory* 12(4): 368–387.

Elford, Gideon. 2013. "Reclaiming Two Concepts of Liberty." *Politics, Philosophy and Economics* 12(3): 228–246.

Ellis, Anthony. 1992. "Deontology, Incommensurability and the Arbitrary." *Philosophy and Phenomenological Research* 52: 855–876.

Elster, Jon. 1983. "Sour Grapes – Utilitarianism and the Genesis of Wants." In Amartya Sen and Bernard Williams (eds.), *Utilitarianism and Beyond*. Cambridge: Cambridge University Press, 219–238.

Ely, Richard. 1902. "Industrial Liberty." *Publications of the American Economic Association, 3rd Series* 3: 59–79.

Esping-Andersen, Gøsta. 1990. *The Three Worlds of Welfare Capitalism*. Princeton, NJ: Princeton University Press.

Feinberg, Joel. 1978. "Voluntary Euthanasia and the Inalienable Right to Life." *Philosophy & Public Affairs* 7: 98–104.

1980. "Legal Paternalism." In *Rights, Justice, and the Bounds of Liberty, Essays in Social Philosophy*. Princeton, NJ: Princeton University Press, 110–129.

Flathman, Richard E. 1984. *The Philosophy and Politics of Freedom*. Chicago: University of Chicago Press.

Forst, Rainer. 2005. "Political Liberty: Integrating Five Conceptions of Autonomy." In John Christman and Joel Anderson (eds.), *Autonomy and the Challenges to Liberalism*. Cambridge: Cambridge University Press, 226–244.

Francis, Leslie. 2009. "Understanding Autonomy in Light of Intellectual Disability." In Kimberly Brownlee and Adam Cureton (eds.), *Disability and Disadvantage*. New York: Oxford University Press, 200–215.

Frankfurt, H. 2004. *The Reasons of Love*. Princeton, NJ: Princeton University Press.

Flikschuh, Katrin. 2012. "Freedom." In Gerald Gaus and Fred D'Agonstino (eds.), *The Routledge Companion to Social and Political Philosophy*. New York and London: Routledge, 562–575.

Freeden, Michael. 2005. *Languages: Ideological Imagination and Twentieth-Century Progressive Thought*. Princeton, NJ: Princeton University Press.

Freeman, Samuel. 2001. "Illiberal Libertarians: Why Libertarianism Is Not a Liberal View." *Philosophy & Public Affairs* 30(2): 105–151.

Fried, Barbara H. 2009. *The Progressive Assault on Laissez-Faire*. Cambridge, MA: Harvard University Press.

Garnett, Michael. 2017. "Agency and Inner Freedom." *Nous* 51(1): 3–23.

Gaus, Gerald. 1985. "On Justice and Community: A Reply to Professor Golding." *Bulletin of the Australian Society of Legal Philosophy* 9: 197–204.

1999. *Social Philosophy*. Armonk, NY: Routledge.

2000. *Political Concepts and Political Theories*. New York: Westview Press.

2010. "The Idea and Ideal of Capitalism." In George Brenkert and Tom Beauchamp (eds.), *The Oxford Handbook of Business Ethics*. Oxford: Oxford University Press, 73–99.

2011. *The Order of Public Reason: A Theory of Freedom and Morality in a Diverse and Bounded World*. New York: Cambridge University Press.

Gaus, Gerald, and Chad Van Schoelandt. 2015. "'Public Reason.'" In James D. Wright (ed.), *International Encyclopedia of the Social and Behavioral Sciences*, 2nd ed. Amsterdam: Elsevier, 591–596.

2017. "Consensus on What? Convergence for What?: Four Models of Political Liberalism." *Ethics* 128(1): 145–172.

Gewirth, Alan. 1982. *Human Rights: Essays on Justification and Applications*. Chicago: University of Chicago Press.

1996. *The Community of Rights*. Chicago: The University of Chicago Press.

Gibbard, A. 2003. *Thinking How to Live*. Cambridge, MA: Harvard University Press.

Gonzalez-Sobrino, Bianca, and Matthew W. Hughey. 2016. "Colorism." In Kofi Lomotey (ed.), *People of Color in the United States: Contemporary Issues in Education, Work, Communities, Health, and Immigration*, Vol. 2: *Employment, Housing, Family, and Community*. Santa Barbara, CA: Greenwood, 70–74.

Goodin, Robert, James Mahmud Rice, Antti Parpo, and Lina Eriksson. 2008. *Discretionary Time. A New Measure of Freedom*. Cambridge: Cambridge University Press.

Goodley, Dan. 2011. *Disability studies: An Interdisciplinary Introduction*. London: Sage.

Goodwin, Barbara. 1985. *Using Political Ideas*. Chichester: Wiley.

Gould, C. 1978. *Marx's Social Ontology: Individuality and Community in Marx's Theory of Social Reality*. Cambridge, MA: The MIT Press.

1983. "Beyond Causality in the Social Sciences: Reciprocity as a Form of Non-Exploitative Social Relations." In R. S. Cohen and M. W. Wartofsky (eds.), *Epistemology, Methodology and the Social Sciences: Boston Studies in the Philosophy of Science*, Vol. 71. Boston and Dordrecht: D. Reidel, 53–88.

1988. *Rethinking Democracy: Freedom and Social Cooperation in Politics, Economy and Society*. Cambridge: Cambridge University Press.

2007. "Transnational Solidarities." *Journal of Social Philosophy* 38(1): 146–162.

2009. "Structuring Global Democracy: Political Communities, Universal Human rights, and Transnational Representation." Special Issue on Global

Democracy and Political Exclusion, *Metaphilosophy*, 40(1): 24–46 [republished as *Global Democracy and Exclusion*, Ronald Tinnevelt and Helder De Schutter (eds.). 2010. Oxford: Wiley-Blackwell].

2013. "Retrieving Positive Freedom and Why It Matters." In Bruce Baum and Robert Nichols (eds.), *Isaiah Berlin and the Politics of Freedom 'Two Concepts of Liberty' 50 Years Later*. New York: Routledge, 102–113.

2014. *Interactive Democracy: The Social Roots of Global Justice*. Cambridge: Cambridge University Press.

2019. "Protecting Democracy by Extending It: Democratic Management Reconsidered." *Journal of Social Philosophy*, 50(4): 513–535.

2020. "Motivating Solidarity with Distant Others: Empathic Politics and the Problem of Global Justice." In ed. Thom Brooks (ed.), *Oxford Handbook of Global Justice*. Oxford: Oxford University Press, 122–138.

Gourevitch, Alex. 2013. "Labor Republicanism and the Transformation of Work." *Political Theory* 41(4): 591–617.

Graby, S., and Greenstein, A. 2016. "Relational Autonomy and Disability: Beyond Normative Constructs and Post-structralist Deconstructions". In R. Mallett, C. Ogden, and J. Slater (eds.), *Precarious Positions: Theorising Normalcy and the Mundane*. Chester: University of Chester Press, 228–259.

Gray, J. 1995. *Berlin*. London: Fontana Press.

Green, Jeffrey. 2016. "Liberalism and the Problem of Plutocracy." *Constellations* 23 (1): 84–95.

Green, T. H. 1924/1907/1890. *Prolegomena to Ethics*, 5th ed., ed. A. C. Bradley. Oxford: Clarendon Press.

1931/1999. *Lectures on the Principles of Political Obligation*. Kitchener: Batoche Books.

1986a. "Lecture on 'Liberal Legislation and Freedom of Contract'." In Paul Harris and John Morrow (eds.), *Lectures on the Principles of Political Obligation and Other Writings*. Cambridge: Cambridge University Press, 194–212.

1986b. "Lectures on the Principles of Political Obligation." In Paul Harris and John Morrow (eds.), *Lectures on the Principles of Political Obligation and Other Writings*. Cambridge: Cambridge University Press, 13–93.

1986c. "On the Different Senses of "Freedom" as Applied to Will and to the Moral Progress of Man." In Paul Harris and John Morrow (eds.), *Lectures on the Principles of Political Obligation and Other Writings*. Cambridge: Cambridge University Press, 228–249.

Gutmann, Thomas 2013. "Some Preliminary Remarks on a Liberal Theory of Contract." *Law and Contemporary Problems* 76: 39–55.

Habermas, Jürgen. 1990. "Discourse Ethics: Notes on a Program of Philosophical Justification." In his *Moral Consciousness and Communicative Action*, trans. C. Lenhardt and S. Weber Nicholsen. Cambridge, MA: MIT Press, 43–115.

1995. "Reconciliation through the Public Use of Reason: Remarks on John Rawls's Political Liberalism." Translated by C. Cronin. *Journal of Philosophy* XCII (3): 109–131.

1996. *Between Facts and Norms*, trans. W. Rehg. Cambridge, MA: MIT Press.

2003. *The Future of Human Nature*, trans. W. Rehg, M. Pensky, and H. Beister. Cambridge: Polity Press.

2008. *Between Naturalism and Religion: Philosophical Essays*, trans. Ciaran Cronin. Cambridge: Polity Press.

Hardin, Russell. 1986. "The Utilitarian Logic of Liberalism." *Ethics* 97: 47–74.

Hawkins, Derek. 2020. "Denied a Diploma, April Dunn Made Sure Other Students with Disabilities Had Options. She Died of Covid-19." *The Washington Post*, April 18, 2020. www.washingtonpost.com/nation/2020/04/18/denied-diploma-april-dunn-made-sure-other-students-with-disabilities-had-options-she-died-covid-19/ (accessed online on April 26, 2020).

Hedrick, Todd. 2019. *Reconciliation and Reification: Freedom's Semblance and Actuality from Hegel to Contemporary Critical Theory*. New York: Oxford University Press.

Hegel, G. W. F. 1965. *Hegel's Philosophy of Right*, trans. T. M. Knox. Oxford: Oxford University Press.

Henrich, Dieter. 2008. *Between Kant and Hegel: Essays on German Idealism*. Cambridge, MA: Harvard University Press.

Hevia, Martin. 2007. "Kronman on Contract Law and Distributive Justice." *Journal of Contract Law* 23: 105–119.

Hirschmann, Nancy J. 1996. "Toward a Feminist Theory of Freedom." *Political Theory* 24(1) (February): 46–67.

2003. *The Subject of Liberty: Toward a Feminist Theory of Freedom*. Princeton, NJ: Princeton University Press.

2008. *Gender, Class, and Freedom in Modern Political Theory*. Princeton, NJ: Princeton University Press.

2015. "Invisible Disability: Seeing, Being, Power." In Nancy J. Hirschmann and Beth Linker (eds.), *Civil Disabilities: Citizenship, Membership, and Belonging*. Philadelphia: University of Pennsylvania Press, Chapter 10.

2020. "What's Right with Positive Liberty: Agency, Autonomy, and the Other." In Daniel Weinstock, Jacob T. Levy and Jocelyn Maclure (eds.), *Interpreting Modernity: Essays on the Work of Charles Taylor*. Montreal, CA: McGill-Queens University Press, Chapter 7.

n.d. "Disability Rights: A Question of Justice? Or a Question of Freedom?" In Malcoml Langord and Michael Stein (eds.), *Disability Social Rights*. Cambridge University Press, forthcoming.

Hobbes, Thomas. 1985. *Leviathan*. Ed. C. B. Macpherson. New York: Penguin.

Hobhouse, L. T. 1921. *The Rational Good*. London: George Allen & Unwin.

1994. *Liberalism and Other Essays*. Ed. James Meadowcroft. Cambridge University Press.

Hobson, J. A. 1974. *The Crisis of Liberalism*. Ed. P. F. Clarke. London: George Allen & Unwin.

Hodgson, Geoffrey M. 2015. *Conceptualizing Capitalism. Institutions, Evolution, Future*. Chicago: University of Chicago Press.

Honoré, A. M. 1987. "Ownership." In A. M. Honore (ed.), *Making Law Bind: Essays Legal and Philosophical.* Oxford: Clarendon Press, 161–192.
Honneth, A. 2007a. "Between Aristotle and Kant: Recognition and Moral Obligation." In A. Honneth (ed.), *Disrespect: The Normative Foundations of Critical Theory*. Cambridge. Polity Press, 129–143.
2007b. "Negative Freedom and Cultural Belonging: An Unhealthy Tension in the Political Philosophy of Isaiah Berlin." In A. Honneth (ed.), *Disrespect: The Normative Foundations of Critical Theory*. Cambridge. Polity Press, 240–253.
2007c. "Post-Traditional Communities: A Conceptual Proposal." In A. Honneth (ed.), *Disrespect: The Normative Foundations of Critical Theory.* Cambridge. Polity Press, 254–262.
2012. *The I in the We: Studies in the Theory of Recognition*. Cambridge. Polity Press.
2014. *Freedom's Right: The Social Foundations of Democratic Life.* New York: Columbia University Press.
2015a. "On the Poverty of Our Freedom: Relevance and Limits of the Hegelian Ethical System." In Paul Dumouchel and Reiko Gotoh (eds.), *Social Bonds as Freedom: Revisiting the Dichotomy of the Universal and the Particular*. New York: Berghahn, 109–124.
2015b. "Freedom, Solidarity, and Democracy: An Interview with Axel Honneth." Conducted by Morten Raffnsoe-Moller. In J. Jakobsen and O. Lysaker (eds.), *Freedom and Recognition*. Leiden: Brill, 260–282.
Humboldt, W. von. 1854/1993. *The Limits of State Action*, ed. J. Burrow. Indianapolis, IN: Liberty Fund.
Hurka, T. 1993. *Virtue, Vice and Value*. Oxford: Oxford University Press.
Hurley, S. 1989. *Natural Reasons: Personality and Polity*. Oxford: Oxford University Press.
Ingram, D. 2018. *World Crisis and Underdevelopment: A Critical Theory of Poverty, Agency, and Coercion*. Cambridge: Cambridge University Press.
2020. "When Microcredit Doesn't Empower Women: Recognition Theory's Contribution to the Debate Over Adaptive Preferences." In G. Schweiger (ed.), *Poverty, Inequality and the Critical Theory of Recognition*. Cham, Switzerland: Springer, 227–260.
Jamieson, Beth Kiyoko. 2003. *Real Choices: Feminism, Freedom, and the Limits of Law.* University Park: Penn State University Press.
Jiang, Tao. 2011. "Two Notions of Freedom in Classical Chinese Thought: The Concept of Hua 化 in the Zhuangzi and the Xunzi." *Dao* 10: 463–486.
2012. "Isaiah Berlin's Challenge to the Zhuangzian Freedom." *Journal of Chinese Philosophy* 39: 69–92.
Kafer, Alison. 2013. *Feminist, Queer, Crip.* Bloomington: Indiana University Press.
2017 "Bodies of Nature: The Environmental Politics of Disability." In Sarah Jaquette Ray and Jay Sibara (eds.), *Disability Studies and the Environmental*

Humanities: Toward an Eco-Crip Theory. Lincoln: University of Nebraska Press, 201–241.

Kaiser, Thomas. 1994. "Property, Sovereignty, the Declaration of the Rights of Man, and the Tradition of French Jurisprudence." In Dale Van Kley (ed.), *The French Idea of Freedom: The Old Regime and the Declaration of 1789*. Stanford, CA: Stanford University Press, 300–339.

Keates, Simeon, and John Clarkson. 2003. *Countering Design Exclusion: An Introduction to Inclusive Design*. London: Springer London.

Keh, Andrew. 2020. "A Lot of Athletes Seem to Have the Coronavirus. Here Are Some Reasons." *The New York Times*, July 10.

Kittay, Eva Feder. 2011. "Forever Small: The Strange Case of Ashley X." *Hypatia* 26(3): 610–631.

Knight, Amber. 2017. "Disability and the Meaning of Reproductive Liberty." *Politics, Groups, and Identities* 5(1): 67–83.

Korsgaard, C. M. 1996. *The Sources of Normativity*. New York: Cambridge University Press.

Kramer, M. H. 2003. *The Quality of Freedom*. Oxford: Oxford University.

Kristjansson, K. 1996. *Social Freedom*. Cambridge: Cambridge University Press.

Kukathas, C. 1994. "Defending Negative Liberty." *Policy* (Winter): 21–26.

Landemore, Hélène, and Ferreras, Isabelle. 2016. "In Defense of Workplace Democracy: Towards a Justification of the Firm–State Analogy." *Political Theory* 44(1): 53–81.

Leland, R. J., and Han van Wietmarschen. 2017. "Political Liberalism and Political Community." *Journal of Moral Philosophy* 14(2): 142–167.

Levy, Jonathan. 2017. "Capital as Process and the History of Capitalism." *Business History Review* 91: 483–510.

Lindblom, Charles. 2001. *The Market System. What It Is, How It Works, and What to Make of It*. New Haven, CT: Yale University Press.

List, Christian, and Pettit, Philip. 2011. *Group Agency: The Possibility, Design, and Status of Corporate Agents*. Oxford and New York: Oxford University Press.

Lister, Andrew. 2013. *Public Reason and Political Community*. New York: Bloomsbury.

Locke, John. 1967. *Two Treatises of Government*. Ed. Peter Laslett. Cambridge: Cambridge University Press.

Lomasky, Loren. 1987. *Persons, Rights, and the Moral Community*. Oxford: Oxford University

1998. "Libertarianism as If (The Other 99 Percent of) People Mattered." *Social Philosophy & Policy* 15(2): 350–371.

2005. "Libertarianism at Twin Harvard." *Social Philosophy & Policy* 22(1): 178–199.

MacCallum, Gerald C. 1967. "Negative and Positive Freedom." *The Philosophical Review* 76(3): 312. doi:10.2307/2183622.

MacGilvray, Eric. 2011. *The Invention of Market Freedom*. Cambridge: Cambridge University Press.

Mack, Eric. 2010. "The Natural Right of Property." *Social Philosophy & Policy* 27 (1): 53–78.
2018. *Libertarianism*. Medford, MA: Polity.
Macpherson, C. B. 1973. *Democratic Theory: Essays in Retrieval*. Oxford: Oxford University Press.
Marneffe, Peter de. 1994. "Contractualism, Liberty, and Democracy." *Ethics* 104 (4): 764–783.
Marshall, T. H. 1950. *Citizenship and Social Class and Other Essays*. Cambridge: Cambridge University Press.
Marx, Karl. 1975. "On the Jewish Question." In Q. Hare (ed.), *Early Writings*. London: Penguin Books, 211–242.
1994a. "Critique of Hegel's Philosophy of Right." In J. O'Malley (ed.), *Early Political Writings*. Cambridge: Cambridge University Press, 1–27.
1994b. "On the Jewish Question." In J. O'Malley (ed.), *Early Political Writings*. Cambridge: Cambridge University Press, 28–56.
Mazzucato, Mariana. 2018. *The Value of Everything. Making and Taking in the Global Economy*. London: Allen Lane.
McCormick, John. 2006. "Contain the Wealthy and Patrol the Magistrates: Restoring Elite Accountability to Popular Government." *American Political Science Review* 100(2): 147–163.
2011. *Machiavellian Democracy*. Cambridge, England/New York: Cambridge University Press.
McKenna, M. 2013. "Resisting the Manipulation Argument: A Hard-Liner Takes It on the Chin," *Philosophy and Phenomenological Research* 89(2): 467–484.
Mensch, Betty. 1980–1981. "Freedom of Contract as Ideology." *Stanford Law Review* 33: 753–772.
Mill, John Stuart. 1978/1859. *On Liberty*, ed. E. Rapaport. Indianapolis, IN: Hackett.
1981/1824. "Periodical Literature: Edinburgh Review." In John M. Robson (ed.), *Collected Works*. Vol. 1. Toronto: University of Toronto Press.
1991. "Considerations on Representative Government." In John Gray (ed.), *On Liberty and Other Essays*. Oxford: Oxford University Press, 205–470.
Miller, D. 1983. "Constraints on Freedom." *Ethics* 94: 66–86.
1989. *Market, State and Society*. Oxford: Oxford University Press.
2006. *Liberty: A Reader*. New York: Routledge.
Mills, C. 1997. *The Racial Contract*. Ithaca, NY: Cornell University.
2005. "'Ideal Theory' as Ideology." *Hypatia* 20(3) (Summer): 165–184.
Mintz, Kevin Todd. 2014. "Sexual Intimacy, Social Justice, and Severe Disabilities: Should Fair Equality of Opportunity in Health Extend to Surrogate Partner Therapy?" *The Journal of Philosophy, Science & Law: Disability* 14(3): 4–15.
Moehler, Michael. 2018. *Minimal Morality: A Multilevel Social Contract Theory*. Oxford: Oxford University Press.
Morgan, Anne. 2008. "Simone de Beauvoir's Ethics of Freedom and Absolute Evil." *Hypatia* 23(4): 75–89.

Motchoulski, Alexander, and Phil Smolenski. 2019. "Principles of Collective Choice and Constraints of Fairness: Why the Difference Principle Would Be Chosen behind the Veil of Ignorance." *The Journal of Philosophy* 116(12): 678–690.

Muldoon, Ryan. 2016. *Social Contract Theory for a Diverse World: Beyond Tolerance*. New York: Routledge.

2017. "Perspectives, Norms, and Agency." *Social Philosophy & Policy* 34(1): 260–276.

et al.. 2014. "Disagreement behind the Veil of Ignorance." *Philosophical Studies* 170(3): 377–394.

Munzer, Stephen. 1990. *A Theory of Property*. Cambridge: Cambridge University Press.

Nagel, T. 2001. "Pluralism and Coherence." In M. Lilla, R. Dworkin, and R. B. Silvers (eds.), *The Legacy of Isaiah Berlin*. New York: The New York Review of Books, 105–111.

Nelson, E. 2005. "Liberty: One Concept Too Many?" *Political Theory* 33(1): 58–78.

Neufeld, Blain, and Chad Van Schoelandt. 2014. "Political Liberalism, Ethos Justice, and Gender Equality." *Law and Philosophy* 33(1): 75–104.

Neufeld, Blain, and Lori Watson. 2018. "The Tyranny – or the Democracy – of the Ideal?" *Cosmos + Taxis* 5(2): 47–61.

Neuhouser, Frederick. 2000. *Foundations of Hegel's Philosophy of Right. Actualizing Freedom*. Cambridge, MA: Harvard University Press.

Ni, Peimin. 2002. "The Confucian Account of Freedom." In Jiang Xinyan (ed.), *The Examined Life: Chinese Perspectives*. Binghampton, NY: Global Academic Publishing, 119–140.

Nicholson, Peter P. 1985. "T. H. Green and State Action: Liquor Legislation." *History of Political Thought* 6(3): 517–550.

1990. *The Political Philosophy of the British Idealists*. Cambridge: Cambridge University Press.

Nicholson, Peter P. (ed.). 1997. *Collected Works of T.H. Green*. Vol. 5. Bristol: Thoemmes Press.

Nietzsche, Friedrich. 1978. *A Nietzsche Reader*, reprint edition, trans. R. J. Hollingdale. Harmondsworth and New York: Penguin Classics.

Nozick, Robert. 1974. *Anarchy, State, and Utopia*. New York: Basic Books.

1981. *Philosophical Explanations*. Cambridge, MA: Harvard University Press.

Nussbaum, M. 2001. *Women and Human Development: The Capabilities Approach*. Cambridge: Cambridge University Press.

O'Brien, Mary. 1981. *The Politics of Reproduction*. London: Routledge.

Okin, Susan Moller. 1991. *Justice, Gender, and the Family*, reprint edition. New York: Basic Books.

O'Neill, Martin, and Thad Williamson (eds.). 2012. *Property-Owning Democracy: Rawls and Beyond*. West Sussex: Wiley.

Ostrom, Elinor. 1990. *Governing the Commons: The Evolution of Institutions for Collective Action*. Cambridge: Cambridge University Press.

Otsuka, Michael. 2005. *Libertarianism without Inequality*. Oxford: Clarendon Press.

Oudejans, N. 2019. "The Right Not to Have Rights: A New Perspective on Irregular Immigration." *Political Theory* 47(4): 447–474.

Owens, D. 2000. *Reason without Freedom: The Problem of Epistemic Normativity*. London: Routledge.

Parent, William A. 1974. "Some Recent Work on the Concept of Liberty." *American Philosophical Review* 11(3): 149–167.

Parijs, Philippe van. 1995. *Real Freedom for All: What (If Anything) Can Justify Capitalism?* Oxford: The Clarendon Press.

2003. "Difference Principles." In Samuel Freeman (ed.), *The Cambridge Companion to Rawls*. New York: Cambridge University Press, 200–240.

Pateman, Carole. 1970. *Participation and Democratic Theory*. Cambridge: Cambridge University Press.

Patten, Alan. 1999. *Hegel's Idea of Freedom*. Oxford: Oxford University Press.

Patterson, O. 1982. *Slavery and Social Death: A Comparative Study*. Cambridge, MA: Harvard University Press.

1991. *Freedom: The Making of Western Culture*. London: I. B. Tauris.

Peters, Bernhard. 1994. "On Reconstructive Legal and Political Theory." *Philosophy and Social Criticism* 20(4): 101–134.

Pettersen, Tove. 2015. "Existential Humanism and Moral Freedom in Simone de Beauvoir's Ethics." In Tove Pettersen and Annlaug Bjørsnøs (eds.), *Simone de Beauvoir – A Humanist Thinker*. Leiden/Boston: Brill/Rodopi, 69–91.

Pettit, P. 1996. "Freedom as Antipower." *Ethics* 106(3): 576–604.

1997a. *Republicanism: A Theory of Freedom and Government*. Oxford: Oxford University Press.

1997b. "Freedom with Honor: A Republican Ideal." *Social Research* 53(1) (Spring): 52–76.

2001. *A Theory of Freedom*. Oxford: Oxford University Press.

2002. "Keeping Republican Theory Simple: On a Difference with Quentin Skinner." *Political Theory* 30(3) (June): 339–356.

2009. "Republican Freedom: Three Axioms, Four Theorems." In C. Laborde and J. Maynor (eds.), *Republicanism and Political Theory*. Oxford: Blackwell Publishing, 102–130.

2012. *On the People's Terms: A Republican Theory and Model of Democracy*. Cambridge: Cambridge University Press.

2014. *Just Freedom: A Moral Compass for a Complex World*. New York: Norton.

Piketty, Thomas. 2014. *Capital in the Twenty-First Century*. Cambridge, MA: Belknap Press.

Pincione, Guido 2007. "The Trolley Problem as a Problem for Libertarians." *Utilitas* 19(4): 407–429.

Pippin, Robert B. 2008. *Hegel's Practical Philosophy: Rational Agency as Ethical Life*. Cambridge: Cambridge University Press.

Pistor, Katharina. 2019. *The Code of Capital: How the Law Creates Wealth and Inequality*. Princeton, NJ and New York: Princeton University Press.

Pitkin, Hanna. 1988. "Are Freedom and Liberty Twins." *Political Theory* 16(4) (November): 523–552.
Pound, Roscoe. 1909. "Liberty of Contract." *The Yale Law Journal* 18(7): 454–487.
Price, Margaret. 2015. "The Bodymind Problem and the Possibilities of Pain." *Hypatia* 30(1) (Winter): 268–284.
Pullen, Graham. 2011. *Design Meets Disability*. Boston: MIT Press.
Quante, Michael. 2015. "Max Stirners Kreuzzug gegen die Heiligen, oder: Die Selbstaufhebung des Antiperfektionismus." In M. Quante and A. Mohseni (Hrgs.), *Die linken Hegelianer*. Fink: München, 245–263.
Quong, Jonathan. 2005. "Disagreement, Asymmetry, and Liberal Legitimacy." *Politics, Philosophy and Economics* 4(3): 301–330.
Radin, Margaret Jane 1987. "Market-Inalienability." *Harvard Law Review* 100: 1849–1937.
Rahman, K. Sabeel. 2017. "Democracy against Domination: Contesting Economic Power in Progressive and Neorepublican Political Theory." *Contemporary Political Theory* 16(1): 41–64.
Railton, P. 2003. "Facts and Values." In *Facts, Values and Norms*. Cambridge: Cambridge University Press, 43–68.
Rawls, J. 1971. *A Theory of Justice*. Cambridge, MA: Harvard University Press.
1999. *The Law of Peoples*. Cambridge, MA: Harvard University Press.
2001. *Justice as Fairness: A Restatement*. Cambridge, MA: The Belknap Press.
2005. *Political Liberalism*. New York: Columbia University Press.
Raz, J. 1986. *The Morality of Freedom*. Oxford: Oxford University Press.
1999. *Engaging Reason*. Oxford: Oxford University Press.
Reeve, Andrew. 1986. *Property*. Basingstoke, Hampshire: Macmillan.
Reich, Charles. 1964. "The New Property." *Yale Law Journal* 73(5): 733–787.
Retief, Marno and Rantoa Letšosa. 2018. "Models of Disability: A Brief Overview." *HTS Teologiese Studies/Theological Studies* 74(1), https://doi .org/ 10.4102/hts.v74i1.4738 (accessed online April 1, 2020).
Ritchie, D. G. 1895. *Natural Rights*. London: Swan Sonnenschein.
Roberts, Dorothy. 2016. "The Ethics of Biosocial Science." In M. Matheson (ed.), *The Tanner Lectures in Human Values*, Vol. 37. . Salt Lake City: University of Utah Press, 99–142.
Robeyns, I. 2011. "The Capabilities Approach." *Stanford Encyclopedia of Philosophy*. http://plato.stanford.edu/entries/capability-approach/#SpeCapApp (August 2020).
2017. "Having Too Much." In Jack Knight and Melissa Schwartzberg (eds.), *Nomos LVIII: Wealth*. New York: New York University Press, 1–44.
Rosenberg, Anat 2013. "Contract's Meaning and the Histories of Classical Contract Law." *McGill Law Journal* 59: 165–207.
Rousseau, J.-J. 1760/1987. *Basic Political Writings*, ed. D. Cress. Indianapolis, IN: Hackett.
1997. "Discourse on Political Economy." In Victor Gourevitch (ed.), *The Social Contract and Other Later Political Writings*. Cambridge: Cambridge University Press, 3–38.

Ruddick, Sara. 1989. *Maternal Thinking: Towards a Politics of Peace*. Boston: Beacon Press.
Scanlon, T. M. 1998. *What We Owe to Each Other*. Cambridge, MA: Harvard University Press.
Schmidtz, David, and Jason Brennan. 2010. *A Brief History of Liberty*. Malden, MA: Wiley-Blackwell.
Schneewind, Jerome B. 1998. *The Invention of Autonomy: A History of Modern Moral Philosophy*. Cambridge: Cambridge University Press.
Schweickart, David. 2002. *After Capitalism*. Lanham, MD: Rowman & Littlefield.
Schweik, Susan. 2010. *Ugly Laws: Disability in Public*. New York: New York University Press.
Sen, A. 1985. "Well-Being, Agency and Freedom." *Journal of Philosophy* 82: 169–221.
1987. *The Standard of Living*. Cambridge: Cambridge University Press.
1992. *Inequality Reexamined*. Oxford: Oxford University Press.
1993. "Capability and Well-Being." In Martha Nussbaum and Amartya Sen (eds.), *The Quality of Life*. Oxford: Clarendon Press, 30–53.
1999. *Development as Freedom*. New York: Knopf.
2009. *The Idea of Justice*. Cambridge, MA: Harvard University Press.
Sensen, Oliver. 2017. "Kant." In Gerald Gaus and Piers Turner (eds.), *Public Reason in Political Philosophy: Classic Sources and Contemporary Commentaries*. New York: Routledge, Chapter 4.
Shakespeare, Tom. 2006. *Disability Rights and Wrongs*. London: Routledge.
Shapin, Steven. 1996. *The Scientific Revolution*. Chicago: University of Chicago Press.
Shue, Henry. 1980. *Basic Rights*. Princeton, NJ: Princeton University Press.
Sidgwick, Henry. 1884. "Green's Ethics." *Mind* 9: 169–187.
1897. *The Elements of Politics*, 2nd ed. London and New York: Macmillan.
Siebers, Tobin. 2010. "In the Name of Pain." In Jonathan M. Metzl and Anna Kirkland (eds.), *Against Health: How Health Became the New Morality*. New York: New York University Press, 183–194.
Simhony, Avital. 1991. "On Forcing Individuals to Be Free: T.H. Green's Liberal Theory of Positive Freedom." *Political Studies* 39: 303–320.
1993. "Beyond Negative and Positive Freedom: T.H. Green's View of Freedom." *Political Theory* 10(1): 28–54.
2019. "MacCallum, Baldwin and Green on Freedom." *Collingwood and British Idealism Studies* 25: 101–128.
Simmons, A. J. 2010. "Ideal and Non-Ideal Theory." *Philosophy & Public Affairs* 38(1): 5–36.
Singer, Abraham. 2018. *The Form of the Firm: A Normative Political Theory of the Corporation*. Oxford: Oxford University Press.
Singer, Peter. 1993. "Taking Life: Humans." In *Practical Ethics*, 2nd ed. Cambridge: Cambridge University Press, 38–50.
2009. "Why We Must Ration Health Care." *The New York Times*, July 19.

Skinner, Quentin. 2002. "A Third Concept of Liberty." *Proceedings of the British Academy* 117: 237–268.
2012. *Liberty before Liberalism*. Cambridge: Cambridge University Press.
Spector, Horacio. 1992. *Autonomy and Rights*. Oxford: Oxford University Press.
2006. "Philosophical Foundations of Labor Law." *Florida State University Law Review* 33: 1119–1148.
2010. "Four Conceptions of Freedom." *Political Theory* 38(6): 780–808.
2013. "Autonomy." In Gerald Gaus and Fred D. Agostino (eds.), *The Routledge Companion to Social and Political Philosophy*. New York and London: Routledge, 573–584.
Stalley, R. F. 1998. "Plato's Doctrine of Freedom." *Proceedings of the Aristotelian Society* 98(2): 145–158.
Steiner, H. 1983. "How Free: Computing Personal Liberty." In A. Phillips Griffiths (ed.), *Of Liberty*. Cambridge: Cambridge University Press, 73–90.
Stemplowska, Z. 2008. "What's Ideal about Ideal Theory?" *Social Theory and Practice* 34(3) (July): 319–340.
Stiglitz, Joseph. 2012. *The Price of Inequality*. London and New York: W. W. Norton & Company.
Stirner, Max. 1995. *The Ego and Its Own*, ed. David Leopold. Cambridge: Cambridge University Press.
Strawson, P. F. 1961. "Social Morality and Individual Ideal." *Philosophy* 36(136): 1–17.
1962. "Freedom and Resentment." *Proceedings of the British Academy* 48: 1–25.
Sunstein, Cass R. 2019. *On Freedom*. Princeton and Oxford: Princeton University Press.
Swanton, Christine. 1992. *Freedom: A Coherence Theory*. Indianapolis, IN: Hackett.
Taylor, C. 1979. "What's Wrong with Negative Liberty?" In A. Ryan (ed.), *The Idea of Freedom*, Oxford: Oxford University Press, 175–194.
1985a. "What's Wrong with Negative Liberty?" In *Philosophical Papers 2*. Cambridge: Cambridge University Press, 211–219.
1985b. "The Diversity of Goods." In *Philosophy and the Human Sciences: Philosophical Papers 2*. Cambridge: Cambridge University Press, 230–247.
1989a. *Sources of the Self: The Making of the Modern Identity*. Cambridge, MA: Harvard University Press.
1989b. "Cross-Purposes: The Liberal-Communitarian Debate." In N. Rosenblum (ed.), *Liberalism and the Moral Life*. Cambridge, MA: Harvard University Press, 159–182.
2006. "What's Wrong with Negative and Positive Liberty." In David Miller (ed.), *The Liberty Reader*. Edinburgh: Edinburgh University Press, 141–162.
Terzi, Lorella. 2015. "Cognitive Disability, Capability Equality, and Citizenship." In Nancy J. Hirschmann and Beth Linker (eds.), *Civil Disabilities: Citizenship, Membership, and Belonging*. Philadelphia: University of Pennsylvania Press, 186–203.
Thaler, Richard H., and Cass R. Sunstein. 2008. *Nudge*. New York: Penguin Books.

2014. *Why Nudge? The Politics of Libertarian Paternalism*. New Haven, CT: Yale University Press.
Thomas, Alan. 2017. *Republic of Equals. Predistribution and Property-Owning Democracy*. Oxford: Oxford University Press.
Thompson, Michael. 2018. "The Political Dimensions of Economic Division: Republicanism, Social Justice and the Evaluation of Economic Inequality." In Lauren Langman and David Smith (eds.), *Twenty-First Century Inequality & Capitalism: Piketty, Marx and Beyond*. Leiden: Brill, 201–221.
Thomson, Judith Jarvis. 1976. "Self-Defense and Rights." The Lindley Lecture, University of Kansas.
1990. *The Realm of Rights*. Cambridge, MA: Harvard University Press.
Thomson, Rosemary Garland. 1997. *Extraordinary Bodies: Figuring Physical Disability in American Culture and Literature*. New York: Columbia University Press.
Tomasi, John. 2012. *Free Market Fairness*. Princeton, NJ: Princeton University Press.
Towle, Evan B. and Lynn M. Morgan. 2002. "Romancing the Transgender Native: Rethinking the Use of the 'Third Gender' Concept." *GLQ* 8(4): 469–497.
Tremain, Shelley. 2001. "On the Government of Disability." *Social Theory and Practice*, October 2001, 27(4) (October): 617–636.
2018. "Philosophy of Disability as Critical Diversity Studies." *International Journal of Critical Diversity Studies* 1(1) (June): 30–44.
Tronto, Joan C. 2013. *Caring Democracy: Markets, Equality, and Justice*. New York: New York University Press.
Tutor, Andrés. 2018. "Isaiah Berlin on Positive Freedom." *International Philosophical Quarterly* 58(4): 407–422.
Tyler, Colin. 2010. *The Metaphysics of Self-realization and Freedom*. Exeter: Imprint Academic.
"Unconscionable contracts." Legal Information Institute, Cornell University Law School at www.law.cornell.edu/wex/unconscionability (August 2020).
Valdman, M. 2010. "Outsourcing Self-Government." *Ethics* 120(4): 761–790.
Vallier, Kevin. 2014. *Liberal Politics and Public Faith: Beyond Separation*. New York: Routledge.
VanDeVeer, Donald. 1986. *Paternalistic Intervention: The Moral Bounds of Benevolence*. Princeton, NJ: Princeton University Press.
Van Meeteren, M. 2009. "Striving for a Better Position: Aspirations and the Role of Cultural, Economic, and Social Capital for Irregular Migrants in Belgium" *International Immigration Review* 43(4) (Winter): 881–897.
Van Schoelandt, Chad. 2015. "Justification, Coercion, and the Place of Public Reason." *Philosophical Studies* 172(4): 1031–1050.
2018. "Moral Accountability and Social Norms." *Social Philosophy & Policy* 35 (1): 217–236.
2020. "Functionalist Justice and Coordination." *Social Theory and Practice* 46 (2): 417–440.

Waldron, Jeremy. 1988. *The Right to Private Property*. Oxford: Clarendon Press.
2005. "Moral Autonomy and Personal Autonomy." In John Christman and Joel Anderson (eds.), *Autonomy and the Challenges to Liberalism*. Cambridge: Cambridge University Press, 307–329.
2006. "Homelessness and the Issue of Freedom." In R. Goodin and Ph. Pettit (eds.), *Contemporary Political Philosophy*. Malden, MA: Blackwell, 432–448.
Wall, S. 2016. "Autonomy as a Perfection." *American Journal of Jurisprudence* 61 (2): 175–194.
Walzer, Michael. 1983. *Spheres of Justice. A Defense of Pluralism and Equality*. New York: Basic Books.
Watson, G. 2004. *The Work of the Will*. In *Agency and Answerability: Selected Essays*. Oxford: Oxford University Press, 123–157.
Weinstein, W. L. 1966. "The Concept of Liberty in Nineteenth Century English Political Thought." *Political Studies* 13: 145–162.
Wellmer, Albrecht 1998. "Models of Freedom in the Modern World". In *Endgames*, trans. D. Midgely. Cambridge, MA: MIT Press, 3–37.
Wendell, Susan. 1996. *The Rejected Body: Feminist Philosophical Reflections on Disability*. New York: Routledge.
Wilson, Robert Anton. 2016. *Prometheus Rising*, 2nd ed. Grand Junction, CO: Hilaritas Press.
Winters, Jeffrey A. 2011. *Oligarchy*. Cambridge and New York: Cambridge University Press.
2017. "Wealth Defense and the Complicity of Liberal Democracy." In Jack Knight and Melissa Schwartzberg (eds.), *Nomos LVIII: Wealth*. New York: New York University Press, 158–225.
Wood, Allen W. 1981. *Karl Marx*. Henley-on-Thames: Routledge.
Zamir, Eyal, and Medina, Barak 2010. *Law, Economics, and Morality*. New York: Oxford University Press.

Index

Milton Keynes UK
Ingram Content Group UK Ltd.
UKHW021949081023
430197UK00012B/35

9 781108 738217